ADVANCE PRAISE FOR *RELEASING HOPE*

Anyone interested in women imprisoned or the value of participatory action research will find this book inspiring. Incarcerated women involved in Women in2 Healing speak clearly and movingly of the challenges in their lives, and the value of the meaningful opportunities they were given to help themselves and others move beyond addictions, grief, and loss, to reflection, forgiveness, and productive lives. They share with us, the reader, their connection to their families and children and ultimately offer insight into the remarkable sameness we share as human beings and how we find meaning in our lives. Nine-in-ten women in Canada who go to jail do so for less than six months. Anyone reading this book can surely not help but reflect on how meaningful change came about for these women—in the community, engaged with others—actively addressing the problems in their lives. *Releasing Hope* illustrates the value of giving individuals the opportunity to have control over the determinants of their health and ultimately their lives.
—SHAWN BAYES, Executive Director, Elizabeth Fry Society of the Greater Vancouver

No one sets out for a life of social exclusion, stigma, shame, or incarceration. The generous sharing of and learnings from these deeply impactful stories compiled by the editors are testimonials to the determination and courage of these women. They clearly express what women need to thrive outside the prison gates and the content will be of enormous value to policy makers, clinicians, system planners, and leaders. *Releasing Hope i*s a must read for people that need or want their heart stirred, their mind stimulated, and their soul refreshed. In these stories, you will see and hear very courageous women and perhaps think of many like them who can change their lives when empathy, trust, compassion, care, and companionship are a clear and present feature. The simple truth of it all is where there is love there is healing, where there is healing there is strength to face the challenges ahead and to sustain hope for tomorrow. As a provider of health services to people in BC provincial corrections facilities, we will proudly use this

book and the first, *Arresting Hope*, to guide our policy development, programming, and service delivery
—CARL ROY, President and CEO, British Columbia Provincial Health Services Authority

The book addresses the difficult journeys women face when released from prison and shows that in our current society, sentences do not stop upon release. The women's stories illustrate this in a sometimes shocking and sad, sometimes encouraging and hopeful, but always very open and honest way. It gives us a true insight into the lives of women released from prison. Great initiatives have been started to help women return to their life in the community in a way in which they can thrive and do well. Participatory health research as well as peer health mentoring are of great value in the period after release and should be conducted on a much broader scale across the world. I highly recommend reading this book to gain a deeper understanding of the reality women face upon their release from prison and of the ways in which we all have an important role in helping them on their journey to freedom.
—BRENDA VAN DEN BERGH, Health Department, DIGNITY Danish Institute against Torture, Denmark

Releasing Hope gives amazing glimpses of anguish and triumph—of women released from prison—one who makes it after thirty years of addiction. Journal entries and poems are interspersed with observations from the physician who treated the women in prison and now guides a novel "Participatory Research" project with former inmates as co-editors and authors. They can write! Some have moved on to degrees and decent jobs. The social scientist in me asks, can this program be tried in other places?
—LYNN MCDONALD, Professor Emerita, University of Guelph, co-founder of the Campaign for the Abolition of Solitary Confinement

RELEASING HOPE

Copyright © 2019 Inanna Publications and Education Inc.

Except for the use of short passages for review purposes, no part of this book may be reproduced, in part or in whole, or transmitted in any form or by any means, electronically or mechanically, including photocopying, recording, or any information or storage retrieval system,without prior permission in writing from the publisher or a licence from the Canadian Copyright Collective Agency (Access Copyright).

Published in Canada by
Inanna Publications and Education Inc.
210 Founders College, York University
4700 Keele Street, Toronto, Ontario M3J 1P3
Telephone: (416) 736-5356 Fax (416) 736-5765
Email: inanna.publications@inanna.ca Website: www.inanna.ca

We gratefully acknowledge the support of the Canada Council for the Arts and the Ontario Arts Council for our publishing program. We also acknowledge the financial support of the Government of Canada.

Note from the publisher: Care has been taken to trace the ownership of copyright material used in this book. The authors and the publisher welcome any information enabling them to rectify any references or credits in subsequent editions.

Cover artwork: Mo Korchinski
Interior black and white illustrations: Mo Korchinski
Cover design: Val Fullard

Library and Archives Canada Cataloguing in Publication

Title: Releasing hope : women's stories of transition from prison to community / edited by Ruth Elwood Martin, Mo Korchinski, Lynn Fels and Carl Leggo.
Names: Martin, Ruth Elwood, 1954– editor. | Korchinski, Mo, 1966– editor. | Fels, Lynn, 1955– editor. | Leggo, Carleton Derek, 1953–2019, editor.
Identifiers: Canadiana (print) 20190157844 | Canadiana (ebook) 20190157852 | ISBN 9781771337052 (softcover) | ISBN 9781771337069 (epub)
| ISBN 9781771337076 (Kindle) | ISBN 9781771337083 (pdf)
Subjects: LCSH: Women ex-convicts—Canada—Biography. | LCSH: Women ex-convicts—Services for—Canada. | LCSH: Women ex-convicts—Health and hygiene—Canada. | LCSH: Women ex-convicts—Mental health—Canada. | LCSH: Women ex-convicts—Canada—Social conditions. | LCSH: Hope.
Classification: LCC HV9505 .R45 2019 | DDC 364.8082/0971—dc23

Printed and Bound in Canada.

RELEASING HOPE

Women's Stories of Transition from Prison to Community

edited by
RUTH ELWOOD MARTIN, MO KORCHINSKI,
LYNN FELS AND CARL LEGGO

INANNA Publications and Education Inc.
Toronto, Canada

We dedicate Releasing Hope *to the inspiration, enduring hopefulness, and memory of Carl Leggo.*

You lived your life making poetic poetry.
Thank you for being there,
for showing me the path
You were by my side
giving me courage to do things I've never done before.
You spoke to me with dignity and respect
without judgement.

You edited the narrative of my life.

You showed me that writing
can heal one's soul
You taught me to see the positive
instead of a broken story.
You believed in me
more than I ever believed in myself

You were the one who pushed me
to reach my full potential
I wouldn't be who I am today if I didn't have you in my life
I wouldn't be the voice of others with broken stories.

We broke the past and build
a future of hope.

I will always hear your voice when
I listen to my poems
No one could read poetry like you.

—Mo Korchinkski

Table of Contents

Acknowledgements

xi

Preface

xv

Invitation to Readers

1

The Editors Are Beset by Questions

11

I. Release

13

II. Women in2 Healing

45

III. Health Goals

101

Hope: Interlude One

129

IV. Mentoring
134

V. Preventive Health
63

VI. Indigenous Healing
201

Hope: Interlude Two
241

VII. Mothers, Babies, and Children
247

VIII. Education
305

IX. Ways Forward
337

Final Reflections
365

Who We Are
393

Appendices
403

Acknowledgements

WE ACKNOWLEDGE THAT OUR WORK AND LEARNING have taken place on the traditional and unceded land of the Coast Salish peoples, including the shared traditional territories of the Skwxwú7mesh Úxwumixw (Squamish), Tsleil-Waututh, and xʷməθkʷyəm (Musqueam) First Nations, as well as numerous Stó:lō Nations south of Fraser River, including the Kwantlen, Semiahmoo, Tsawwassen, Katzie, Kwantlen, Kwikwetlem, and Qayqayt First Nations.

This book would not have been written without the support, commitment, and dedication of many people. We heartily thank the expansive community who contributed to this work.

We acknowledge the women who, within these pages, have shared their experiences of being incarcerated and of leaving the gates.

We acknowledge all those who have worked and those who continue to work towards a new understanding of community for women following their release from prison. We recognize the challenges experienced by women who have been incarcerated, their stories, and the hope that is released into our stewardship.

We acknowledge organizations and individuals whose support provides invaluable affirmation of the women's research work and advocacy: Brenda Tole, and other wardens who support her vision; Alison Granger-Brown, Lara-Lisa Condello, Linnea Groom, and the Woman to Woman (W2) workers, whose compassion and commitment extends beyond the gates into the community; the late prison Chaplain Henk Smidstra and Elder Mary Fayant ("Holy Cow"), who have provided inspiration and solace; Debra Hanberg, Kate Roth, and the project staff of the Collaborating Centre for Prison Health and Education, for their determination and dedication; and all the academic faculty who have journeyed as co-investigators in this work.

We also acknowledge the readers of *Arresting Hope*, who have encouraged us during the preparation and publication of the manuscript of *Releasing Hope*.

We acknowledge the funding organizations that believed in this work and provided operating and program grants for Women in2 Healing, the *Doing Time* research project, the Unlocking the Gates Peer Health Mentor Program, and preventive health projects for individuals with incarceration experience. We have included a list of the funding organizations, project titles, and dates in the Appendix. We are particularly grateful for the ongoing collaboration provided by Michelle DeGroot of the First Nations Health Authority.

We also acknowledge the individuals, some of whom wish to remain anonymous, who generously donated funds so that women with incarceration experience can take educational courses, present their work at conferences, host networking events for women with previous incarceration experience, and support venues for women as they transition from prison.

We thank the Nicola Valley Institute of Technology (NVIT) for their support. In particular, we acknowledge NVIT for hosting monthly support meetings of Women in2 Healing and the writing workshops that inspired the work in *Arresting Hope* and *Releasing Hope*. In addition, we are indebted to the University of British Columbia School of Population Health, Department of Family Practice, the Women's Health Research Institute, BC Women's Hospital, and the Provincial Health Services Authority for providing practical support such as office space, fiscal hosting, and human resources and administrative support.

Finally, we thank Gerda Wever, Director of The Write Room & The Write Room Press, for her thoughtful and insightful attention to the manuscript. We thank Ruth and Lynn's book group members for their invaluable suggestions following their reading of the first draft. And we thank Luciana Ricciutelli, Editor-in-Chief of Inanna Publications, for her faith in the manuscript, her expertise, and her thoughtful oversight of *Releasing Hope*.

We have a chance as women with lived experience to help women being released from prison. As peers, we understand the emotions and fears that build upon our release. When the gates open, a person has a choice: to give in to the old way or walk alongside a peer who will guide you to freedom.
—Mo Korchinski

In between arrest and release there is a space ... and in that space, there is the opportunity to choose. The support needed is simply to help during the choosing process, because in that choice lies freedom.
—Alison Granger-Brown

When you listen carefully, you can hear a resonant song of hope.... To live with hope requires immense courage, forgiveness, and patience.
—Carl Leggo

Preface

IMAGINE THAT A GATE IS OPENING and that you are stepping beyond the gated barriers into a new reality. Who is waiting for you? What opportunities are offered? Who reaches out to welcome you?

Releasing Hope was born out of our first book *Arresting Hope*, which describes participatory health research and the experience of women incarcerated inside a British Columbian provincial correctional centre from 2005 to 2007. Readers of *Arresting Hope*, moved by the stories written by incarcerated women, would ask us, "What happened next?" and, "How are the women doing, now that they are released from prison?"

Starting in 2007, women who were released from prison formed a network called Women in2 Healing because they wished to continue participatory health research in the community. Their overarching research question was, "How can we improve the health of women in prison and following their release?" *Releasing Hope* emerged iteratively over the ensuing eleven years of community-based participatory health research. The University of British Columbia Behavioural Research Ethics Board provided certificates of approval for each of the research projects described in this book.

Releasing Hope describes the journeys of formerly incarcerated women and their encounters with the barriers (financial, emotional, familial, systemic) that they confronted during their reintegration into the community. *Releasing Hope* touches on the stories of individual women and the participatory health research that made their lives, their hopes, their dreams, and their fears visible. Upon release, the challenge is to reimagine lives that have been interrupted beginning anew.

Releasing Hope is a compilation of women's stories, of those who were released and of those who strived to walk alongside us; the book represents a learning journey that we hope to share with you.

We repeat here what we wrote in the preface for *Arresting Hope*: it takes tremendous courage for women to go back in time, to dig into their memories, to re-live traumatic formative years, and to write. They travel back because they want to make sense of their present; they want to understand, so they can heal and move forward; and they want to contribute to the learning of others.

Ruth Elwood Martin led the book project, and she was the principal investigator of the participatory health research projects. She also guided the formation of the Collaborating Centre for Prison Health and Education, a network that is committed to encouraging and facilitating collaborative opportunities for health, education, research, service, and advocacy, in order to enhance the social wellbeing and (re)integration of individuals in custody, their families, and communities.[1] Mo Korchinski took a leadership role in the book. She edited the evolving manuscript and contributed reflections, poetry, and narratives. In addition, Mo created all of the book's illustrations using lead pencil and charcoal on paper. Lynn Fels and Carl Leggo, academic co-investigators in the prison health research projects, edited and shaped the writing as the book project began to unfold.

We donate all royalties and net proceeds from the sale of both books, *Arresting Hope* and *Releasing Hope*, to the Vancouver Foundation Arresting Hope Education Fund.[2] The Education Fund provides educational awards for women with incarceration experience and their children; the awards are administered and selected by a committee whose members have many years of experience in community service, corrections, and education. The selection committee is hosted by Nicola Valley Institute of Technology, British Columbia's Aboriginal public post-secondary institute.

NOTES

[1] See www.ccphe.ubc.ca.
[2] See www.vancouverfoundation.ca/arrestinghope.

Invitation to Readers

CARL LEGGO

FOR OVER TEN YEARS, we have been engaged in a life-changing collaboration of research, writing, teaching, and activism focused on prisons and people with incarceration experience. In 2014, we co-edited the book *Arresting Hope: Women Taking Action in Prison Health Inside Out*, which narrates a story about women in the Alouette Correctional Centre for Women (ACCW), a provincial prison in Maple Ridge, British Columbia, Canada. *Arresting Hope* tells a story about how creative leadership fostered opportunities for transformation and hope, and about how engaging in research and writing contributed to healing.

Arresting Hope narrates the experiences of women in a minimum-security prison, and demonstrates how courageous and innovative leadership created opportunities for significant change, both in the ways a prison can be imagined and in the lives of individual women when they are invited to be researchers, teachers, and activists who collaborate and support one another. The book describes participatory health research that ran inside the British Columbia provincial correctional centre from 2005 to 2007. Outside the prison gates, starting in 2008, women who were released into the community formed a network called Women in2 Healing. They created a closed Facebook group to provide peer support, and the Unlocking the Gates to Health Peer Mentor Program, which supports women during the immediate days following their release from prison.

Arresting Hope includes poetry, stories, letters, interviews, reflections, memories, journal entries, and research findings. The book records the warden's vision for an effective prison, the prison doctor's exploration of what health means for women in prison, and the narratives of some incarcerated women, including Mo Korchinski, who emerged from prison as a writer, researcher, and community leader. *Arresting Hope* reminds us that prisons are not only places of punishment, marginalization, and trauma. They can also be places of hope, where people with difficult lived experiences can begin to compose stories of healing, anticipation, communication, education, connection, community, and hope.

Releasing Hope: Women's Stories of Transition from Prison to Community is our second book about research connected to experiences of women with incarceration experience. While *Arresting Hope* narrated the experiences of many women with incarceration experience, the book focused on four singular women: a doctor, an inmate, a warden, and a recreation therapist. Dr. Ruth Elwood Martin was the medical doctor in the prison. Mo Korchinski was an inmate. The book also narrated the collaboration that occurred between incarcerated women and prison staff, community activists, and academic researchers, to plan and conduct participatory health research projects that had a profound impact on the lives of many people. After Mo was released from Alouette Correctional Centre for Women in 2006, she completed a Bachelor of Social Work at Nicola Valley Institute of Technology. She now is the project manager of Unlocking the Gates, a peer health mentoring program. Ruth and Mo have engaged in numerous health research projects in the community that arose from research questions that incarcerated women asked, including several projects that are narrated in *Releasing Hope*. For example, in Doing Time, we interviewed women following their release from prison to ask about their experienced barriers and about what they found helpful in achieving their health goals.

Releasing Hope is not an epilogue to *Arresting Hope*, but a second volume of an expansive story that needs to be shared. When we composed *Arresting Hope*, we understood that we would need a second book to narrate the many experiences of researching and living outside the gates. Therefore, in *Releasing Hope*, we narrate the stories of women after they leave the prison. Many women with incarceration experience understand the notion of the revolving door of prison. They enter prison, they leave, they return. What do women with incarceration experience need to find hope in shaping healthy lived experiences after they have been released from prison?

Like *Arresting Hope*, this new book includes poetry, stories, letters, interviews, transcribed conversation, reflections, memories, quotations, journal entries, creative nonfiction, and scholarly research. And like *Arresting Hope*, this new book presents a carefully chosen sequence of texts that have been aesthetically organized much like a documentary filmmaker composes a story. There are many kinds of texts in *Releasing

Hope, and many of these texts are like fragments of coloured glass that reflect and refract the light in different ways as the glass is turned and seen from different perspectives. The invitation we offer in *Releasing Hope* is to linger with the fragments of stories, to respond with heart and imagination, to empathize with the stories of incarceration, renewal, forgiveness, grief, loss, fear, love, and hope that shape the lives of so many people.

To attend to *Releasing Hope* as patient and empathetic readers, it is important to understand that this book does not narrate a specific temporal story. Instead, it represents a series of ruminations and narratives about what it means to release hope, to generate hope, to sustain hope. The book could be subtitled *Fifty Ways of Listening to Hope* or *Countless Ways of Listening to Hope* because *Releasing Hope* is a manifesto to hope and living hopefully. The words of women with incarceration experience, and the words of others who have journeyed with them, are full of hope. But the main hope invested in this book is the hope that will be generated when readers take up the book, when they commit themselves to careful and thoughtful conversations, and when the conversations turn to social activism to support women with incarceration experience.

Releasing Hope presents a compelling testimony to what women with incarceration experience need to thrive (not just survive) outside the prison gates. Women have shared their needs, fears, and hopes in the research and storytelling that is the foundation of the book. Unlike *Arresting Hope*, which tells the story of ACCW in a particular place in a particular time, *Releasing Hope* is focused on comprehensive research in health goals and what contributes to and supports hopeful engagement with daily living to achieve these goals. Wonderfully, during research, individual women have arrived with heart, determination, compassion, and willingness to offer what is needed in the hopes of sharing what they have learned and what is yet to be learned amongst us all.

NARRATIVE FRAGMENTS AND LINGERING

As researchers, writers, co-editors, and activists, we are always eager to avoid presenting a narrative about the lives of women who have been incarcerated and released in ways that might be construed (and subsequently dismissed) as naïve, sentimental, or delusionary. We want to present a multi-faceted narrative that elicits differences among women's experiences. We seek to sidestep stereotypes, clichés, and conventional images in order to recognize the diversity of stories lived by women in and out of prison. How then do we narrate complex experiences in ways that recognize that such experiences cannot be contained in simple categories that produce the illusion of coherence, unity, and explanation?

Our strategy in composing both *Arresting Hope* and *Releasing Hope* was to attend to the discourse of the narrative. In narrative research, there are three main dynamics. *Story* focuses on what happened. *Discourse* focuses on how the story is told. *Interpretation* addresses questions like, "Why is this story meaningful?" and "What can I learn from this story?" While all three dynamics of story, discourse, and interpretation are integrally important in narrative research, we purposefully focus on discourse because we are especially eager to invite readers to slow down, to linger with the texts, to read with imagination and heart. We have carefully and creatively composed *Releasing Hope* as a collection of fragments, poems, quotations, excerpts, and stories that intersect in order to shape a text that is a *métissage* or braiding of many texts.

In *Belonging: Home Away from Home*, Isabel Huggan discusses the value of writing fragments, which she calls "the random mode of composition" (223) that does not "impose pattern on experience" (224). Instead, the reader moves "from one subject to another, enjoys tracing subtle links between them. The work of making patterns is left to the open-minded reader" (224). As Huggan suggests, this kind of reading experience invites the reader to generate "an infinite number of variations" (224). We are keenly interested in creative approaches to researching lived and living experiences.

In 1985, Gregory Ulmer announced "the collapse of the distinction (opposition or hierarchy) between critical-theoretical reflection and creative practice" (225). He promoted a practice of scholarship that recognizes how the critical and the creative need to be braided together. *Métissage* is a way of creatively braiding diverse kinds of texts, of composing stories in creative performances.[1] In *Releasing Hope*, we braid stories, poetry, art, ruminations, journal writing, and citations to create a complex chorus of voices that sing out and invite conversation with others. Our diverse voices evoke multiplicity, and through the text, we enter creative relationships full of mystery where we learn to trust that the artful process of engaging together teaches us how to live well together. *Métissage* connects the mind, imagination, heart, and body in a holistic celebration of interconnections, and *métissage* invites possibilities for radical and transformative learning, for new beginnings.

In the way of *métissage* and braiding, *Releasing Hope* presents a story metonymically. Where metaphor expresses how one thing is like something else (for example, *my love is a rose*), metonymy is a trope of contiguity where one thing comes alongside something else. People with incarceration experience come alongside people in positions of authority and privilege, and people without incarceration experience come alongside those with incarceration experience. In the metonymic relationship there is communication, sharing, and action. The two words most often used in the English language are the pronouns "I" and "you." So often the relationship between "I" and "you" is expressed as opposition and fear, but in a metonymic relationship, the relationship between "I" and "you" is nurtured.

Consider one of the most challenging fears that is terrorizing the world today—xenophobia—the fear of the stranger, the foreigner, the other. What might our lives be like if we replaced "phobia" in xenophobia with another Greek root *"philia"* which means, not fear, but love. Xenophilia is the love of the stranger, the foreigner, the other. There is an ancient Greek word, *paraclete*, which means "the one who comes alongside" or "the comforter." The *paraclete* walks with you, interceding, advocating, calling, comforting. The people whose stories and voices sing out in *Releasing Hope* have come alongside one another.

Like Gregory Ulmer, we are committed to both creative discourse and critical discourse. We are steeped in the arts as a way of knowing, being, and becoming. And here we pause, for ways of knowing are borne of a multiplicity of experience, perspectives, communal rituals, and ethical stances that remind us of the vast complexity that is the human experience and expression. If we understand that ways of knowing embody ways of doing, being, creating, not-knowing, undoing in our becoming here and now (Frantzich and Fels), then we understand that our actions through the arts are an invitation not to reproduce or represent but to re-perform what is and what might become possible.

As a research process, *métissage* evokes and provokes possibilities for meaning-making, full of startling surprises. By naming our creative composition of *Releasing Hope* a *métissage*, we are honouring the elusive, intangible way that memory works. In *Threading Light: Explorations in Loss and Poetry*, Lorri Neilsen Glenn writes that "memories ground us, even as we know they are fleeting and flawed constructions that slip through our consciousness; ghosts of ghosts" (79). She also reminds us that "memory is a cracked bowl, and it fills as it empties. Memory is what we create out of what we have at hand" (80).

In *Releasing Hope*, we do not claim to tell the stories of the many women who have participated in the different research projects that span a decade. Instead, we are eager to present fragments and traces that are sensual, imagined, and physical, heartful memories that trail from the past into the present. Marlene Kadar notes that "memory registers what it felt like, not exactly what it was like" (224), and she promotes the value of understanding "traumatic events" through fragments that do not pretend to tell the definitive and comprehensive story. *Releasing Hope* is composed in a discursive way that invites engagement, conversation, and empathy. The narrative is always open to multiple interpretations. There is no conclusion. The narrative of *Releasing Hope* is always in process. The story continues.

A RESONANT SONG OF HOPE

As co-editors, we have journeyed as companions. We have lived the research, activism, and writing that now sing out in *Releasing Hope*. Our intention is that the new book will be, like *Arresting Hope*, both an inspiration and a challenge. We hope *Releasing Hope* will generate new visions, bold commitments, complex conversations, and energetic action for change. Not only does *Releasing Hope* offer an invitation to look at the stories from many different perspectives, but *Releasing Hope* invites you to listen, to hear the stories, especially to hear the stories as we have never heard them before. In particular, *Releasing Hope* sings with the voices of women, and those voices are startling, diverse, heartful, and human. When you listen carefully, you can hear a resonant song of hope. As Sandra Finney and Jane Thurgood Sagal understand in *The Way of the Teacher: A Path for Personal Growth and Professional Fulfillment*, "hope is not wishful thinking but an orientation to a life of doing our best and doing what we can" (133). All the people whose voices are included in *Releasing Hope* are committed to living hopefully as an orientation to living well in the midst of challenges, both past and present. To live with hope requires immense courage, forgiveness, and patience.

So, Ruth writes in her journal about the tangled experiences of being a medical doctor turned researcher and advocate. Mo writes poetry and stories about her life. In *How Poetry Saved My Life*, Amber Dawn asks, "What does it mean to be given the rare and privileged opportunity to have a voice?" (13). Like Mo, Amber understands how calling out in your unique voice "means possibility and responsibility. It means nurturing ... creativity and playing with personal storytelling" (13). And like Amber, Mo knows how "the written word can be a faithful witness ... if you're willing to show yourself" (56). Mo is willing to share her stories, and in sharing her stories as poetry and carefully constructed narratives and images, she invests an aesthetic order and dynamic that holds her life experiences in hopeful ways.

In *Women's Lives: The View from the Threshold*, Carolyn G. Heilbrun comments on how writers re-create "themselves even as they write; they are not only retelling the past" (73). Henk Smidstra, the chaplain for many years in Alouette Correctional Centre for Women, writes about hope, as does Alison Granger-Brown, the former recreation therapist in ACCW, and a significant leader in the story of the prison recounted in *Arresting Hope*. A circle of women with incarceration experience who have collaborated on many research projects, and who have supported one another as a community connected by shared experiences and Facebook and intrepid hope, are represented in *Releasing Hope* with stories, ruminations, and poems.

As co-editors, we are especially eager to draw attention to a series of nine found or erasure poems in the book. The found or erasure poem is composed out of texts that others have written. Found or erasure poems are often written out of texts as diverse as newspapers, magazines, advertising, Internet sites, bureaucratic memos, and regulation manuals. In composing a found or erasure poem, the writer finds an interesting text, and shapes the words into a poem. The shaping might include erasing words to represent a responsive engagement with the original texts. Some people ask, "Is a found poem really a poem? Is a found poem a form of plagiarism? Doesn't a found poem blow a big hole in the traditional myth of the original poet inspired by an unseen Muse?" Found or erasure poems remind us that poems are everywhere, just waiting to be found (Walmsley, Cox, and Leggo "'It's a trash'"; "Reproductive tourism"; "Listening deeply"). In *Releasing Hope* the data from several research projects were explored to compose found or erasure poems that represent the voices of women with incarceration experience. In one research project titled Unlocking the Gates, women with incarceration experience were asked, "What would you like people to know that would be helpful for women being released?" There were many responses from 257 women. The following lines are part of a found poem composed from the women's responses.

We're all human
We're only human

We all make mistakes
We just made bad choices

We are trying to change
We deserve a second chance

In *Teaching Community: A Pedagogy of Hope*, bell hooks claims that we must "cultivate a spirit of hopefulness about the capacity of individuals to change" (73). hooks promotes several commitments that are all connected to the living experiences narrated in *Releasing Hope*. First, hooks advises us to refuse simplistic binaries. Instead, she recommends that, "we refuse to allow either/or thinking to cloud our judgment" (10). Instead, we need to "embrace the logic of both/and, and to "acknowledge the limits of what we know" (10). Second, she recommends that the sharing of personal narratives is essential to raising consciousness and determining "the best action to take" (107). Third, hooks promotes love as the way that "will always challenge and change us" (137). With consummate hopefulness, hooks claims that "to be guided by love is to live in community with all life" (163). *Releasing Hope* is a testimony to the value of complex thinking, personal sharing, and loving with hopefulness.

In an extract from her poem "Jail," Mo writes,

most people think jail is hard
a sad place to be
but jail saved my life
jail gave me hope

Mo reminds us constantly in her courageous writing and loving leadership that hope is always possible. In a twist of irony, Mo can claim that "jail gave me hope." To understand the lived experiences of women with incarceration experience, we need to listen to their stories. We need to hear their voices. In collaboration, we can continue to seek ways to release hope so that we can learn together how to live with wellness in the world.

NOTES

[1] See Hasebe-Ludt, Chambers, Oberg, and Leggo; Chambers and Hasebe-Ludt; Hasebe-Ludt, Chambers and Leggo; Leggo.

REFERENCES

Cynthia M. Chambers and Hasebe-Ludt, Erika with Dwayne Donald,

Wanda Hurren, Carl Leggo, and Antoinette Oberg. "Métissage." *Handbook of the Arts in Qualitative Social Science Research*. Eds. Adra L. Cole and J. Gary Knowles. Thousand Oaks, CA: Sage, 2008. 141-153.

Dawn, Amber. *How Poetry Saved My Life*. Vancouver, BC: Arsenal Pulp Press, 2013.

Finney, Sandra and Jane Thurgood Sagal. *Way of the Teacher: A Path for Personal Growth and Professional Fulfillment*. Lanham, MD: Rowman & Littlefield, 2017.

Frantzich, Kirsten and Lynn Fels. "Embodied Theater Ecology: Illuminating the Gap through Bridging Depth Psychology's Encounter with Performative Inquiry." *British Journal of Guidance & Counselling* 46.3 (2018): 272-281.

Hasebe-Ludt, Erika, Cynthia M. Chambers, and Carl Leggo. *Life Writing and Literary Métissage as an Ethos for Our Times*. New York: Peter Lang, 2009.

Hasebe-Ludt, Erika, Cynthia M. Chambers, C., Oberg, A., and Carl Leggo. "Embracing the World, With All of Our Relations: Métissage as an Artful Braiding." *Being with A/r/tography*. Eds. S. Springgay, R. Irwin, C. Leggo, and P. Gouzouasis. Rotterdam, NL: Sense, 2008. 57-67.

Heilbrun, Carolyn G. *Women's Lives: The View from the Threshold*. Toronto: University of Toronto Press, 1999.

hooks, bell. *Teaching Community: A Pedagogy of Hope*. New York: Routledge, 2003.

Huggan, Isabel. *Belonging: Home Away from Home*. Toronto: Vintage Canada, 2003.

Kadar, Marlene. "The Devouring: Traces of Roma in the Holocaust. No Tattoo, Sterilized Body, Gypsy Girl." *Tracing the Autobiographical*. Eds. M. Kadar, L. Warley, J. Perreault, and S. Egan. Waterloo, ON: Wilfrid Laurier University Press, 2005. 223-246.

Leggo, Carl. "Writing a Life: Representation in Language and Image." *Transnational Curriculum Inquiry* 7.2 (2010): 47-61.

Martin, Ruth Elwood, Mo Korchinski, Lynn Fels and Carl Leggo, eds. *Arresting Hope: Women Taking Action in Prison Health Inside Out*. Toronto: Inanna Publications, 2014.

Neilsen Glenn, Lorri. *Threading Light: Explorations in Loss and Poetry*. Regina, SK: Hagios Press, 2011.

Ulmer, Gregory L. *Applied Grammatology: Post(e)-pedagogy from Jacques Derrida to Joseph Beuys*. Baltimore, MD: Johns Hopkins University Press, 1985.

Walmsley, Heather L., Susan Cox, and Carl Leggo. "'It's a Trash': Poetic Responses to the Experiences of a Mexican Egg Donor." *Art/Research International: A Transdisciplinary Journal* 2.1 (2017): 58-88.

Walmsley, Heather L., Susan Cox, and Carl Leggo. "Reproductive Tourism: A Poetic Inquiry." *Cogent Arts & Humanities* 4.17 (2017): np. Web.

Walmsley, Heather L., Susan Cox, and Carl Leggo. "Listening Deeply: Understanding Experiences of Reproductive Tourism through Poetic Inquiry." *Creative Approaches to Research* 8.3 (2015): 15-43. Web.

The Editors Are Beset by Questions

Who is served by incarceration?

Who are you?
Who are you becoming?
Who do you want to be?

Who has agency over writing your story?

Who is being released without any consideration for who will receive them?
What networks of support exists for those being released?
Where are the gaps?

Who is waiting for you?

What is hope?
What sustains our hope in this work?
What does it mean to be a part of a community?
What does it mean to write a story?
What does it mean to offer a story?
What sustains health outside of prison?
What am I supposed to be learning?
What are the women given when they are released?
What can people do to better their lives coming out of prison?

How does telling one's story support healing?
How are you received?
How do you create a life?
How will you respond?

How are you seen?
How can you change how you are seen?
What's waiting for you?

How are you going to respond?

How can we learn to be present to one another?
How do we sustain hope?
How do we find voice?
How do we nurture voice?
How do we sustain voice?

To what have I given my heart?

I. Release

Keys to the Gates

MO KORCHINSKI

I've been watching women struggle with bridging the gap
between a life focused on crime, drugs and prison
and a life

                where they fit into mainstream society.

People need to know

it's not as simple as putting down the drugs
and getting on with your life.

The key to the gates of prison represents far more than just turning
the lock to open it on the days you are incarcerated or released.

For me, the day I was released
was the beginning of many unknown challenges
that I would have to face as I tried to find my place
in mainstream society.

So many barriers to moving forward in one's life
after many years of addiction that led to crime.

Always on the outskirts of society and not sure where I fit
into this big wide world we live in

Doctor's Journey

RUTH ELWOOD MARTIN

WORKING AS A PRISON PHYSICIAN, I am privileged to journey with the women I meet in the prison medical clinic.

Once a woman leaves the correctional facility, I lose contact with her—I hope that she is doing well beyond the gates, despite the odds, but I never know how things are going for her. I only see a woman again when things have not gone well for her, when she returns to prison. I welcome her back, not because I am happy that she has been re-arrested, but because I am relieved that she survived—she survived the ravages of violence and addiction; she has not died of an overdose or of other trauma. Her re-incarceration offers another opportunity for health intervention.

As I reflect on my emotions, I wonder about the paradox, that I should be pleased when a woman is re-arrested and returns to prison. I consider a woman to be safe only when she returns to prison—what nonsense, absurdity, injustice!

And when I say goodbye to a woman who is being released from Alouette Correctional Centre for Women, I hold onto hope, despite my fear, because maybe this time she will make it.

—*Journal entry*

After their release from prison, women face harsh barriers to (re)integrating into the community, including poverty, homelessness, stigma, difficulty finding employment, and little support to raise children. Leaving prison is a high-risk situation that can lead women to return to substance use, or worse, to giving up on life. Incarcerated women have a higher prevalence of trauma and adverse childhood events compared to the general population, and the transitions in and out of prison can be re-traumatizing. This is consistent with international health literature that documents the barriers to health care and adverse health outcomes for individuals following their release from prison (Kinner and Wang).

As a prison physician, I listen to the stories of women who have revolved in and out of provincial corrections. Many women tell me that they only receive medical care when they return to Alouette Correctional Centre for Women because beyond the gates they focus on survival only. Over the years, I have developed a trusting relationship with many women who cycle in and out of the prison: I have become their default family physician as I seek to provide them with continuity of health care.

In medical school, we were taught about boundaries, about how to keep our personal lives separate from our clinical professional lives, so that we could remain objective when trying to sort out patients' diagnoses, and when advising patients about treatment options. It was all about boundaries—establishing them, maintaining them, and never breaking them—which translated into how to maintain one's distance, one's emotional distance, from patients. Over the years since my graduation, I have wrestled with this way of teaching about boundaries, as it felt contrary to my own experience of learning to be a physician, and counter to my own intuition.

Jack Coulehan explained that we need to teach medical students about "emotional resilience," and we can do this by using the humanities—literature, poetry—and by mentoring. Physicians need to develop emotional resilience so that they can express empathy and compassion. When I first came across Coulehan's article and read his poetry, I felt liberated and affirmed because his writing resonated with my experience. Now, working as a community-based participatory health researcher, my approach to "boundaries" has diverged further from the teaching that I received in medical school.

Community-based participatory health research centres on relationships—long-lasting and trusting relationships. This approach contrasts the helicopter approach to doing research within the traditional medical paradigm, with boundaries intended to foster objectivity, where researchers swoop in, gather data, and leave, without communicating again with their "subjects."

And so, in this book, you will read about a form of research based on relationships between women with incarceration experience, community members, and academics. In our work, women with incarceration experience generated research questions that were driven by the urgent need to improve the situation facing women who are released from prison—not only for themselves, but also for their peers and friends, and for their children and families.

REFERENCES

Coulehan, John L. "Tenderness and Steadiness: Emotions in Medical Practice." *Literature and Medicine* 14.2 (1995): 222-36.

Kinner, Susan A. and Emily A. Wang. "The Case for Improving the Health of Ex-Prisoners." *American Journal of Public Health* 104.8 (August 2014): 1352-1355. Web.

Jail

MO KORCHINSKI

most people think jail is hard
a sad place to be
but jail saved my life
jail gave me hope
a sense of belonging
a purpose to life
a new way to live
jail gave me a job
three meals a day
a warm bed to sleep in
clean clothes to wear
friends by my side
growing and healing
from the beat of the drum
on this new journey
called life

Inside the Gates

BRENDA TOLE, FORMER WARDEN, ACCW

WITH THE ENDURING AND RESILIENT SPIRIT of the women in custody at Alouette Correctional Centre for Women (ACCW), and a unique and dedicated team of correctional and contracted staff, we challenged several perceptions of women in custody. Women are less violent than men both in the community and in a correctional setting, but they are consistently over-classified to more secure settings than required. Remanded[1] women and women detained on immigration holds were always held in secure institutions in the provincial system. We were able to negotiate the transfer and management of these women to ACCW, a medium-open setting, without incident.

At ACCW we initiated the First Nations Women's Studies Program in conjunction with Nicola Valley Institute of Technology. This program included discussions about current and historical issues affecting the well-being of First Nations women, including health, family, education, art, spirituality, and culture. Aboriginal women are over-represented in all prison systems throughout Canada. Sadly, this is an issue that is far from being understood or corrected. The discrimination towards this population is systemic in the justice system. It will take huge efforts by all stakeholders in the system to address this tragedy.

Women who are incarcerated have consistently been offered employment programs that involve work in areas that are not consistent with the current job market such as service industry employment (i.e., tailoring, kitchen services, janitorial services). These programs rarely resulted in employment, and if they did, the wages were minimal. We offered programs such as first aid, flagging, developing resumes, and keyboard skills, and we attempted to set up light trade programs that the women could complete in a short time to give them a better chance for reasonable employment.

Correctional centres are generally closed off from their communities, creating even more isolation for the women and staff. Isolating correctional centres from their local communities does not allow the community to understand the needs and potential of people in custody. We found ministries and community agencies who were more than willing to work with the women in the centre and in the community, and to help them plan for their return to the community upon release. We also found that the women volunteering with a variety of non-profits in the community benefited everyone. The safety of the community was not compromised. The women gained a great deal from access to programs and activities outside the centre, and it gave them a sense of accomplishment and community involvement.

NOTES

[1] According to the *Collins English Dictionary*, "If a person who is accused of a crime is remanded in custody or on bail, they are told to return to the court at a later date, when their trial will take place.... "Remand" is used to refer to the process of remanding someone in custody or on bail, or to the period of time until their trial begins."

My New Start

MO KORCHINSKI

I KEEP HEARING MY NAME. The loudspeaker is calling me to go to records—the final stop—to sign the paperwork and collect the personal belongings I had on me when I was arrested. I feared leaving ACCW. The women are waiting by the front gate to drum and sing me out. It's a tradition our Elder Holy Cow taught us, so women leave in a good way. Last night Holy Cow gave me a beautiful eagle feather and told me I had one more lesson to learn, but she wouldn't tell me what that lesson is. She said I will know when the lesson is taught to me.

I feel many emotions as I say goodbye to what has been my home for so long. Feeling sad, nervous, and scared, I am leaving behind many great memories, a comfortable life, and the friends who have become my family. They always have my back and they always bring joy.

I am saying goodbye to start my new life.

All I have are the jail clothes on my back and a small welfare cheque to start over. I have no ID to even cash the cheque, so I'm not sure what I'm going to do. I stop at the local second-hand store on my way to treatment and the store donates an outfit to me. Well, at least I have something to wear. The anxiety I am feeling is overwhelming; I feel like I am having a heart attack. I sit outside the treatment centre having a smoke, not sure if I'm doing the right thing. How do I start over with no family or my old friends to help me? I slowly smoke my cigarette before I walk in. But is it the right door I am walking through?

I'm met by a staff member who gives me a hug and says they will love me until I can love myself. *Well, that's going to be a long time because I don't think I can ever love myself.* I turn around and all the other clients are sitting down to dinner. They all turn to look at me. I want to run out the door; I feel out of place. I go into the office and do all the paperwork to start my journey in treatment.

As I walk out of the office with my head down on the way to my room, I hear someone call my name. I slowly look up and see a friend from jail sitting on a couch in the hallway. "Wow, it took you a while to get out," she says.

I ask, "How did you know I was coming?" She says all she knew was that somebody from ACCW was coming, but she didn't know it was me. *Great, everyone knows I'm from jail.* Still I'm happy to know someone here.

I go to my room and look at the dresser where my clothes would go if I had any clothes. I look at the closet where things should be hung. *How the hell will I survive with only the clothes on my back? What will I wear when I have to wash my clothes? How am I going to live without money and no way to support myself? Who is going to hire me when I have no job experience and a criminal record?* So many questions and fears swirl around me. I wonder if I'm doing the right thing. When I lived in addiction, I never questioned how to support myself; I didn't rely on anyone for anything.

I hear a knock at my door, and I am told I have to go upstairs to the office since it is time to do Step[1] work. I go up to the office and get a big book, and the first assignment is to write about my last ninety days. Well, during my last ninety days I was locked up in jail, and those ninety days were great. The purpose of the last ninety days assignment is to remind you of how bad it was out there when you were using.

During the years I spent at ACCW, I lived in a community of renewal and compassion where women learned to stand in leadership. We learned to be present with those who have been abused. Together we found the strength and imagination to create a vibrant community of women. The warden, and those who worked with her, dreamed of a new community on the edge of the forest—a series of bungalows, a recreation building, offices, a gym, an Eagle Hut.

This community blossomed in the presence of women who have been incarcerated for a variety of crimes, including selling drugs, violence, and prostitution. At ACCW, a provincial corrections centre, our crimes warranted two years less a day. The warden of ACCW, and her support team, recognized the trauma in the stories of our lives, and created a place of renewal, beginnings, possibilities, and reciprocity. Above all, ACCW was a place where women were invited to find ways into healing, to speak, and to know new ways of being in relationships with themselves and one another based on recognition and respect.

ACCW was especially inspired by three women: a warden who wanted to reimagine incarceration for women; a prison doctor who initiated a participatory health research project where women were co-researchers; and a recreation therapist who believed in homemade cookies and running outside the gates. ACCW was a place where women were assigned jobs, including opportunities to work with the research team. The women worked in the garden and the kitchen, cared for dogs, and sorted clothes in a volunteer centre. Through the research project, they researched issues that mattered to them, such as parenting teenagers, life of addiction, grief, SARS, diabetes, exercise, proper diets, fitness and nutrition, shoplifting, heroin, Lupus, and HIV.[2] At community gatherings in the gym, they shared their stories and learning. One correctional officer said, "I learned more about drugs from you and your presentation than from all the workshops I've taken." A few women went out into the community, into high schools, to share their stories because they wanted to give back.

The warden created a committee where the women could present their concerns. Leadership among the women emerged, along with Halloween parties, Easter egg hunts, workouts in the gym, and women laughing, and creating memories, and becoming friends. For many women, ACCW was a home, a relief from being homeless, from the streets of drugs and abuse. ACCW was a place of compassion, care, and hope. Women became hopeful in their abilities, in the promise that renewal was possible.

Nevertheless, for all the hope that was nurtured at ACCW, it was still a prison where women wore blue uniforms and where headcounts interrupted the rhythms of the day, including night rounds when flashlights shone on women to make sure they were asleep in their beds. It was a place filled with women who had experienced heartbreak and trauma, betrayal, and broken trust. It was a place where women came in and out of the gates again and again, unable to break the cycle; a place where women, once released, were often lost in illness, drugs, and violence. Many women disappeared. Their names were written on a board, more than six hundred names. Still, we nurtured hope at ACCW. Being at ACCW has been an amazing part of my life. I learned so much about myself while serving my time. ACCW gave me hope and made me feel valued, seen. At ACCW, I found the value of a community.

After I was released, the new warden moved in, the memorial board was removed, the walls of her office were painted brown, and the mother and babies program was cancelled. Everything changed.

The staff at the treatment centre doesn't want me to write about my last ninety days in prison. They want me to write about my last ninety days of using drugs. I can't even remember when I had ninety days of using when I wasn't arrested. I would only last out in the real world for thirty to sixty days before I was arrested again, but that was okay by me—I wanted to go back to jail. I knew who I was and how to function inside the prison walls. I just didn't know how to live in society.

I loved the life of a drug dealer, and I loved who I became when I was high on crack cocaine. But I didn't like who I was when I was sober. I was scared and insecure. When I was not high I felt like the little girl my parents didn't want and didn't love. I felt society didn't want a loser like me in it.

What am I doing here? Who am I kidding? I'm scared, but at the same time I don't want to let down all those people at ACCW who believe in me and believe that I can do great things out here.

I decide to pull up my big girl panties and give this recovery and new life all I have.

I have no money, but I get some clothes from a friend. Her mom also sends me clothes and a care package. Being able to change my clothes is good, but I still have no ID to cash the cheque in my pocket. It's not a big cheque ($180.00), but that money feels like a million bucks to me. I can buy myself smokes and some clothes and feel like I have a bit of control over my life. The owner of the treatment centre learns about my situation and wonders why I haven't asked for help—they have a donation room. No one told me, yet everyone knew I had no clothes when I walked in. Then she says that the staff have been waiting for me to reach out and ask for help.

Asking for help is not something I do. I learned a long time ago to only rely on myself. They give me a work assignment that is all about asking for help. I learn from the assignment that my childhood played a big part in how I view life. I don't trust others because I fear rejection. Why wouldn't I fear rejection when I was rejected by my parents?

Drugs gave me a sense of power, and I came out of my shell. I spent much of my childhood in my room, which became my safe place—as long as I was locked in my room I wasn't getting hit or put down. And that is why being locked up in jail was comfortable for me. I felt safe being away from people.

NOTES

[1] The twelve steps were created by the founders of Alcoholics Anonymous to establish guidelines for the best way to overcome dependence to alcohol. The 12-Step Program was adapted by other support groups for their own needs, including Narcotics Anonymous, substance use, and behaviour programs.

[2]For a full list, see Martin, Korchinski, Fels, and Leggo.

REFERENCES

Martin, Ruth Elwood, Mo Korchinski, Lynn Fels, and Carl Leggo, eds. *Arresting Hope: Women Taking Action in Prison Health Inside Out*. Toronto, ON: Inanna Publications, 2014. 139-141.

Amber's Story
"My Heart Broke"

AMBER CHRISTIE

SLAM! HEARING THE DOOR SLAM behind me has always caused fear and anxiety.... I know what is coming and I know it isn't going to be fun.... I was fourteen when my aunt stuck the first needle in my arm.... I'd never drank alcohol or smoked pot. I went straight to cocaine.... I wanted to know why people gave up everything to get high.[1]

When I was twelve, my parents split up. My sisters lived with Mom, but my relationship with my mom was strained. I wanted to live with my dad, but my dad had a drug problem and was an alcoholic. I couldn't live with him until he completed drug therapy and a parenting course. In the meantime, I was placed in my first foster home until my dad finished therapy and coursework and I moved in with him.

One night my dad came home from the bar. He wasn't alone. I walked into the living room to see a bunch of drunk people, including my uncle. I noticed my dad and a girl go into the bathroom. Why was he going into the bathroom with this girl? I peeked in the keyhole and saw the girl shoving a needle in my dad's arm. I screamed and smashed the door until it opened. I grabbed the girl by the hair and dragged her out. My dad chased me, yelling, "Leave her alone!"

A few seconds later he dropped to the floor. He was convulsing and foaming at the mouth. I was the only one who was sober. I had taken a CPR course in my swimming club. I grabbed my dad, tipped his head back, and started CPR. I called 911 with the phone pinned to my ear while I pumped his chest with both hands. The ambulance showed up seconds later. As the paramedics came in, my uncle pushed me into the bedroom to hide me so social services wouldn't be called. They narcaned my dad, and he started screaming, "Where's my daughter?" I ran out and told him I was okay and that he needed to go to the hospital. I sent him there with no shoes, no jacket, no wallet. That way he couldn't take off from the hospital and do it all again.

He came home in a cab, and I paid for it and then hid his wallet. He was exhausted. We just grabbed some couch cushions and made a little bed on the floor. Even though that night caused me so much fear, that night was also one of the best nights of my life. We sat for hours, and he told me all these stories about when he was in the Little League World Series and hit the home run that won the game. We talked and talked and we finally fell asleep. The next day, I woke up to a hard knock on the door. I got up to open the door, but my dad grabbed my foot and said, "This is your decision now."

I didn't know what he meant until I opened the door to see two social workers. They asked to talk to me, and I said no and slammed the door.

A few days later, I was told to go to my grandparents for Christmas, which we did every year. Our family tradition is to all sleep over at Grandpa's and wake up together Christmas morning. I didn't want to go. I didn't want to leave my dad, but I had no choice.

On December 19, 1993, my mom came to get me. My sisters and I were going to the mainland with my grandpa a few days earlier than she was. My sisters and I hugged my dad and cried, and he cried. It was hard to leave, but we did and a few days later my mom came for Christmas and I noticed she had been crying. She hugged us and then brought us all into my grandparents' room and sat us down and told us that there had been an accident and that my dad was dead. My heart broke.

NOTES

[1] In my last piece, for *Arresting Hope*, I didn't really scratch the surface, so I wanted to provide an accurate description so that if one day anyone needed help, they could come to me knowing that I was once there too.

Stigma

PAM YOUNG

I GREW UP IN A SMALL CITY on the east coast, and every time someone went to court, it would be in the newspaper the next day. I ran into someone from my old neighbourhood growing up and I went to say hi. He said, "Hey, how's it going?" but before I had a chance to respond, his mother came along and gave me the dirtiest look. Then she grabbed his arm and marched him off. He looked confused because maybe he didn't read *The Daily Gleaner*, the paper in my hometown, but I heard his mom say to him, "She's a jailbird." I felt hurt. It made me wish I could move away where everyone didn't know my business. I began thinking about my family who had to read about my charges in the paper, and I wondered if people treated them differently too. I wanted to leave my home town so my family wouldn't have to be affected by my poor choices. And when I made it to the big city, I never told anyone.

Stuff Happens

LYNN FELS

I'M IN A QUEUE FOR X-RAYS, waiting for the nurse to call my name. A young woman, escorted by a police officer, enters the room. She is bruised, and she has a cut on her lip.

"Sit here until they call you," he says to her. She slumps in a chair, a clear plastic garbage bag dropped at her feet, crumpled clothing crammed inside. *Just out of jail and already in trouble.* She's been recently released, probably from ACCW, where we are doing research with incarcerated women. Dropped off at the bus stop with a bus ticket and a plastic garbage bag filled with her belongings. That's how the women are released at the end of their jail sentence, those who have no one to shepherd them home. They catch the bus into the city, the plastic bag signalling where they have come from, and pretty much advertising where they are going. No one picks them up. They're on their own. And stuff happens.

I watch her as she exchanges words with the officer, words barely audible over the noise of the waiting room. I watch her, wondering if I should say hello. I'm not sure how to start a conversation with the officer standing by and her bruised eyes focused on the floor. *What is she thinking? How did she get into trouble so quickly? Who gave her those bruises? Does she have somewhere to go? Should I get involved?* I check my watch and say nothing.

Solitary
My Spiritual Retreat

COLBY

ON MARCH 15, 2015, I WAS FOUND GUILTY of an institution charge and sentenced to solitary confinement. After spending forty-three life-altering days locked up in segregation cell 18 at Alouette Correctional Centre for Women, I now know how strongly our brains affect our reality. I took a place perceived by society as the darkest, dreariest place in prison, as well as one of the saddest, loneliest places on earth, and turned it into a spiritual retreat.

Built to house the worst of the worst, segregation is a major deterrent used to keep inmates from misbehaving. Most people cringe at the thought of having to spend even one hour locked in an eight-foot by eight-foot cell alone with their thoughts. You are forced to either confront yourself head on or curl up and hide, terrified of what you might discover. The soul-searching I took part in throughout these days gave me the opportunity to meet Me. Not the facade I had created but the true Me I was intended to be. Through prayer and meditation, I no longer felt lonely, and yet I was all alone.

The days flew by. Then about thirty days into my sentence, something happened within me. It was as if the dark cloud I could not get out from underneath started to separate, allowing some light to shine through. I grasped onto that bit of light, and like a tree that wakes up when you touch it, I began to flourish, every day a new blossom. I began to journal and discovered I had a passion for writing. I began to see things from a new perspective, and for about a week, I woke up religiously at four in the morning feeling rejuvenated and ready to start my day. I began to meditate and pray every morning. I enjoyed the sound of the birds chirping at the first sight of light in the morning. I began to wonder if I was going insane, but truthfully I did not care. If this was the feeling you encounter when you go insane, sign me up because I had never felt so good in my life. In all my years of coming in and out of jail, I felt less locked up than I had ever felt before. I began to reach out to people. I began to work closely with the mental health team, the psychologist, and the drug and alcohol counsellor, and I explored my spirituality.

I will be released from jail tomorrow. I am leaving this place with a purpose. My purpose is to tell my story to other women struggling with addictions and to pass on my newfound knowledge of the importance of finding life's purpose. I am excited to move on in my journey of recovery and no longer fear the unknown. I cannot wait to watch it all unfold.

Amber's Story
"My Heart Broke"

AMBER CHRISTIE

I STAYED WITH MY DAD'S FAMILY during the funeral, and then I went to my grandparents' house. Not long after my dad died, my mom also started using drugs. She had never touched drugs in her life. My mom took off sometimes for days and would come back all messed up. Eventually, I had to call my aunt and uncle on my mom's side to come help us because my mom had been gone so long that our hydro and our water went out. They came and took my sisters over to the mainland. There was no way that I was leaving my mother. I learned from the last time with my dad, and I didn't care what I had to do. I was not going to let her die too. Her drug habit got worse and worse, but she kept me with her, so at least I knew that she was okay. Then one night I was going to bed and she was high and brought some flowers into my room and kissed my head and said she loved me and shut the door. When I woke in the morning, she was just gone. I waited for a few days and then ran out of food. I went to my aunt's house. She started doing drugs as well, and one day I wanted to know what this drug that had ripped my life apart was all about.

That day she stuck a needle in my arm.

I was a slave immediately.

I was willing and ready to do anything to get that next fix.

I went back and forth from her house.

I met a girl who helped take me out of my depression for a while.

I started drinking and I slowed down on the drugs.

When I was fifteen, I met a guy who was twenty-one. I had lost my dad, and here was a man willing to take care of me. He showed up at my aunt's house and walked in, picked me up, and carried me out of the house. He put me in his car and put a cigarette out on her face, saying she was evil and would have to deal with that one day. He had pawned his TV to get some rent to bring me to this new apartment to help me detox. I was in love, or so I thought. I thought I had found my soulmate. Slowly things started to deteriorate. I was his possession. I went back into foster care. I would go back and forth from foster care to living with him. Then I got sick of being in care, so I went to the mainland with this man and moved into my aunt and uncle's house where my sisters were living. My uncle made it clear to my new boyfriend that he was too old for me. I woke up one day and he was gone.

I then went back and forth between the mainland and Victoria, between foster homes and family. I was doing drugs almost daily.

A family friend invited me to go to a Christian retreat. I decided why not. I went and I had a good time, so I stayed in Alberta for a week. One night, I was drinking at the bar and I went home with some guy who said he had coke. When we got to his house he threw me in the basement with a bunch of other girls who had been there for a few days. The guy pulled out a gun, and I was trapped in his basement. I was caught in a human trafficking ring! The difference between me and the other girls was that I had had many fights in my last four years, and I was not going to go down without a fight.

After a few hours in the basement I said I had to use the washroom, which was upstairs. Some guy with a gun grabbed my arm and pulled me upstairs and said not to try anything. The second he said that I kicked him in the balls and opened the door and just ran. I ran until I couldn't run anymore. I saw a house and started banging on the door and thankfully they opened it and called the police. I took them back to the house to show them, and they went and got all of the girls out. Ten men were arrested. It was about eleven in the morning. I called my friend to come get me from the police station. He came and brought me back to his house until my family friend could get back to Alberta to get me.

I went back to BC and went back and forth between foster care and my boyfriend and Victoria for about a year.

Born with a Conscience

COLBY

Born with a conscience, I knew right from wrong
One sip out of the bottle and I was gone
Don't worry! I'm fine, got this under control
Everything in moderation is what I've been told
Although this may be true for some
Others are doomed after the first one
Blessed with the powerful disease of addiction
With feelings of guilt, shame, and denial
Only humility and faith can put into remission
My life defeated, took a downward spiral
I put down the bottle, picked up crystal meth
Been to jail, institutions, next step death
With this harsh reality, there's no happiness in sight
My prayers become pleas to replace darkness with light
For years I lived in fear of the unknown
Now I live in wonder as I watch it unfold
I left behind a life of habitual hate
I entered an eternity of infinite grace
Immense goodness I intend to maintain
After deliverance from a state of hopeless pain
The adrenaline we feel on the whoosh of arrival
Kick starts our instinct to win at survival

First Year

MO KORCHINSKI

THE FIRST YEAR AFTER BEING RELEASED from prison was the hardest time in my life. I had to make so many changes to break free of the life I had known for so many years. The biggest change was with my thinking. I had to change all my old beliefs about myself and about mainstream society. I never believed that I was good enough or that I deserved to have a good life.

I had to learn to live with the guilt and shame that came with all the stupid stuff I did in my addiction. I turned my back on my young children to get high. What kind of mother chooses drugs over her children? I knew in my heart that they were better off without me in their lives. Raising children when I was not emotionally present or able to care for them did harm too.

The power of addiction is so strong that a good person can make so many wrong choices. The power that the drugs had over me was crazy. I became a person that I was ashamed of, but I also knew that, without the drugs, I was not that person

Step by Step

MO KORCHINSKI

I SLOWLY START TO FEEL THAT I CAN do the treatment and that life can get better. Working the twelve steps of AA, I feel a bit more at peace with who I am. I still struggle with major anxiety when leaving the house, so I avoid doing it. I am uncertain where I am going after treatment. The treatment centre has a second stage house for women to go when they finish the program, but the house is full with a wait list.

I start Job Club, where we work on our resumes and interview skills so we can be work-ready after treatment. I feel like a fraud. Who am I kidding? I screwed up my life for so long, I have never held on to a job for long, and I haven't worked in over ten years. I feel discouraged and in a dark place. One of the staff at Job Club pulls me aside and tells me that he was in prison for years and that he can help me make a resume with the skills that I learned on the street. It gives me a little hope that he has a job even though he had been in prison.

At the treatment centre, they have a huge yard with lots of gardens, which reminds me of my time at ACCW. I used to spend twelve hours a day doing horticulture, and I loved being able to keep busy. While keeping busy I could look outward, not at myself.

I spend many hours cleaning up the gardens and hiding away from everyone. I am always the first person to volunteer my time to do extra jobs around the treatment centre so I don't have to look at myself. I don't think I will ever be able to look at myself in the mirror and like what I see.

I have to start Step 4, which is about writing about all the people I resent and looking at my part in the resentments. My biggest resentment is towards my mom. How can a mother not feel a loving bond with her child? How can I forgive her for a life full of pain? I can never ask her, since she has been gone for many years. I feel like my relationship with my mom is unfinished.

She asked for my forgiveness when she was dying from cancer. Even though I couldn't forgive her for the years of abuse and the hurtful things she said to me, I still tried to be the best daughter by dropping everything I was doing in my life to come to her bedside. I left my children with their fathers and went to be with her. I never felt like I belonged, or that I should even be by her side, as no one else in my family would talk to me. I guess I resented her even after she died because the night she died I picked up the crack pipe and smoked crack cocaine for the first time.

The day she died, I found out that I had lost custody of my children. I fell in love with how the crack made me feel—all warm and fuzzy. Like I didn't have a worry in the world and all my pain was gone. But it wasn't long before it started to control my life and I just left everything behind, including my children.

I go to the office with my write-up for Step 4, and one of the staff reads about mom's resentment and tells me that I had no part in that resentment. I look at her and say that I had a huge part in that resentment. I allowed my mom's abuse to live on for twenty-eight years after she hit me for the last time. I let it relive in me every day. It controls me and affects every part of my being. That afternoon, we go to group and the assignment is to write our own obituary. I thought I didn't have to write one because no one would care if I died. There would be no write-up in any paper when I died, but I still have to write one. That is a big reality check for me. I have no one in my life who cares about me or loves me. Since I have screwed up every relationship because I don't love myself enough, how can I love another person? I don't think I have ever known what love is, but I am slowly going to try and learn how to love me for me.

The treatment centre calls me into the office and says that because I spend so much of my time working on getting over being in prison for so many years that I am not working on my addiction problems. I'm a little confused as I have not used any drugs in a year and have no urges to use. What I need to work on is being able to function in the real world. If I can't get over the anxiety of being away from the house, then I am not going to change my life for the better.

I do find out that I get to move into the second-stage house, so my life is slowly falling into place. I get to move next week. I'm a little scared to move away from the treatment centre as it has been my safe place. The only other time I felt safe was at ACCW. But I do have a newfound hope that I am going to make it.

I move to the second-stage housing and start being a house mom back at the treatment centre, where I get to work watching the clients at night when there is no staff working. I am paid twenty-five dollars a night, and that feels like a lot of money.

Prison Aboriginal Day

COLBY

ON A BEAUTIFUL SPRING DAY, I sat in the shade beneath a big oak tree listening to the native Elder talk about the Aboriginal program he ran at ACCW. I couldn't help but notice the number of dragonflies and hummingbirds that had joined us to celebrate Aboriginal Day. The smell of fresh bannock and smoked salmon wafted by every so often, catching my stomach's attention. He announced that he was looking for a volunteer to share how the sweat lodge had affected her stay in jail. I knew I should stand up, but my legs wouldn't move. I felt paralyzed. But after the third plea for someone to volunteer, something inside me shifted. "I'll share." I couldn't believe I had done that, and as I walked past the 150 spectators, most of whom were my peers, I felt my face get hot. I felt like running back to my seat, but something kept pushing me forward. As I grabbed the microphone and the Elder passed me his medicine bag to help me through the process, I instantly burst into tears. Through my tears, I managed to explain how the sweat I took part in only three months earlier had changed my life. After I finished, everyone cheered and applauded. I felt empowered. Not only had I faced my fear of public speaking, but I had also fought the social anxiety I've lived with my whole life, and I won.

Right or Left

MO KORCHINSKI

Which path shall I follow?
What route should I take?
Should I go left or should I go right?
Will I fall back into the dark bliss?
Make the same mistakes or try something new?
Move far away and start over again?
All I really know is the life of crime.
I know too much about the game.
The lifestyle. The people.
It's all about money and drugs.
For me it has to change.
So what do I do?
I've made big mistakes for many years.
It's either this way or that way.
I'm going to change and try something new.
The unknown has to be better than the past.
I have been lost for many years.
I guess I am going to change.
Follow the right path.
And hope it leads to happiness.

What are you feeling most hopeful about?[1]

I Am Hopeful About

everything:

changing
being free
being happy
finding a job
being a mom
losing weight
going to college
doing things right
getting on my feet
getting healthy again
beginning a new life
getting my life on track
having a life without drugs
learning more about spirituality
working things out with my family
moving forward with my life
putting my record behind me
regaining my husband's trust
keeping my shit together
maintaining a steady life
staying out of jail
living a good life
taking care of me
supporting peers
taking initiative

being content
staying clean

everything:

NOTES

[1]Found poems were created from responses, provided by women who were recently released from prison, to the survey question of the title. Each chapter of *Releasing Hope* ends with a found poem.

II: Women in2 Healing

We are not going to arrest our way out of these issues.
—Mo Korchinski

I never thought I would ever be working alongside a doctor, nor have my words be of account for anything!
—Lora "Koala" Kwandibens

Doctor's Journey

RUTH ELWOOD MARTIN

TODAY, KELLY SHOWED UP AT UBC.
Several women in prison have previously said to me, "When I get released from here, I want to do research work with you." But then I don't hear from them. The logistics never work out for them. Getting (re)settled in the outside world is so complex, and, with reason, there is not much time left over in their day to "do research."

So, when Kelly phoned me at my UBC office and said, "I got out last week and I'm living in Vancouver and I'm coming to UBC," I didn't really believe it. When she arrived today, I was thrilled for her—that she had been able to follow through with her decision; that it was important enough for her to be able to come.

Kelly was clearly somewhat anxious and uncomfortable, but she also appeared quite elated about having made it this far. And, for myself, now that Kelly has arrived at UBC, I am wondering, what will I do with her? I'm not really set up at the university to handle women recently released from prison who arrive wanting to do research.

I'm not sure where this will take me.

—Journal entry

Participatory health research (PHR) engages the "subjects" of the research as equal partners in all aspects of the research process, including generating the research questions, deciding the research design, collecting the data, conducting the data analysis, and interpreting and disseminating the research findings (ICPHR).

In *Arresting Hope*, we describe the first prison participatory health research forum in October 2005, a day-long event in which incarcerated women came to the microphone, as if using a talking stick, to share their ideas for the research. Incarcerated women, who are normally silenced, came up to the microphone to give voice to their hopes and passions for change, their wish to help with improving health for their families and for each other. During that forum, five values emerged as important underpinnings of all future PHR activities: transparency; breaking the code of silence; respect for diversity; building on strengths; and access for all who wish to be involved.

Arresting Hope tells some of the stories of the prison PHR. Incarcerated women in prison considered this work meaningful, and they convinced the warden that health research work should become a prison work placement position. During the following two years, as more than two hundred incarcerated and formerly incarcerated women engaged in participatory health research and as they followed their research passions, they compiled life stories, paragraphs of passion, surveys, focus group transcripts, art, and letters. We also shared the story of this work in medical journals, in media interviews, at conference presentations, and in film.[1]

When the prison PHR project was shut down and the warden retired, Kelly arrived at the University of British Columbia and initiated a network of formerly incarcerated women, ACCW alumni, who wanted to continue the prison PHR work outside the prison gates. Then, the ACCW alumni PHR project was offered an office at BC Women's Hospital.

As women were released from ACCW, their unanswered PHR questions moved with them. Women from prison brought to the outside their passion for asking questions and for developing initiatives to improve the health of incarcerated women, their children, and their families. Renamed as Women in2 Healing, we became a network of formerly incarcerated women, academics, and volunteers, who upheld the values of collaboration, reciprocity, respect, transparency. We focused on strengths and were committed to furthering the achievement of nine health goals in order to improve spiritual, physical, emotional, and mental health for incarcerated women and their families.

When we started Women in2 Healing, we were excited and hopeful, but unsure about where the work would take us. We had differing visions and priorities. Lots of ideas emerged from those early days, some of which morphed into projects that endure to this day. Women's PHR became action advocacy initiatives. Throughout this chapter and the ones that follow, we describe how our PHR project moved from inside the prison walls to the outside, released beyond the gates.

NOTES

[1] For more details, see Appendices.

REFERENCES

International Collaboration for Participatory Health Research (ICPHR). *Position Paper 1: What Is Participatory Health Research?* Berlin: International Collaboration for Participatory Health Research, 2013.
Martin Ruth Elwood, Mo Korchinski, Lynn Fels and Carl Leggo, eds. *Arresting Hope: Women Taking Action in Prison Health Inside Out.* Toronto: Inanna Publications, 2014.

Early Meeting of Women in2 Healing

MO KORCHINSKI

I HAVE A FRIEND FROM PRISON named Kelly. She contacts me about a group that is starting up called Women in2 Healing. Dr. Ruth Elwood Martin is the doctor at Alouette Correctional Centre for Women (ACCW). She started participatory health research inside ACCW. Women got to research issues and experiences they were passionate about. Now Dr. Martin wants to pursue research on the other side of the prison walls. Women in2 Healing is a group of women from ACCW who I served time with. I am excited to see everyone but also scared to leave the safe haven of the treatment centre. I have just changed one safe place for another, and I'm not sure I am ready to expand out of my safe place. A friend is going to pick me up the next day to drive to Abbotsford for the meeting. I come up with every excuse not to go, but I know I have to push myself to join people more. I walk into the room, and it feels like I walked into my own home. All the people that I have seen for years as my family are sitting around laughing and having fun.

As the meeting begins, another friend, Christine, walks into the room. We spent almost two years at ACCW working in horticulture together. When Christine showed up at ACCW, she was as straight as they come. At first everyone thought she was an undercover cop, hired to discover some big dark secret behind the walls of ACCW. Christine was the first white collar criminal I ever met while serving time, but it wasn't long before she got caught up in jail-house life. Christine wasn't a drug addict; she wasn't a typical criminal like the rest of us at ACCW who did crime to support a drug habit. Christine was in jail for identity fraud.

I look over at her as she sits at the table with all of us; I can tell she is using drugs. She hides it well, but I know her so well that I can see she is not herself. I pull her aside and ask her, "What the heck are you doing? You watched so many women who wrecked their lives, their health, and relationships for drugs, and you come out of prison and start using.

How many women do we know who are dead because of drugs? What can I do to help you?" When I look up, I see tears in her eyes.

She tells me, "It was so much harder getting out than I thought it would be. I thought it would be a piece of cake to just pick up my life once I got out."

I ask her if it is okay to tell Dr. Martin. When she says yes, I hug her. "I want to be whole again," she says.

As I walk towards Dr. Martin, Christine adds, "I sure needed to run into you today. This is a wake-up call."

Over the next few months we meet every two weeks to support each other. A few of the women start to transcribe the data from the ACCW research team, and others write letters to women still inside the prison to offer their support. We get a small grant from the Vancouver Foundation to put together a newsletter that we can mail to the women inside.

Introducing the Newsletters
Excerpt, Women in2 Healing Newsletter, Issue 1

THIS IS THE FIRST ISSUE of our newsletter, so we beg of you to be patient with us.

This is a newsletter to connect women inside prison and those who have left (and anyone else who might be interested), so we need you to submit articles, poetry, art, jokes, jail-house recipes, and anything else that you might think to put in here.

This way, it becomes everyone's newsletter, not just something put out for no apparent reason (We all have too much going on around us that happens for no apparent reason).

And, just to be clear: We will not publish anything demeaning to anyone.

Where We Are At Now
Excerpt, Women in2 Healing Newsletter, Issue 1

WE HAVE SINCE MOVED out of the gates of ACCW (the gates just couldn't contain us anymore) and are now operating from an office at BC Women's Hospital on Friday mornings, from the M2/W2–Restorative Christian Ministries offices in Abbotsford, and daily in Maple Ridge, which is connected with Alouette Addictions on Lougheed Highway. And many of us work part-time from our homes.

We have been very busy getting into more of an "action phase," trying to improve our own lives, the lives of women who have left prison, and the lives of women who will be leaving prison. We have collaborated with academics to create this vision statement for our project: "The empowerment of women inside and outside of prison in their emotional, physical, mental, and spiritual healing through participatory research processes."

Here is a very incomplete (we are doing so much, I find it impossible to say it all) list of what we are doing now as we work towards our vision:

- We have changed our name from ACCW Alumni to Women in2 Healing.
- Four women who have been in prison have been hired as "peer researchers" on a part-time basis.
- We are continuing to lend our expertise to academics and service providers to collectively find feasible solutions to the problems faced by women inside prisons, as well as by those women who have left "the system."
- We are using the pre-existing informal network of ex-inmates to gather resource information from across the province, and to share hope with one another.
- We are creating a website containing all of these resources and a blog where we share ideas.

- We have created flyers containing housing resources for women leaving prisons.
- We are regularly interacting on a Facebook group exclusively for female ex-prisoners.
- We are operating a recreation program on Fridays at a rec. centre in Abbotsford for women who have left prison (and any other women who want to hang out with us).
- We are holding weekly web-based meetings for women who have left prison, service providers, and academics.
- We are speaking at public education events sharing who we are and what we do.
- We have obtained significant CIHR (Canadian Institute for Health Research) funding for a special project called Doing Time to interview women three times during the first twelve months following their release from prison. We are asking what helps and hinders them in attaining the nine health goals mentioned earlier. We will use the interview data to help develop an action health strategy with government policy makers, community agencies, and health authorities to improve health.
- We are now producing this newsletter trying to engage women from both sides of the fence.

Value of Women in2 Healing

RUTH ELWOOD MARTIN

DURING A PARTICIPATORY HEALTH RESEARCH meeting at Nicola Valley Institute of Technology, we embarked on a discussion of the five values that were generated during the first research forum inside ACCW in October 2005.

What do these values—transparency; breaking the code of silence; respect for diversity; building on strengths; welcoming all who wish to be involved—really mean when you dig down into them, when you are working in the real on-the-ground messy task of doing PHR in the community?

For example, when we received some PHR funding, some formerly incarcerated women were employed by University of British Columbia as part-time community-based research assistants and a salaried faculty member was the principal investigator. Other women who were recently released from prison were invited to join the project as volunteer participants. At this point, the dynamic became messy—how do we continue to espouse "all who wish to be involved" and "transparency of all information"?

Amber offered to write an annotated explanation of the five values of the PHR of Women in2 Healing.

Annotated Values

AMBER CHRISTIE

TRANSPARENCY OF ALL INFORMATION

We strive to practise a transparent process, which involves equality for all participants; a non-adversarial, supportive, nonjudgmental atmosphere; consensus-based decision-making; and collaboration on research findings.

BREAKING THE CODE OF SILENCE

To me this means no longer living in the mind frame of isolation. Today we choose to be heard and no longer be silent. We lived for much too long in the silence of addiction, and old behaviours kept us sick. Today we are being heard and breaking the code of silence.

RESPECT FOR DIVERSITY: LISTEN AND BE HEARD

Today we have come together as a group from all nations and life experiences to support each other through good and bad. Respecting each other's thoughts and goals is part of our day-to-day. We listen to what the other is saying and collaborate on ALL of our ideas to make sure that OUR voices are heard.

BUILD ON STRENGTHS

All of us have spent way too much time focusing on the negativity in our lives. Today we choose to focus on the positive, which keeps us where we are. We share it with each other. We all mentor one another and lend an ear, a hand, or an email "lol."

ALL WHO WISH TO BE INVOLVED IN THE RESEARCH PROCESS MAY BE INVOLVED

Women in2 Healing was formed inside the walls of ACCW. We are a group of women who encourage all incarcerated women to better each other's health and wellness and join us in our journey. We also encourage you to participate in the research process. We all have learned so much from each other and look forward to continuing to be creative and to heal together.

My Passion
Excerpt, Women in2 Healing Newsletter, Issue 6

LORA "KOALA" KWANDIBENS

WHY I JOINED WOMEN IN2 HEALING: For one thing, I never thought I would ever be working alongside a doctor, nor have my words be of account for anything! Considering my lifestyle, I was destined for hell ... sort of. The work I'm involved in now helps me make changes for "inside coming out." I look forward to this so much. I've seen the cruel side of prison, not just the cruelty of the inmates, but also the cruelty of the people who run their prison—right or wrong. Having been victimized all over again by the system that is supposed to protect people from being victimized, I want to help the persons who are committing these crimes.

Dialogue

RUTH ELWOOD MARTIN

WE'VE BEEN GATHERING TOGETHER for monthly meetings at Nicola Valley Institute of Technology, and today I suggested that we do an activity. I thought we could all write on post-it notes some activities that we have been doing over the past year for Women in2 Healing; then, in turn, come up to a whiteboard, on which we would draw a bubble diagram of the nine health goals, and stick our post-it notes on the most applicable health goal; then, share with the group about our experiences of participating in Women in2 Healing.

As I listened to each woman share, I felt immense awe that they are so passionate and enthusiastic about the work that they were now engaged in. As a health researcher, I recognize that this is significant and innovative work, but the fact that women themselves, who had previously been incarcerated, today recognize that what they are doing is meaningful, and will make a difference, and will effect change, was profoundly impactful for me.

We video-recorded the meeting and transcribed our words verbatim. I wrote the annual progress report for our funder, Vancouver Foundation, based on today's dialogue.

Dialogue

MO KORCHINKI'S REPORT

"I HAVE BEEN DOING RESEARCH on our mother-baby program, research on housing, finding a mother-baby house. I've been visiting women in prison—I go every second week and visit inmates in there."

Someone asks, "Why do they let you in there?"

Mo responds, "That's a really good question! It's really surprising, the response I get when I do go in—officers and inmates, really supportive. They say, 'Keep going.'

I've been doing media interviews for newspapers, and I'm working on my education, taking a research course here at Nicola Valley Institute of Technology. I've been writing my story for the orientation package and for the Women in2 Healing newsletter. I've been writing letters to women in jail. I've spent many hours painting, so we can auction off the paintings and raise funds for the education bursary."

Dialogue

LORA "KOALA" KWANDIBENS'S REPORT

"THERE IS SO MUCH ABOUT THIS INITIATIVE that I love. I love people, bringing people into this project. I love talking to a lot of people—funders, other organizations—I love doing that! I also love attending meetings. I love writing out my orientation package introduction. And speaking at the prison health conference. I like coming to the 'in-house' meetings because I can plan in advance and bring ideas to the table. These meetings are where we get to educate ourselves and talk about health. I love learning computer skills and adding stuff on the internet—I had never done it before and it's a lot of fun. Also, the public speaking, especially speaking to organizations. I spoke to a lot of organizations in Mission: Fraser Health, the police community, the friendship centre, the resource centre, and Triangle. I spoke to a lot of people, and they're interested in the project. They want to know more—they want to have an info fair, and they want to learn what Women in2 Healing is about. They know it benefits women with incarceration experience, and they want to know what they can do to be a part of it, and to help out.

"I think that is what a community is about. It's about sharing and coming together and bringing resources to one area and having a big talk about what to do for women in the community. Community support is so important for women who are high risk and violent, who aren't allowed to access the services in Mission. I do peer support—I go talk to them. Then I go to the organizations who don't want the women around, and I say, 'Why don't you want that woman around? She's still a woman.' I took that media training program. The Women in2 Healing project is having its own group January 8 in Mission. We will be trying to bring the local women who were in prison together into one room, so we can discuss our experiences. Our goal is to find out what we can do to access the services that are available in Mission. It's just a start. It will be helpful to introduce these women to other women in the community who are doing well, so we can all share our ideas. We'll say, 'Wednesdays we go here, and there's a car that passes through here on these days to give you a ride.' The friendship centre will be a safe place to hold these meetings. Some places won't welcome high risk women, but the friendship centre will—as long as you are clean for that day, they don't care if you were using yesterday. Our goal is to find out where these women are at, and to find out how Women in2 Healing can make Mission a stronger and healthier place for you.

"I am looking forward to going into the youth custody centre—I'm going to give them all my secret tips! (no just joking...). I want to be supportive and to talk to them at their level. I want to talk to them about FASD and the effects of drugs and alcohol on youth. If you're going to have a baby, wait until you're older. I think I can do that, talk with them at their level. I'm not just a book worm—I can be a good sister. I know some of the girls call me sister on the street in Mission. One girl that I hang out with sometimes is a DJ. She's twenty-one and she can't access some of the programs in Mission. She's drug addicted and she's on the street. She's twenty-one and she's already seen three murders. There's something wrong with Mission—why isn't it working?"

Dialogue

AMBER CHRISTIE'S REPORT

"I'VE BEEN PUTTERING AWAY OUT IN MISSION. I presented at a crystal meth awareness conference in Mission and Chilliwack. I've written submissions to the Women in2 Healing newsletter. I did an interview with *Vancouver Sun*. I've been helping other women just released, a few of whom are pregnant, find housing and get stability in their lives. I've run two NA (Narcotics Anonymous) meetings in Mission at the Union Gospel Mission building—I open the doors, make the coffee, put the chairs away. I've attended our Women in2 Healing WebEx meetings. I showed up and mingled at a W2 Meeting. I presented at a mother-baby conference at UBC. I gave birth to a healthy baby boy! I gave a presentation on the Seabird Reserve about drug addiction and grandparents' parenting."

Dialogue

KELLY MURPHY'S REPORT

"I'VE PRESENTED AT CONFERENCES: at the Women's Health Research Institute, at the Department of Family Practice, and with Dave Adams at Douglas College. We took a media advocacy workshop. I attended an urban health conference as a representative of Women in2 Healing. I did a media interview about the mother and baby unit; the interview will go on the media webpages and we can download it. I have a relationship with my daughter now. I also work on my own health and wellness therapy, so I can be in this group. We wrote a letter to the government with Dr. Amy Salmon, advocating for the prison mother-child units. I took part in the Galiano retreats. I participate in the weekly WebEx Women in2 Healing meetings."

Post Incarceration Syndrome

MO KORCHINSKI

I AM NOT SURE IF I CAN CONTINUE this journey of recovery. The anxiety is out of control. I have panic attacks unless I am at Hannah House, the treatment centre, or in my bedroom with the door shut. I feel like I am locked in a third-rate horror movie with no ending in sight. This is no way to live. No one understands what I am going through. People are like, "Just get over it," or, "It's not that bad." They ask me, "Would you rather be back in jail?" In all honesty, yes, I would rather live my life behind the tall chain-link fence watching the sharp razor wires looming high up, keeping all the nightmares away. I feel like I am going crazy. I am pissing people off because of the fear I am living with every time I have to leave the treatment centre. I am frozen with fear.

Leslie, one of the staff members at Hannah House, brings me into the office and says that she lives with anxiety too and that she learned to work through the fear and panic attacks and so could I. There is an addiction agency in town, Alouette Addictions, that has an anxiety and depression support group that she would like to take me to. At this point I'm willing to try anything to get over these panic attacks. I hate that something is still controlling me. All I want is to move forward in my life, but it seems like I keep going backwards. I have been stuck with something always controlling me—everything from childhood abuse, being raped, and then my addiction to escape all the pain that lives inside me. I just want to be the best me that I can be. Just me without having a noose around my neck pulling tighter, slowly ready to hang me any second.

She says that there is a group meeting at three o'clock at Alouette Addictions. She says that the meetings have helped her lots with dealing with her panic attacks. I say I am willing to do anything, that I want to be able to live my life without fear. I have lived too many years scared, and I can't keep going with this fear that controls me. As the time gets closer to three o'clock, I wonder why I agreed to go. I am having a hard time breathing, and I feel like I am having a heart attack.

Alouette Addictions is close to Hannah House, which is good since I don't have time to think too much about how I am again walking into unfamiliar territory. Leslie knocks on my door and smiles at me. She says to take a deep breath and that she will be with me the whole time. We drive into town. As I slowly walk up the stairs I feel a sudden surge of overwhelming anxiety and fear. My heart pounds and I can't breathe. My legs are shaking and my hands are sweating as I get to the top stairs.

A cute blonde woman behind the counter smiles at me and says, "Hello, can I help you?" Her smile helps to calm me a little, and Leslie says we are here for the anxiety and depression group. We sign our names, and then we go into a large group room with ten other women sitting in a circle. We sit down. The counsellor talks about taking small baby steps, like if you need to clean your room, pick up one item. If you have to make phone calls, look up the number and write it by the phone. Take slow and easy steps to help you towards your goal. She asks what steps each of us is going to focus on over the next week. I sit there and listen to everyone check in on how they are doing that week. Everyone knows each other and is very supportive.

I sit with my arms crossed over my chest willing myself not to have a heart attack. My heart is beating so fast and just keeps beating faster as the women talk around the table, the talk getting closer and closer to me. I want to run away. I didn't know I would have to talk to others in a group. I just thought we were going to check it out. Oh my God, I want to die, I can't breathe. I am holding my breath, and I can't get my brain to work to take in a mouth full of air. Leslie reaches over and touches my leg and smiles, and that helps me catch a breath of air. I slowly take another breath, and I'm not so light-headed anymore. The circle gets to Leslie and she says she is here just to listen. A huge relief comes over me as I hear myself say, "I am here just to listen, thanks."

After the group meeting ends we walk out and I hear someone call my name. I turn around and there is Julia. She used to work at the prison, and she was a great support and super easy to talk to. She walks up to me and gives me the biggest hug. "What are you doing here? I am so happy to see you." I tell her that I have been out of jail for four weeks and that I am having a hard time dealing with anxiety. She asks if I have a few minutes to talk in her office. Leslie says, "Go ahead. I will check my email on my phone." We go to Julia's office and she says, "Wow! I can't believe you are here." I tell her, "I am at Hannah House and having a really hard time functioning on this side of the gate. I really want to make this work. I am so sick of being in and out of jail. I want to live. I want a good life. But I am afraid that this feeling of not being able to go outside without having a panic attack will never stop. I feel like I am going crazy sometimes."

She says what I am going through is normal for someone who has spent lots of time in jail. She tells me about Post Incarceration Syndrome (PICS). PICS is present in many recently released prisoners, and is caused by being subjected to prolonged incarceration in environments of punishment with few opportunities for education, job training, or rehabilitation. She pulls an article about PICS up on her computer and starts to read a little.

PICS is most severe in people incarcerated for longer than one year. There are six stages to PICS. The first stage is marked by helplessness and hopelessness due to the inability to plan for community re-entry. Stage two is marked by intense and immobilizing fear. Stage three is marked by anger and rage with flashbacks similar to those that people with PTSD experience. Stage four is marked by a tendency towards impulsive violence upon minimal provocation. Stage five is an effort to avoid triggering violence by seeking isolation. The last stage is marked by the intensification of flashbacks, nightmares, sleep impairment, and impulse control problems caused by self-imposed isolation.

I am like, "Wow, that's me in a nutshell. So I am not going crazy."

Julia laughs and says, "I have worked with many women who have gone through what you have gone through, and, no, you are not going crazy." We set up a time for me to come back and see her one-on-one after the anxiety and depression group in two days.

I walk out of Alouette Addictions feeling hope for the first time since leaving ACCW, hope that I can beat this feeling of hopelessness and immobilizing fear. I continue to make small steps toward learning to live life with anxiety by telling myself that I am not going to die over and over when I am out and about. I have learned that these panic attacks are going to be a part of who I am, which really sucks as I can come up with many reasons why I can't leave the house. I am back in jail. Just this time there are no chain link fences keeping me locked— just my own fear.

For the first time since my release, I have hope. I am not crazy. Just knowing that what I am going through is common for someone who has spent a long time in prison is helpful. I walk out of her office feeling lighter on my feet and looking forward to the days ahead of me. I know I am going to be okay.

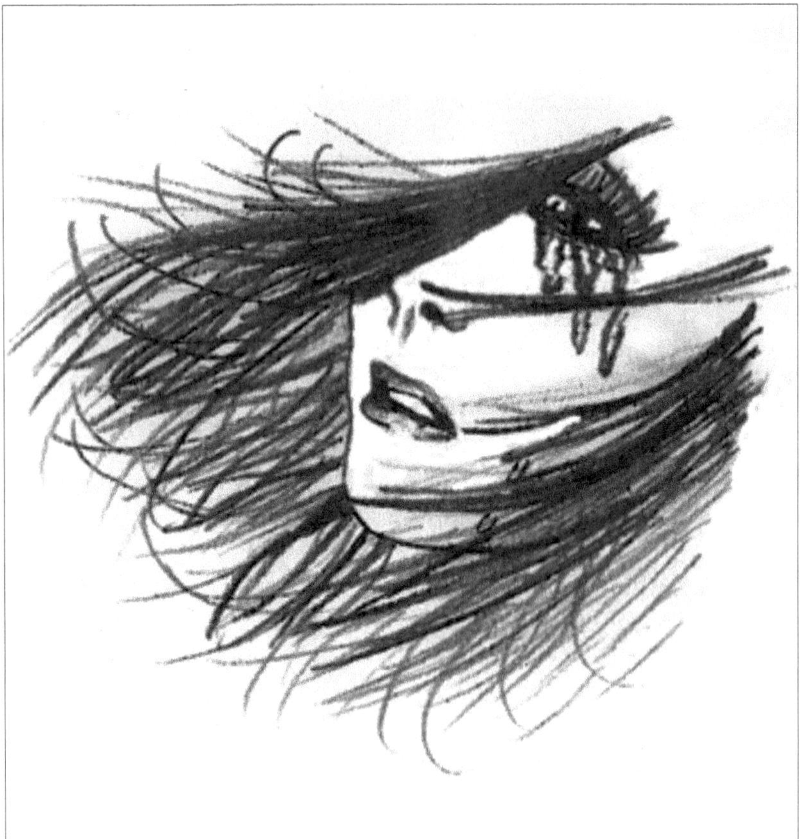

Great Intentions

PAM YOUNG

THE ENTIRE TIME I WAS IN JAIL, I had great intentions for when I got out. But about a week before my release date, I'd start to isolate myself and cut ties with people. All I could focus on were drugs—*how am I going to make some quick money to buy drugs?* But the last time I left jail on June 15, 2009, everything changed. I was picked up and driven to a recovery house. The woman who ran it was nice. She bought me smokes and a coffee. I arrived at the recovery house having the old feelings of doubt and insecurity, but when I saw that an old friend was running the recovery house, I wanted to be there. I started my first set of NA steps. Slowly, the old feelings dissipated.

Revolving Door

MO KORCHINSKI

I REMEMBER THE FEELING I WOULD GET two weeks before I was to be released. The dreams of using would start and all I could do was think about wanting drugs. It's weird since during the rest of my sentence, I wouldn't even think about using drugs. All of a sudden the thought would start to take over my mind. I dreamed about using drugs and I could almost taste the drugs on the end of my tongue.

The last time I was released I did not have those dreams or the thought to use. I was done.

I was sick of going in and out of jail and having to start all over again when I got out.

I realized that there had to be more to life than the revolving door of prison and addiction.

First Job

MO KORCHINKSI

I HAVE NO EXPERIENCE, but I am offered a part-time job. Cleaning toilets and floors a few nights a week helps me to keep pocket money for cigarettes and food, but the biggest pay-off is learning the true meaning of earning your way in life. After so many years of selling drugs and spending money like I was a millionaire, and then having nothing but a jail-house outfit, learning to ask for help is not easy.

Galiano Island

RUTH ELWOOD MARTIN

WE ARE FINDING IT INCREASINGLY DIFFICULT to meet face-to-face because of individual schedules, long commutes, and varying childcare needs. I begin to wonder if I should offer our family home on Galiano Island as an option for Women in2 Healing—a weekend away together—but I wrestle with this idea.

Even though our home is part of a community that provides retreat for others, I am uncertain how others in our Galiano community will respond if I invite a group of formerly incarcerated women to stay in our home. Even more, I wrestle within myself, questioning if this is the right thing for me to do. How would this impact my relationships and my "professional boundaries" with members of Women in2 Healing? Would a weekend in our home in Galiano nurture women's healing, or hinder it? How much additional work would I be getting myself into?

During the uncertainty of my Galiano decision, a family physician colleague offers to donate old office chairs. We could restore the wood, re-upholster them, and sell them to raise funds to support the work of Women in2 Healing and provide educational awards for women. I consult with mentors and colleagues—Viv, Lynn, Alison, Lara-Lisa. Where would we find enough space—physical and temporal—to do chair restoration work together? Our Galiano home seems like the right, and the inevitable, space for this work.

We come together on Galiano, with our children and partners, to restore old office chairs, to write and reflect about our participatory health research experiences, to brainstorm a storybook for children of incarcerated parents, and to just be together. We cook together, eat together, swim in the ocean, paddle in kayaks, watch movies, sing and drum, go for walks, watch the sheep. We discuss and argue and reminisce. We laugh and we weep together.

Catching the Ferry

MO KORCHINSKI

I'M SUPER EXCITED AS WE ALL LOAD ONTO THE FERRY to Galiano Island. Dr. Ruth Elwood Martin has a house on the island, and we are heading over to refinish a bunch of office chairs to resell as a fundraiser for our education bursary. My daughter and granddaughter are with me for the weekend, plus my two roommates Rose and Cat. I'm guessing there must be fifteen of us. Women have their spouses with them, their children, and Linnea and Alison are here too.

The ferry trip is only forty-five minutes, so I don't really get a chance to catch up with everyone. But man, is it great to see so many of us make this trip! The best thing that could have happened to me was finding Women in2 Healing. To have the support of all these great women who I get to call my friends is what helps me to keep moving forward. Not sure how we all are getting to Ruth's house, but when we walk off the ferry, Ruth is there with a couple of her friends to help get us all to the house. The house is on a fifty-acre farm where there are ten other houses.

At the house, Ruth says, "Find a room where you want to sleep. You can go upstairs or downstairs." My group goes upstairs, and we find a room with two single beds and two bunk beds. Then I look way up and there is a ladder built into the wall that takes you to a loft with more beds. So far, this room alone can sleep eight people, and there are two more rooms upstairs! It turns out the house can sleep twenty-five people!

We have time to unpack our stuff and head downstairs to have a snack and relax with a visit. Looking around the room and seeing everyone who is here, I can already predict that there is going to be conflict this weekend.

I worked all day today, and I am pretty tired. I decide I will take my granddaughter upstairs and lie down with her for a bit.

The next thing I know it's morning, the sun is shining, and I am looking out over a cliff to the ocean glittering from the sun reflecting in the morning breeze.

I go downstairs to put on the water to have a cup of tea and walk outside to have my morning smoke. It isn't long before everyone is up and about, kids are running around, and chairs are being brought outside onto the deck. The refinishing of the chairs begins.

It isn't long before people start to disappear from the back deck. Refurbishing chairs is a lot of work, and it stops being fun after we sand the first chair. I decide to grab my granddaughter and go for a walk to the beach.

I reflect on how quiet it is as I walk through the trees, looking around at the scenery. I reflect on how much my life has changed. To be at Dr. Martin's house is just crazy.

Other women, who are part of the farm community, come by the house to bring food for us and to help us with reupholstering the cushions and the backs of the chairs. This part of the work I enjoy, and have done before, so I find a place to work inside. The weekend goes pretty well. There are only a few disagreements, which is good with this group of headstrong women. Not saying this is something I would jump at doing again, but I would love just to come back to Galiano Island.

Galiano Retreat

LYNN FELS

I'M WATCHING A TODDLER toddling precariously up and down the stairs, my hands raised, prepared to catch her. It's the first time this child is navigating the ups and downs of stairs. Climbing up is easy; it's the turning around and coming down that has me anxious. First steps, tentative, bold, cautious, daring—a toddler's trust in descent, the turning, and doing it again, and again.

How do we learn to navigate stairs, when the journey throws us off balance? Will there be someone there to catch us if we fall?

On the patio, they are working on the chairs, some muttering under their breath, and others more vocal about the challenge of preparing the chairs for sale. Sanding and varnishing and upholstering requires time and patience. And it takes imagination to see these chairs in someone's home, a doctor's office, or, here, as I now realize, as I sit typing these words, in one of the cottages on the farm where the final pages of *Releasing Hope* are being edited.

Some of the chairs remain captive on the island.

Kindness

RUTH ELWOOD MARTIN

THE ANGEL WORD[1] I PULLED OUT of the basket on Galiano was kindness. I find it really difficult to watch when women aren't kind to each other. I remember Alison inside the prison giving out bracelets that read "doing kindness." They were black bands with white lettering, I think for World Kindness Day. I think the Christian phrases, "Love the Lord God," and then, "Love your neighbour as yourself," exemplify the attitude of kindness that I aspire to. Instilled into me as a child, "Love your neighbour as yourself." But it's hard. And when we watch women not being kind to each other, and hurting each other, how do I respond? Is it my role to respond?

NOTE

[1] Incarcerated women introduced "angel words" as part of the daily routine of their prison participatory health research team. Each person in turn randomly selected a card with an "angel word" on it from a closed bag and then shared with the group what their word meant to them that day. We often adopted the "angel words" tradition during Women in2 Healing meetings.

Galiano Writing

LYNN FELS

I'VE JUST ARRIVED AT THE FARM, for one of our writing retreats on Galiano. I head down the stairs and deposit my sleeping bag and suitcase in one of the various empty rooms in the basement. Upstairs, I hear laughter, as rooms and beds are claimed.

"Anyone for the top bunk?"
"I want the room closest to the bathroom."
"Too late, I've already got it!"

I am nervous. I am always nervous around those whose experience is so different than mine. What do I have to offer?
   Writing words on a page is a dangerous act.
   Reciprocity requires that I too be vulnerable.
   Silence holds untold stories.
   Releasing mine would be a relief, yet the page remains blank.

"Here, I'll write down your words, as you speak." I offer my assistance to Amanda. She is struggling to put words on paper. I sit next to her, fingers poised for action on my computer keyboard.
   She's a poet. Metaphors fill the page as she speaks about her life on the run.

Moments call me to attention....

> • Sharing angel words, pulled randomly from a box. Each word invites us to be present, to speak to what matters, to listen with our hearts.
> • The women's bantering, bold laughter, and teasing.... I wonder when we ever laugh in our faculty, restrained as we

are by academic competitiveness, the constant anxiety—*is this good enough? Am I good enough?*
- Holding hands, at the table, speaking of grace and kindness, and the sharing of good food and friendship in difficult times.

After writing all day, we sit in the dark together, watching Brad Pitt being washed downstream in an icy British Columbian river, juxtaposed with darkness outside, stars quilting the sky, knowing that somewhere a woman stands on at the edge of a highway, arm outstretched, thumbing a ride home.

I Wasn't Going to Be a Victim[1]

AMANDA STALLER

Searching for connection—running was my only companion.
After more than three years clean,
I competed in races,
earned a diploma
(Addictions Community Support Worker),
re-created my life.

But I was lonely.

Then something happened.

I found another woman named Amanda.
She was like my reflection;

she too had heartbreak and loss.

Our relationship was equal.
We started a journey on her couch,
                      where I cried, where I dug deep.

She too was finding her way, and I walked back
into the rooms where addicts come together to find a new way to live.

I cried lots of tears, went to meetings, and kept showing up for my life.

I felt like a badass.
I got a car.
I got a job.

It wasn't easy; no one told me it was easy.
It was the hardest thing I've done in my life.

I persevered.
I wasn't going to be a victim.

My son, Terence, is recovering too.
My first love, my son.
We re-connected in those rooms.

The journey continues.
I completed the twelve steps.

Now I walk into the federal prison with a message:
I have my freedom.
I use my freedom.
My recovery is to give back.... I made my mess into a message.

NOTES

[1] During our Galiano retreats, women would slip away to quiet corners to write about their lives, their concerns, what they wanted to share to be published in the book. Lynn and Amanda sat together for several hours. Amanda shared her story, while Lynn typed her words into a laptop.

Why Do I Do This?

RUTH ELWOOD MARTIN

LAST NIGHT WE SAT AROUND the dining room tables on Galiano and brainstormed memories of moving from corrections to the outside. There were lots of stories, compelling and sad. Many women were in tears as they remembered their many challenges. One woman asked me, "What do you think about when you hear the stories?" I wondered, "Why do I do this?" And I remembered Renee.

Renee was an active member of the prison participatory health research team. At that time, we held weekly research team meetings inside the prison. After women were released, I encouraged them to phone in to this weekly team meeting if they could. Renee said she would—she'd had such a difficult time leaving prison before, falling right back into addiction.

She phoned in to the weekly meeting. "I made it!" she told us. "I managed to rent a room in a basement of a house! I'm not on the street. I have a room. I have no furniture. I don't know what to do next. I don't know anyone here. There's a guy in the basement and he seems kind enough. I miss you guys. What do I do next? Where do I go?"

We were so thrilled to hear from Renee. And I knew there was still so much to do.

Happy Birthday
Excerpt, Women in2 Healing Newsletter, Issue 5

AMBER CHRISTIE

IT GIVES ME HOPE that we will continue to reach out to other women and help them help themselves. Our goal from the beginning has been to continually support each other. I feel that we are accomplishing that. And every time I go to a meeting, it's always great to see a fresh new smiling face and to hear a different perspective brought to the table; just having those new faces shows me that we are doing what we need to do. We had so much fun that day, spinning each other around and playing pin the tail on the donkey. It is so great to be able to share these milestones with each other.

The Power of Words

AMANDA STALLER

My boss is amazing!
She founded Talitha Koum, a recovery home for women dealing with addiction.
She loves to be in service to organizations and people who mean something to her.

She holds up the mirror to me.
I get to discover parts of myself I didn't know were there.

She is a hard worker, a high achiever;
she is smart and she uses words I adopt.

My language is transforming.

You see, I will always be a raw edge
and say it like it is!

It takes practice and skill to use the power of words.
My voice will be heard.

On the frontlines, on the street,
I will use the language that will reach women.
I hear them.

A lot of professionals don't know their language,
don't hear their cry.

There are a lot of languages.

Go hiking with them. Walk around the block. Listen to them.

Honesty…. I've found the language
with which I can talk to them,
with which I don't break their spirit.

Newsletters

RUTH ELWOOD MARTIN

MEMBERS OF WOMEN IN2 HEALING are creating newsletters in order to publish the writings of women who have encountered the correctional system in British Columbia. The newsletters are becoming an invaluable resource for women to share personal and community stories of success and strife, experiences in the correctional system, and information from other agencies and service providers. Through the newsletters, women can reach out to other women who have also experienced incarceration and social exclusion, thereby extending the support network of Women in2 Healing beyond their invitation-only Facebook group, emails, and texts. In the newsletters, women express themselves, demonstrating to readers that it is possible to break the cycles of addiction, crime, and incarceration.

The newsletters contain articles written by women who are still in the correctional setting as well as those who have been released; information from appropriate interested agencies, mainly regarding diseases and infections commonly associated with drug addiction; references to research reports and projects that were co-authored by co-investigators, research students, and women associated with Women in2 Healing; information from appropriate resources and support agencies within the community; and educational tips for healthy living, such as nutritional advice and tips for finding a family doctor.

Two hundred and fifty printed copies of each issue are produced and distributed to women inside and outside of prison, community organizations, and academic, government, and community stakeholders. The newsletters have also become an important means for community agencies and other collaborators to learn more about Women in2 Healing.

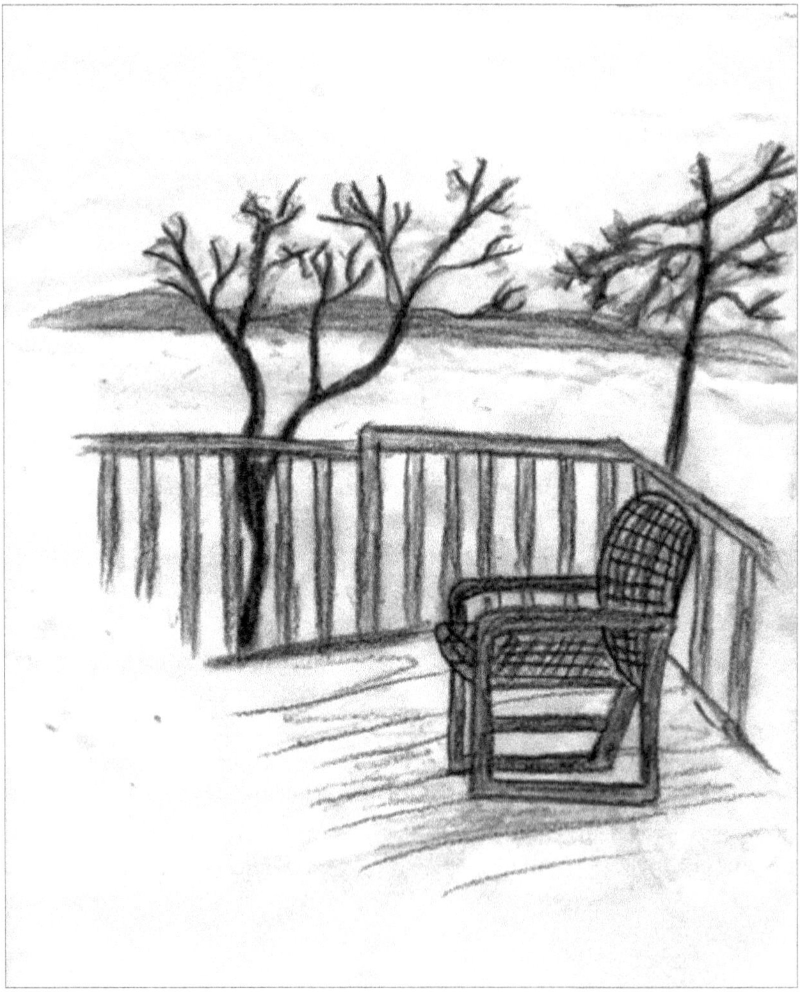

Chairs

RUTH ELWOOD MARTIN

WE SOLD NINE CHAIRS following a silent auction at the Inaugural Prison-Academic-Community Conference at UBC, in December of 2008. We sold eight more chairs to Nightshift Street Ministries in Surrey nine months later. We used the money to help some women with educational expenses, and, in so doing, we developed the idea of a more sustainable fund to support women's educational goals.[1]

NOTES

[1] See Chapter Eight, Education.

Still Running

AMANDA STALLER

For the first time since the injury
I ran, through the forest, on the edge of the ocean....
It was great! I saw three little girls hiding in the woods
I saw ferns and stinging nettles and wild roses.
The trees are tall and big.
Running up that hill was hard. I'm going to look at myself as a beginner....
I'm going to run where my feet are ... because the last time....

It was raining, it was cold, I was running with my marathon training group, it was a Sunday morning. I had to run nineteen kilometres, I hurt myself, I walked it out a bit.
I ran another five kilometres, my coach came up, I said I was not okay.
My coach went back to get a vehicle, I started hitchhiking, I was picked up, my coach asked how I'd gotten there so fast, I said I'd hitch-hiked.
When I got home, I just collapsed.

The next day I went to work, I was overmedicated, there was no one to replace me.
I had ripped a lower muscle, the pivoting one in my hip.
It was the day my son phoned me, he was twenty-eight, he wanted to make amends.
He told me, "I want a step nine from you."

Painful endings are new beginnings,
kind of like when I run, the finish line can be the life of me.
EVERY TIME I CROSS THE LINE I'M REBORN.
I just keep dying to my old self, but I am awakened to my new self, who I really am....

I'VE BEEN RUNNING MY WHOLE LIFE from myself, my feelings, my own life, my own self. I couldn't stand being in my own skin; no matter where I went, I just wanted to lose myself. Running to dope deals with all my money, couldn't get that fix in me fast enough. Running to men, giving them all of me just like I did to the dope. I'd lose myself on the streets for years at a time, the lights, the seasons, the smells of puke, urine, garbage.

Regardless, the longest run of my life was from 2000 to 2011.... I used until I couldn't use anymore. I thought I would die, but I just didn't die. I suffered.

In that time, I went to prison. I did some running inside and had running club twice a week, I believe. Just being outside the gate along the river, the ferns and forest were nice.

At one time, I used running to get away from myself. I ran to stay thin. I was this crazy mom in a dysfunctional marriage, and I thought that as long as I looked after my body, he would look after me.
Running was my drug when I wasn't using.
I'm an addict. I love getting high. It's what I do, or so I thought.

Running doesn't keep you clean, not when you're running from life.

My story is about recovering from my broken life and my broken heart, about putting the pieces back together. I didn't know where to start, so I started to run. I started to run for my life. I ran because I didn't know what else to do; the pain was too great, and my body hadn't felt pleasure in a long time.... I felt pleasure, I felt alive, I felt like I could live without dope. So I started to run, I ran home to myself, I ran home to my self. I was running to new beginnings, putting my troubles beneath my feet, moving forward, breathing in and breathing out, my past behind me where it belonged. I picked myself up off the street and started to run. I cried a lot. There were days when I wanted to give up, and running was my friend. When I run, I see Amanda. I talk to her, we reflect, I let go, I die to my old self....

I found HOPE in my HOPELESSNESS.

I saw the children playing in the trees.
I could feel my heart and I was breathing.

Reflections

RUTH ELWOOD MARTIN

ALTHOUGH THE WOMEN WHO GET INVOLVED are enthusiastic, the logistics of our getting together are complicated. I realize that doing participatory health research inside a prison, with no travelling involved, is easier in some ways than doing it outside the gates. We've tried regular meetings at Nicola Valley Institute of Technology, but women have to rely on rides from those with cars. We've held face-to-face meetings, both in Greater Vancouver and during some research retreats on Galiano Island. Women have established a closed Facebook group to provide support for one another. We've tried to connect with women who live remotely by having regular WebEx online meetings using the UBC computer system, but these WebEx meetings are challenging because it is nearly impossible to understand non-verbal nuances and to provide emotional support to one another. And the technological challenges are so great.

I try to mentor the research processes without taking over. I seek to come alongside women, observing and "bearing witness" to much sorrow amidst some joy. Compassion and empathy are foremost for me. I find myself continually reflecting and questioning my role, what it is and what it should be. Regardless, I am separate; with my education, financial security, and supportive family, I am coming from a different place. It is complicated interpersonal work; I feel like I am muddling through, often not sure whether I am doing it the "right" way.

For example, I find myself in an ethical quandary over finances. While engaged in PHR, the values of which espouse equal participation and voice, I am engaging with women newly released from prison with no source of income. They are struggling to find a place to live and food to eat, grappling with the stresses of transition. And here I am, in my place of privilege, inviting women to essentially volunteer their time, voices, and energy to our ongoing PHR project to improve the health of incarcerated women. I have to realize that one of my new roles will be to secure funding to compensate women for their time. I wrestle with this aspect of my new role, feeling quite ambivalent, thinking that this is beyond what I had expected to be doing as a researcher.

We started an educational bursary fund to provide awards for women with incarceration experience, and their children, who wanted to further their education. We sought donations from philanthropic individuals and organizations to support travel for women presenting their research work at conferences, and to support the educational bursary fund. We organized fundraising activities, such as a silent auction and a car wash. A physician colleague donated waiting-room chairs, which we re-upholstered, re-stained, and sold to raise funds. We sought donations in the form of recycled computers, so that women could learn computer skills.

The Vancouver Foundation provided a grant for the PHR inside the prison, and some of these funds remained after our research agreement with BC Corrections Branch had ended. Using these funds, we were able to provide a small honorarium to women for their time doing research work. But we also tried to build accountability and transparency into the process for everyone. We asked women, including volunteers (academics and community members) who did not have incarceration experience, to complete weekly accountability forms in order to account for the hours that they had spent on project work.

But here is the blessing and curse of funding. I am sure that I don't understand exactly what happened, but we began to have messy discussions about the "value of the dollar," and some of our volunteers (who themselves were community volunteers, not previously incarcerated) expressed feelings that we are enabling behaviours that weren't healthy. We decided to stop the accountability forms and to stop reimbursing women for their project work. In fact, by this time, the funding was used up, and I was almost relieved by this—somehow, the presence of funding had shifted everyone's focus and priorities.

I am now beginning to focus on writing funding applications that include budget lines to employ formerly incarcerated women as project research assistants (i.e., community-based peer researchers). Some of the funding applications are successful. In fact, when we received funding for the Doing Time project from CIHR, we employed Kelly as a research assistant along with ten formerly incarcerated women as interviewers, and we made history—it was the first time that CIHR funds had been used to employ formerly incarcerated women.

I originally thought my prison health research would likely focus on HIV, Hepatitis C, injection drug use, and the effectiveness of prescribing methadone inside prison because I thought that these were the most urgent medical issues facing incarcerated women. If I had followed these research questions, my life would not be what it is today.

When I embarked on PHR, I had no idea what I was getting into. By taking the chance of exploring the unknown with PHR, I have opened my life to new possibilities, new ways of knowing, and new relationships. I was, and continue to be, transformed through the process.

Letter from Anna
Excerpt, Women in2 Healing Newsletter, Issue 2

A UBC STUDENT WHO VOLUNTEERED WITH WOMEN IN2 HEALING

WORKING WITH WOMEN IN2 HEALING has been nothing short of extraordinary! Before I began working with this incredible team as a research assistant, I had no preconceived ideas, no expectations about what this job would entail. My desire to work with them was purely driven by an innate desire to help my fellow women, as well as by curiosity—I was curious to see how women in prison could act, simultaneously, as researchers as well as research participants. To me, as a biologist, it was like asking a rat to dissect itself. The concept of participatory health research was completely foreign to me.

I primarily worked with the recorded face-to-face interviews and forum discussions where the women discussed their ideas, concerns, and experiences. Although the tasks of transcribing and analyzing them were at times tedious, it was well worth it to listen to such intimate and, at times, overwhelming details of the women's personal stories. Though I heard their personal stories without ever meeting them, they have made such an impression on my life that it feels as if I know them.

To say the least, these women inspire me. Although they have committed crimes and have been held accountable for their actions, I've learned about the forces that brought them to such low points in their lives. It's amazing to me how these women have found hope, despite the hate, oppression, and abuse they have endured. They have begun to see their worth, their potential for great and beautiful things. From once having nothing and no one, these women now have each other—a camaraderie based on support, trust, and, above all else, love for themselves and for each other. I know that wherever life takes me, I will always hold these women in my prayers, and I will always remember their fearlessness and perseverance during times of hardship.

Amber's Story
"Three Pounds and Nine Ounces"

AMBER CHRISTIE

ONE DAY, AT MY GRAMPA'S HOUSE, my sister said my boobs looked big as we were walking to the store. I didn't think anything of it for a few days. I had noticed that whenever I used drugs, I would throw up. My family friend wanted to take me back to Alberta for a few days, so I went to dry out. On our way there, we stopped to eat. There was a drug store next door and I needed new makeup, so I went to buy some. I saw a pregnancy test that was on sale—two for one. I remembered that Ashley had told me that my breasts looked bigger, so I bought the tests and went to the bathroom. Immediately the test went positive—not only was I pregnant, but I was very pregnant!

When I went back to BC a few days later, I went to a doctor and found out I was five months pregnant. I was scared because I'd been using drugs the whole time. I stopped that day and decided to move back to the mainland with my boyfriend to live with my grandparents so they could help me with the baby. As much as I wanted him to be the father, I really wasn't sure if he was. I didn't tell him. I was allowed to move to the mainland if I went on methadone. That was the ministry's request. So I did it.

At thirty weeks, I went into labour. I had my beautiful daughter at 9:04 p.m. on November 23, 1999. She was three pounds and nine ounces. Right after I held her for the first time, she was sent to the NICU. I was discharged the next day, but I couldn't bring her home. She was too small.

The ministry said I was unfit and removed her from my care. Nevertheless, I stayed at the hospital all the time. I slept on the bench outside the NICU. My Gramma stepped up to help me. I was able to bring my baby home to my grandparents.

I lasted a few days, then I drank.

Later that night, I was arrested and taken away from my baby.

A Time of Giving
Excerpt, Women in2 Healing Newsletter, Issue 2

KELLY MURPHY

CHRISTMAS IS A TIME OF GIVING; even people who might be Scrooges have been known to open their hearts during this festive time of the year. Last year the women of Women in2 Healing made a trip to downtown Vancouver, to the lower east side, and handed out various articles of clothing to those who were in need. This year we are sponsoring a family; we're hoping that we might help make Christmas special for a single mother and her children. We're inspired by the thought of children possibly opening that one special gift that makes a difference, a gift that they might remember for years to come, and knowing that the meal they will have on the table on Christmas day will be turkey and not TV dinners.

The birth of Jesus and the spirit of giving is what Christmas is all about to me. So it shouldn't matter where a person is at geographically—we are all able to celebrate Christmas in our hearts.

With your release from prison, what are your hopes for the next three months?

Hopes for Release

stay clean
        stay clean
stay clean
        stay clean

stay out of jail
        stay strong
stay out of trouble
        stay focused
stay out of jail
        stay healthy
stay out of trouble
        stay connected

stay alive

be a mom
be happy
believe in a higher power

find a home

gain independence
gain trust back

get a job
get a tooth out
get in shape

go to school
        grow up

make amends
        make art
make better choices
        make money

        see my children
talk to people who actually care about me

get the hell out of here
        move to Winnipeg

III. Health Goals

I would like to ask you some questions about your health, based on the nine topic areas that women in prison told us were important to their health. Some questions will invite you to tell me your story in your own words. Some questions will invite you to reply on a scale of one to five....
—Interviewer for Doing Time project (survey upon a woman's release from prison)

I was comforted to know that I haven't become apathetic to the lives of women who are entrenched downtown. I look and see myself in their lives.
—Kelly Murphy

Giving a woman in prison a welfare cheque and saying, "Be on your way," is not rehabilitation. The gaps in the system need to be closed.
—Amber Christie

Doctor's Journey

RUTH ELWOOD MARTIN

I WISH WE'D HAD THE TAPE RECORDER TODAY. But I'm writing in my journal now. During our research meeting, Mo (one of the peer research assistants) told us that a woman with incarceration experience, whom she was mentoring as a project assistant, has disappeared, and she fears that she has relapsed into substance use. Mo says that she is trying to not take it personally.

The woman had been passionate, motivated, hopeful. She had supports in place, and she was being welcomed into the community. In fact, all of her nine health goals were achievable—everything looked promising. But clearly the nine health goals were not enough and something was missing—she was not done yet.

We all feel devastated. I feel like the rug has been pulled out from under me. I asked, "What are we doing with this PHR in the community? Are we deluded?"

We then had a deep discussion about whether we should bring this up in the research interview, if we should ask participants, "Are you done yet?" That discussion led to the question, "What brings you to the point in your life where you feel you are done? What leads you to it? Is it a spiritual awakening?" We then decided to add a question about spiritual health in the Doing Time research interview, because we thought that maybe this was the missing piece.

During our meeting, women peer researchers shared that their mental obsessions with substance use persist long after their body physically finds it repulsive. I didn't know this. Then, during the meeting, we talked about the Indigenous medicine wheel, and about ways that we each need to learn to integrate spiritual, physical, mental, and emotional health.

I am now reflecting on the factors that lead people to that place in their lives where they can finally feel like they are done. We need to *introduce these factors into our prison systems—maybe it relates to hope?*

—*Journal entry*

Participatory health research projects *inside* prison were constrained as to what they could do to improve the health of incarcerated women. Through analysis and synthesis of all of the prison PHR data, incarcerated women identified nine health goals as necessary:

1) improved relationships with children, families, and partners;
2) improved peer and community support;
3) increased access to safe and stable housing;
4) improved access to individualized healthcare;
5) increased job skills, relevant education, and employment;
6) improved dentition and oral health;
7) improved health awareness and integration;
8) improved health and disease knowledge; and,
9) increased ability to contribute to society. (Martin et al.)

Look again at these nine health goals the women identified. Don't we *all* want these?

However, it became apparent that the majority of these nine health goals were dependent on conditions that women would face *after* their release from prison. Therefore, our research question became, "What are the facilitators and barriers for women in achieving their health goals following their release from prison?"

Our third application to the Canadian Institute for Health Research (CIHR) was successful, and we received funding for Doing Time at about the same time that the PHR project ended inside the prison. Therefore, the funding enabled us to employ women who were released from ACCW as the project coordinator and as part-time community-based project assistants. We trained women with incarceration experience as research interviewers.

Together, we developed an interview guide that asked about barriers and facilitators to the nine health goals for women when released from prison. We interviewed 400 women immediately following their release, and we re-interviewed them at intervals during the following eighteen months. Our analysis demonstrated that good nutritional health, positive spiritual health, and high school graduation protected women against committing future crime (see Janssen et al.).

The overall conclusion of this research project confirmed what we were already so familiar with—that health-related strategies are urgently needed to support women who are released from prison.

REFERENCES

Janssen, Patricia A., Mo Korchinski, Sarah L. Desmarais, Arianne Y.K, Albert, Lara-Lisa Condello, Marla Buchanan, Alison Granger-Brown, Vivian R. Ramsden, Lynn Fels, Jane A. Buxton, Carl Leggo, and Ruth Elwood Martin. "Factors that Support Successful Transition to the Community Among Women Leaving Prison in British Columbia: A Prospective Cohort Study Using Participatory Action Research." *CMAJ Open* 5.3 (2017): E717–E723. Web.

Martin, Ruth Elwood, Kate Murphy, Debra L. Hanson, Christine A. Hemingway, Vivian R. Ramsden, Jane A. Buxton, Alison Granger-Brown, Lara-Lisa Condello, Marla Buchanan, Nancy Espinoza-Magana, Gillian Edworthy, and T. Greg Hislop. "The Development of Participatory Health Research Among Incarcerated Women in a Canadian Prison." *International Journal of Prisoner Health* 5.2 (2009): 95-107. Web.

Letter to Martina

MO KORCHINSKI

Dear Martina,

Thanks for returning my phone call. Sorry it has taken a little longer to get the information to you. I was hoping to be cleared last week to visit, and I had planned to drop this off then. As I was telling you on the phone, I now work at UBC as a research tech for a project called Doing Time. As you know, it's very hard to break the cycle of jail. The obstacles that we face once we're back in the community play a big part in the life choices we make for ourselves. And like most things in life, if people don't know where to find help to make the changes, then they can't make the changes.

Doing Time has received funding through the Canadian Institute of Health Research (CIHR) to conduct a survey for three years with women when they are released from prison. I do interviews with the women the day they are released at Alouette Addictions Services, and then I do follow up interviews with the women at three, six, nine, and twelve months after their release. Our goal is to understand the factors that contribute to their physical, spiritual, emotional, and psychological health in order to develop a community-based action health strategy

---

DOING TIME INVITATIONAL INTERVIEW 1
(baseline)

ACCESS TO INDIVIDUALIZED PRIMARY HEALTH CARE

How satisfied were you with your access to health services, over the last 4 weeks (scale 1-5)?

How much do you need any medical treatment to function in your daily life (scale 1-5)?

Tell us about your plans for finding health care now you are released.

that will support their successful re-integration back into society.

As you know well, that was a huge problem for me, but with help and support from various organizations, I've managed to beat the cycle. There is still so much more that society can do to help us women break free. Alouette Correctional Centre for Women gave me hope and lots of support when I was in there, and now we need to extend that outside the walls to give people back their daughters, sisters, grandchildren, wives, and mothers.

I know we can make a difference, and I know the women can change—I'm living proof that the cycle can be broken. I'm enclosing the handout that I was hoping the jail could give to the women on release. As well as explaining the Doing Time project, it also includes a phone number where women can reach other peer researchers for information or just support as they get through the hard times and make the transition back into society.

Thank you for taking the time to read this letter and if you are requiring more information, please call me at Alouette Addictions.

Sincerely,
Mo Korchinski

Amber's Story
"They Said I'd Never Get Her Back"

AMBER CHRISTIE

AFTER I GOT OUT OF JAIL, the ministry gave me visits with my daughter but told me multiple times that it would be better for her if I just put her up for adoption. I loved her so much, and I said no. I was so crippled by what these social workers said and did that I started using again. They had kept their word. They said I'd never get her back. After almost a year of their threats, I decided it was best for my daughter to be taken out of foster care and adopted into a new home. The social worker already had a place for her to go. I hated them for what they had done, but I never wanted my daughter to go through what I went through in foster care. I signed the papers. That day my life stopped. I took the Skytrain to Vancouver's Downtown Eastside and the real abuse began.

I was under the impression that I was on methadone for my cocaine addiction. It wasn't until I got down there that I found out I was not just addicted to cocaine, but that because of the methadone, I needed heroin to stop being sick. Within two weeks I was a full-blown heroin junkie.

Life in Vancouver's Downtown Eastside was a

DOING TIME INVITATIONAL INTERVIEW VIII (BASELINE)

RELATIONSHIPS WITH CHILDREN, FAMILY AND PARTNERS

How satisfied are you with your personal relationships (on a scale of 1-5)?

How satisfied are you with the support that you get from your family members (on a scale of 1-5)?

Can you tell me about children: do you have any (yes/no)? If yes, how many and what ages?

Would you like to share your plans/hopes about your future relationship with your family and your children?

whole different world. I met a drug dealer who took care of me, but after a year he would only give me so much, so it was my turn to start feeding this ugly monster inside me. I did things that I swore I would never do. I was willing to do anything not to feel.

My mother had gotten clean just a few months before my daughter was born. For once I was just worrying about my own pain and not hers. I remember going to the Downtown Eastside a couple of times the year before to see her. She was a mess, and I never thought I could or would ever be able to live down there. Just a year later, I was down there myself, and I was doing whatever I had to do to feed this monster. I would occasionally see a family friend who came down.

Even though my baby was no longer mine, I still celebrated her birthday at a restaurant I always went to with a friend. We talked about old times, my daughter, and many other things. I would leave those meetings more and more pained. My daughter was my heart. I had to use like mad to try to dull the pain. I can't count how many nights I slept in an alley on a box with my legs stuck in my shirt because I was cold and had rats running across my feet.

Process Notes from Co-Investigators' Meeting
"An Authentic Conversation Breaks Out"

KELLY MURPHY

AS WE GATHER AROUND the pretentious boardroom table, I contemplate the anxiety that I consistently encounter, before, during, and after these Doing Time monthly meetings of the co-investigators. It has occurred to me that it might be the setting, the boardroom, and the vast distance around the table. Or could it be the name "co-investigators;" just that word makes me want to hire a lawyer. My thoughts are wandering, and I am visualizing a different meeting place. The local pub perhaps, or the back of a coffee house, surrounded by the smell of fresh ground beans and baked goods. What would the atmosphere feel like then? Would there be the obvious distinction between academics, peer researchers, and project staff?

Yes, I can envision it now, everyone dressed in jeans, T-shirts, and flip-flops; many of the academics looking like a throwback to the sixties. One would not be able to differentiate between PHD, CSC, MA, or MLA, in fact letters would be of no concern. Bumptious academics would come together with the struggling students (the peer researchers) in a meaningful, participatory way. That is not to say that this is not happening, it's just that there is also tension, evident and uncomfortable. Now keep

---

DOING TIME INVITATIONAL INTERVIEW III
(BASELINE)

ACCESS TO HEALTH EDUCATION

On a scale of 1-5, how available was the health information that you need in your day-to-day life (over the previous 4 weeks)?

Tell me about the information or education you have had about your health (over the past 4 weeks).

Please tell me about plans you may have to learn more about health.

in mind that this is my perspective, my interpretation of an environment that is still quite foreign to me. I consider that if I can't manage to navigate through two hours a month of seeming pleasantries and play-acting, then how will I ever manoeuvre through the ranks of UBC academia?

I bring myself back to the room. The co-investigators are in mid conversation, speaking a language that is completely alien to me: SPSS, SAQ, group force method, and the ever so popular psychometric properties. With notable frustration in my voice, I kindly interrupt the speaker, so that the terms being used might be clarified. As my frustration escalates, I struggle to stay in the room, to remain cognitively present. My thoughts keep wandering to the Women in2 Healing members and wondering how they are digesting all of this over-the-top language. Maybe I am just trying to care for their feelings, being a recovering co-dependent and all. *Labels, shit!*

I'm not entirely certain as to what is transpiring for the other members of Women in2 Healing until a door is opened into the conversation regarding the values of the project. I have never been a person that could just sit back and allow the elephant to tromp around the room without naming it. I feel the need to say something, anything, in order to dispel the obvious tension. *But what, what am I going to say that wouldn't make me look like an idiot?* As I sit there praying, asking God to provide an opening, my will takes over. *Who cares?* Sometimes I forget that this is participatory. There is no such a thing as a wrong way to approach the process. And more than anything, I want the other women to feel safe to speak out also, to come forward if they feel the need to do so. I risk my face for the sake of the others; after all it is only false pride and ego. It wouldn't be the first time in my life that I make a fool of myself, and after all, who am I judging here but myself? *Stop it, step up, step out!*

As I'm working to validate my process, an authentic conversation breaks out—the real deal. Unfortunately, it arrives so late in the meeting that it feels somewhat restrained from its full potential. It is, however, a beginning. I wonder what a meeting might look like if Women in2 Healing had the opportunity to actually process for an hour. Would it bridge the gap of tension? Or is the tension only mine?

Tackling the Impenetrable

MO KORCHINSKI

I'M INVITED TO THE Doing Time co-investigators meeting at UBC. I'm not sure what to expect, but Kelly will be there so it should be fine. I still struggle with anxiety. The people who will be sitting around the table are all smart people. They are university teachers and doctors. I am an ex-con, but I also know that my experience is something no school can teach. The knowledge that I bring to the table is important; I have a valuable perspective on how we can approach the research we are doing with women coming out of jail. The questions, the wording, everything needs to be easy for women to be able to connect with and answer the question.

As I walk into the room, I'm not expecting such a large table with people in business clothing sitting around it. The setting feels so serious. I find a chair next to Kelly. She is feeling out of place too, and that makes me feel a bit better. The meeting starts, and I'm lost right out of the gate. I have no idea what they are talking about when it comes to quality versus quantity research, force, and controlled groups. Kelly looks at me, and I can tell she doesn't understand any of this either.

I sit through the meeting. When it's over I leave the room, unsure about what had happened. I realize that if research is something I plan to do in life, then I better figure out

> DOING TIME INVITATIONAL INTERVIEW IV
> (BASELINE)
>
> **DENTITION AND ORAL HEALTH**
>
> Tell me about your access to dental care (if any) over the previous 4 weeks (scale 1-5)?
>
> Are you able to accept your dental appearance (scale 1-5)?
>
> Please tell me about your plans (if you have some) for your dental care?

the language of research. I stop to talk with one of the co-investigators, Lara Lisa, who teaches at Nicola Valley Institute of Technology. I tell her that I didn't understand one word in that meeting and that I want to find a course that I can take to learn more about research and the terms that are used. Well, it just so happens that Lara Lisa teaches a research method course and it starts next month! I ask if I could take just one course at the college, and she says that she will look into it for me.

Well, it turns out that Nicola Valley Institute of Technology will let me take the course with Kelly, and Christine is going to take it too! I'm super nervous because I was never good at school; I'm just not that smart. I never would have believed that I would ace that course, and that it would be my introduction to a four-year college degree.

Project
Excerpt, Women in2 Healing Newsletter, Issue 2

KELLY MURPHY

TODAY NANCY ESPINOZA AND I had our first interview appointment booked at the Downtown Eastside Women's Centre. I didn't sleep very well last night in anticipation. Although I have experienced a renewing of the mind when it comes to addiction, I still get anxious about entering the world I once knew intimately.

DOING TIME INVITATIONAL INTERVIEW II (BASELINE)

YOUR PERSONAL HEALTH

Thinking about your health over the last 4 weeks (on a scale 1-5):

a. How satisfied are you with your health?
b. How would you rate your quality of life?
c. How often do you have negative feelings, such as a blue mood, despair, anxiety, or depression?
d. How satisfied are you with your sleep?
e. How well are you able to concentrate?
f. Do you have enough energy for everyday life?
g. Are you able to accept your physical appearance?
h. To what extent do you feel that physical pain prevents you from doing what you need to do?

Now that you are released, to what extent will you have the opportunity for leisure and recreational activities (scale 1-5)?

Please tell me about ways that you find healing for yourself in your spiritual, emotional, mental, physical health.

We headed down early with our baseline interview questions, confidentiality forms, and the digital recorder. We got there about fifteen minutes early, only to be bombarded by a bunch of women asking us if we were the ones who were doing the survey. Instantly, I felt overwhelmed. The Downtown Eastside Women's Centre was loud and packed with women. It was apparent that we weren't going to be able to conduct interviews in this environment. We selected five women who had been released recently, and then we gathered at a nearby café. They didn't have a problem with us being there as long as we made a purchase.

Despite the skills that I have acquired as a counsellor, interviewing the women was an emotionally exhausting experience. I was comforted to know that I haven't become apathetic to the lives of women who are entrenched downtown. I look and see myself in their lives.

I offered comfort, care, and concern. My last interviewee stated that I gave her hope, and that I was a "beacon of light." I had an epiphany as to why we were connecting with each other. It was because we had a personal relationship inside the gates of Alouette and had already established a sense of trust.

It's not the easiest gig though; I felt exhausted the next day. I am really thankful that I have support in my life and that I have the discernment to know when to use it. All in all, it was pretty exciting to get a response from women downtown.

Sitting at the Bus Loop

MO KORCHINSKI

SITTING AT THE BUS LOOP interviewing women for Doing Time teaches me that women need much more support the day they get released. Women are dropped off at the bus loop in Maple Ridge in a cab, carrying all their belongings in a clear plastic bag. Most women have no idea how to get back home; they just have a bus ticket back to where they were arrested.

I remember how scary it was the first time I was dropped off at the bus loop. I had no idea how to get home or even where to begin. I didn't make it very far before I ran into someone I knew, and the next thing I knew I was getting high. The minute I was released, I was set up to fail.

I hope that my success in changing my life gives women at the bus loop the hope that they can change too, that they they can leave their old lives behind.

DOING TIME INVITATIONAL INTERVIEW V (BASELINE)

ACCESS TO STABLE AND SAFE HOUSING

Living conditions for 4 weeks prior to arrest:

a. Before your arrest, how satisfied were you with the conditions of your living place (scale 1-5)?
b. Before your arrest, how safe did you feel in your daily life (scale 1-5)?
c. Would you like to share more about your living conditions before your arrest?

Living conditions you plan to go to:

a. How satisfied are you with the conditions of the living place that you plan to go to (scale 1-5)?
b. How safe will you feel in your daily life where you plan to go (scale 1-5)?
c. Would you like to share more about the living conditions you plan to go to?

Answers

MO KORCHINSKI

Research
Data
Voices
Heard
Listen
Knowledge
Power
Experts
Learning
Unsilenced
Valued
Stories
Questions
Unknown
Findings
Sharing
Speaking
Policy
Change
Truth
Participates
Answers
Researchers

Doing Time Complexities

RUTH ELWOOD MARTIN

THIS DOING TIME PROJECT seems so complex, especially compared with my experience of doing participatory health research inside prison. Inside prison, women had time on their hands, and they could choose to become involved in the research project as much or as little as they wanted. And, because we had minimal funding for the work, there was no financial incentive for people to become involved, so everyone volunteered—incarcerated women, other organizations and agencies, and academic faculty—all motivated by hope and passion. An added bonus was that the research office was right there in the middle of the prison, so that there was no travel time involved for women on the research team.

But I am realizing that Doing Time is more complicated. Firstly, I hadn't quite thought through the practicalities of doing community-based participatory health research in a hierarchical academic setting supported by Canadian Institutes of Health Research (CIHR) funding. As much as we embrace our PHR values—for example, the tenant, "all voices are equal," which would see us sitting equitably around a circle together—the reality is that the CIHR funding structure puts the responsibility and authority with myself, as a co-principal investigator, to ensure that the funding is spent in the way that we outlined in the original proposal. And I now have an employee/employer relationship with women who are working as Doing Time peer research assistants, which means we must shift our relationship again. Women whom I knew previously as patients in the medical clinic, have now become peer researchers on the prison health research team.

Secondly, the Doing Time project is more complicated emotionally. Inside prison, despite the hardship of being incarcerated, many women experience some respite from the relentless traumas and challenges of their everyday survival in the outside community. But, in the

Doing Time project, we are observing daily, and vicariously experiencing, the emotional reality of women's trauma and challenges. The peer research assistants who interview women leaving prison experience this most acutely. We have learned that peer research assistants need to work in pairs for their own safety and to provide mutual support, because every Doing Time interview can trigger painful memories for them. And we have learned that it is logistically difficult to interview women for up to eighteen months after their release from prison, because so many of them are "lost to follow up." Despite building trusting relationships with peer research assistants, they often drift away due to homelessness and poverty, their relapse back into drug use, and their eventual re-incarceration or worse, death.

DOING TIME INVITATIONAL INTERVIEW VI (BASELINE)

JOB SKILLS, TRAINING AND RELEVANT EMPLOYMENT

How satisfied are you with your capacity for work
(scale 1-5)?

Will you have enough money to meet your needs
(scale 1-5)?

How satisfied do you think you will be with your transport (scale 1-5)?

How well will you be able to get around (scale 1-5)?

Tell me about your skills training and/or education over the past 4 weeks.

Would you like to share with me your plans for skills training/education/employment?

Gaps in the System
Presentation to the Federal Standing Committee, Ottawa[1]

AMBER CHRISTIE

I AM A RESEARCH ASSISTANT for the University of British Columbia. I work in community-based participatory research. I am employed by the project called Doing Time, and I interview women who have been incarcerated in a provincial institution within the last year. We interview women at zero, three, six, nine, and twelve months after their release from prison and ask them about how they are achieving their nine health goals. We ask them questions about health care access, housing, community resources, drug use, spirituality, self-esteem, employment, etc. Our team has interviewed over four hundred women.

Some of the biggest challenges that we are seeing with women when they are released—and I want to stress this—is that they do not receive housing referrals upon their release, and therefore become homeless. Of 400 women, forty percent leave prison homeless. Forty percent. Many more, an even bigger majority, end up homeless within one month.[2] This must change. These women are also not getting the proper drug and mental health treatment that they need and want. There are

---

DOING TIME INVITATIONAL INTERVIEW IX
(BASELINE)

ABILITY TO CONTRIBUTE TO SOCIETY

How satisfied are you with yourself (scale 1-5)?

How much do you enjoy life (scale 1-5)?

To what extent do you feel your life to be meaningful (scale 1-5)?

Tell me about activities and roles that you found meaningful and/or you felt were valued by others over the previous 4 weeks?

Please tell me about your plans for the future regarding meaningful activities?

not enough places that take in women from prison. Most centres will not accept these women just because they've been in prison, and then the ones who do have a long waiting period. Giving a woman in prison a welfare cheque and saying, "Be on your way," is not rehabilitation. The gaps in the system need to be closed.

NOTES

[1] Amber Christie, Brenda Tole, and Ruth Elwood Martin presented to the Standing Committee on Public Safety and National Security, Federal Corrections: Mental Health and Addictions, Ottawa, March 2010.
[2] Another forty-five percent of women have insecure housing, such as couch surfing at friends' houses (Janssen et al.).

REFERENCES

Janssen, Patricia A., Mo Korchinski, Sarah L. Desmarais, Arianne Y. K, Albert, Lara-Lisa Condello, Marla Buchanan, Alison Granger-Brown, Vivian R. Ramsden, Lynn Fels, Jane A. Buxton, Carl Leggo, and Ruth Elwood Martin. "Factors that Support Successful Transition to the Community Among Women Leaving Prison in British Columbia: A Prospective Cohort Study Using Participatory Action Research." *CMAJOpen* 5.3 (2017): E717–E723. Web.

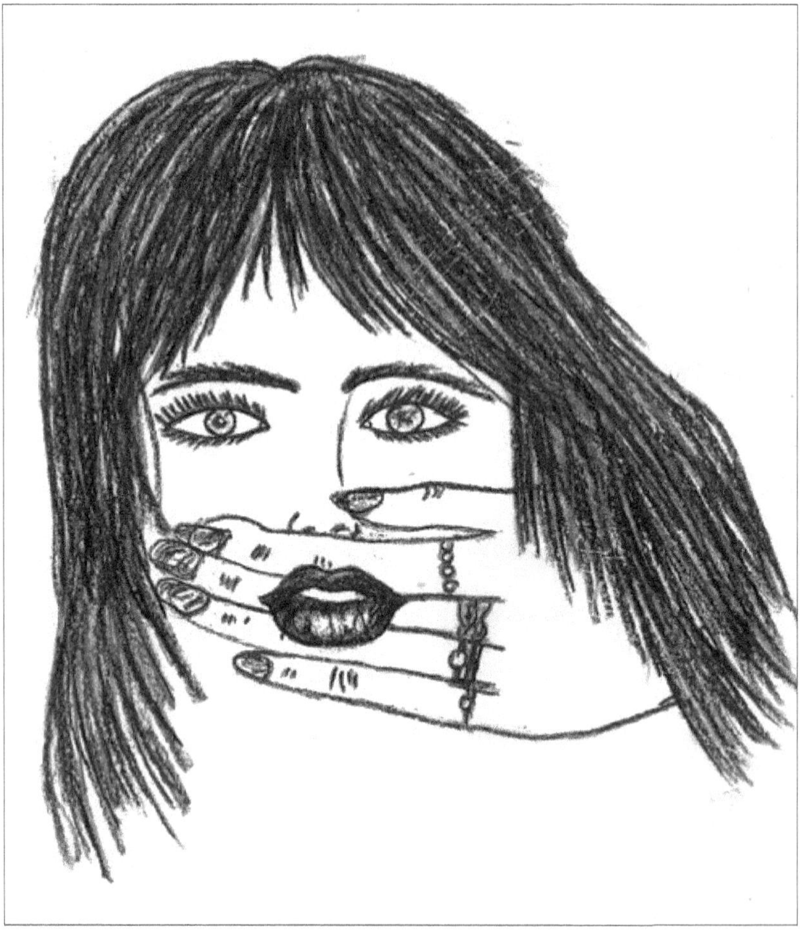

Women Who Didn't Make It Out

MO KORCHINSKI

WHEN I STARTED DOING INTERVIEWS for Doing Time at the bus loop in Maple Ridge, I wanted to take all the women home with me. How do you keep someone from going back into addiction and crime when they have no hope? I want everyone to find what I did when I let go of the drugs and started to heal from years of abuse. I know how hard it is to live in addiction. I know the dangers. The women are like family to me; I spent years doing time with them. I want them to have what I have: inner peace, a purpose, and most of all HOPE. But where do you start when no one believes in you, when you don't even believe in yourself?

I took it very personally the first time a woman whom I helped at the bus loop died later that day. I questioned what I could have done differently. What could I have done to be more supportive? What could I have said to be more helpful? Over time, more and more women I served time with lost their battles to addiction. Many women—mothers, sisters, and daughters—are no longer with us. How do we help someone who feels like she is worthless and unlovable? While I was living with my addiction, I felt that way for many years.

> **DOING TIME INVITATIONAL INTERVIEW VII (BASELINE)**
>
> **PEER AND COMMUNITY SUPPORT**
>
> How satisfied are you with the support you get from your friends (on a scale of 1-5)?
>
> How satisfied are you with the support your get from your community (on a scale of 1-5)?
>
> Would you like to share your future plans and hopes for friend/community support?

Too many who have served time in prison lose the battle with addiction. What can we do differently? Women with so much to offer society don't know where they fit in. Bridging the gap from prison to mainstream society is so hard. You leave the prison with nothing but your stuff in a clear plastic bag. You are leaving behind a safe place for a place where you do not feel like you belong.

What do you want people to know about women leaving prison?

we are not stereotypes

it is possible
        to turn your life around

it is possible
we like having jobs
        going shopping

        we have nowhere to go
and no means to go anywhere

we should not be judged

jail sucks

        a shitty place
we are scared
        life is hard

we need somewhere safe to go
we need resources

we need support
we need skills
we need love

we deserve the same
chances as others

we aren't bad people

just because we made
        a few mistakes

doesn't make
us bad people
we aren't bad people

just because we
did a little time

we made some bad choices

we're not monsters
we're people
we're women
we're human

we can recover
we can change

life after jail
new meaning
we aren't alone

shit happens
        there is hope!

Hope: Interlude One

Thoughts on Hope in Prison

CHAPLAIN HENK SMIDSTRA

Hope is a gift to all who have ... a powerful wish for life to be better than it is, the imagination to look beyond the bad that is to the good that can be, and the faith to believe that the good they imagine and wish for is possible.
—Lewis Smedes (10)

HOPE ARISES FROM A MYSTERIOUS, spiritual source beyond our understanding, and wells up from a deep latent capacity within us. Lewis Smedes suggests that to keep hope alive we need three ingredients: wishing, imagining, and believing (18). Hope, he suggests, is an innate capacity within us as we travel into an unknown future that is not in our control. "Hope is the fuel for the journey. As long as we keep hope alive, we keep moving. To stop moving is to die of hope deficiency" (9).

I was privileged to witness many times the return of hope when all hope was lost, especially during my years as prison chaplain at the Burnaby Correctional Services for Women (BCCW), Surrey Pre-Trial, and Alouette Correctional Centre for Women (ACCW) (from 1991 to 2014). Looking back, there were usually also relational or environmental connections, perhaps an empowering presence or word from another kind, caring person, or a transforming experience, such as watching a sunset. Some attributed the return of hope to a power greater than themselves. Often in retrospect I would hear, "If it had not been for that, I would not have made it."

That said, I certainly did witness the capacity of innate personal character—courage, strength, determination, and perhaps sheer stubbornness ("I'll show them...!")—to make changes during oppressive, tragic life situations. When all hope is gone, a new hope, a new meaning and purpose must be found in order to go forward. The human spirit, the inner will to live, to overcome challenges, is immense;

however, chronic long-term adversity, especially in cruel, demeaning, abusive situations that seek to destroy the spirit of a person can often succeed, and that is tragic. People then say, "What's the use?" Hope can be arrested by chronic toxic adversity and abuse, but in a loving and safe environment, it is possible to find it again.

Hope is the rebirth of a person's diminished spirit. Hope and spirituality are enmeshed. The return of hope is the quickening of a person's very spirit, their soul, or that deepest part of their consciousness and personality. It is the return of belief in themselves when they had given up; it is the return of hope when they have given up on any meaning and purpose to life, or on any transcendent power for good in their lives. If condemnation and ridicule have stolen the vitality of a person, love and affirmation of their human worth gives motivating life to the spirit. Sometimes one affirming word from another person can make all the difference in the world. Sometimes in a transformational moment of deep inner renewal and hope, the realisation dawns that, "I am not alone on my life's journey. My higher power, my God, has not left me and will not abandon me."

Hope and imagination open a creative, positive attitude to the future, the realization that no matter what, I have the power within me to accept the future as it comes. Renewed or new relationships are more likely to come into being with a hopeful posture than with continued self-loathing, despair, and hopelessness. A new sense of connection and self-confidence in all relationships arises in hope from within. The past cannot be changed, but the future is open, and a new hope can be birthed to meet us there in joy.

Modern security-focused, sterile, law-and-order prison regimes are not appropriate environments for healing, empowerment, or the rebirth of hope. Empowering, humanizing environments and resources are needed. These include spiritual resources, through which the mysteries of hope and its depths far beyond the limits of ordinary human rationality can be explored. As a wounded healer myself, I believe in the relational affirming process of healing to hope. I believe in an arresting hope, a hope that surprises us and picks us up so we can flourish on our life's journey.

To revive the wounded spirit, an empowering, therapeutic, relational environment is necessary. The journey toward healing often passes through a long wilderness of loneliness, grief, and sorrow, with no hope for goodness imaginable. Human beings at such a time need affirming relationships and strength-based approaches; they do not need more rejection or psychic-sensory deprivation. Both at BCCW and ACCW, there were supportive, affirming staff. If a woman was struggling, she could also often find other supportive people on her unit. This was a comforting reality that was allowed in the prison environments at that time. However, a law-and-order agenda that wished to see incarceration as a harsh experience for the prisoner proceeded to nip at the heels of those of us who affirmed therapy and education over punishment.

Hope does not come immediately, with the flip of a mental switch or by sheer control of all thoughts; one must allow one's self to feel, to sometimes hit an emotional bottom. However, the amazing thing is that facing the bottom is not at all what we feared it would be. A new hope dawns on us, meets us there—a new freedom and perspective—and strips away the stories and values that had eroded our self-respect and self-worth. We can admit that we are not perfect, that it is human to make mistakes, and to forgive. We may come to see that our humanity is worth way more than the worst thing we have done; we find the courage to make amends and forgive ourselves. This is not done with a demeaning admission of worthlessness, but instead with a new-found self-respect and strength. Having gone through the challenge and transformation of our self-image through suffering, we gain courage and hope. We know that since we have endured what we just went though, we can face the future no matter what it will bring. We know that we are a better person and a better parent for it. It was not all wasted time.

REFERENCES

Smedes, Lewis. *Standing on the Promises: Keeping Hope Alive for a Tomorrow We Cannot Control.* Nashville, TN: Thomas Nelson, 1998.

IV. Mentoring

*Peer mentors are like angels.
They make the difference
between the old life
and new beginnings.*
   —Respondent from Peer Health Mentoring Interviews

When I wake up every morning, over my morning tea, I look on Facebook and I see RIP on the women's page. Just before Easter in 2017, five women died of opiate (fentanyl) overdoses in Maple Ridge in twenty-four hours. It's become the norm. When we first started the peer health mentor program, we wanted to know how to stop women from relapsing and using. Now we want to know how to stop women from dying.
   —Mo Korchinski

Doctor's Journey

RUTH ELWOOD MARTIN

*T*HERE WAS A BAPTIST CHURCH SERVICE *in Maple Ridge this evening. It wasn't a usual church service, or a wedding service, or a funeral. I've never experienced a church service like it before.*

Women with incarceration experience organized the service as a memorial for their peers—to honour their lives and to remember them. Women who, like them, were once incarcerated, but who are now dead.

These women didn't make it; they didn't survive. Each woman was someone's mother, someone's sister, someone's daughter, someone's friend. I can't get my head around this. Young women dying alone in our communities, overdosing.

The invitation read, "Each time one of our beautiful sisters passes on, we see ourselves in grief for not just that one woman, but the many women who have touched our lives in the context of incarceration. We hang on to the memories. Our lives came together in adversity, and through that journey we saw beauty."

I am more convinced than ever that peer support is part of the key.
—Journal entry

Internationally published literature confirms that individuals are at increased risk of adverse health outcomes, including increased risk of overdose and death, following their release from prison (See Kinner and Wang; Groot et al. Binswanger et al.).

Incarcerated women, who originate from communities across the province, are transported from ACCW to the Maple Ridge bus loop, given a bus ticket, and expected to find their way back to their community. The Doing Time research demonstrated that eighty-five percent of women leaving the provincial prison system are homeless or have unstable housing (see Janssen et al.). There is a lack of safe housing for women throughout the province of BC, but this lack is even more extreme for women who are leaving prison. Most treatment centres require that women be on the street for thirty days before they can be admitted, a practice that excludes women who are released from prison. Without safe housing, women after release get caught back up in the revolving door of homelessness, substance use, crime, and prison.

Incarcerated women, during the prison PHR project, gave voice to their vast fears about the first few days following their release from prison. They told us that they needed support from someone who understood what they were experiencing, someone to hold their hand as they transitioned from prison to the outside world. After we completed the Doing Time study, we obtained CIHR funding for a knowledge-translation initiative, which women with incarceration experience co-created and coordinated. This led to the establishment of the Unlocking the Gates peer health mentor program, an initiative that helps women through their immediate transition from inside prison to the outside community.

REFERENCES

Binswanger, Ingrid A., Marc F. Stern, Richard A. Deyo, Patrick J. Heagerty, Allen Cheadle, Joann G. Elmore, and Thomas D. Koepsell. "Release from Prison — A High Risk of Death for Former Inmates." *The New England Journal of Medicine* 356.2 (2007): 157-165. Web.

Groot, Emily, Fiona G. Kouyoumdjian, Lori Kiefer, Parvaz Madadi, Jeremy Gross, Brittany Prevost, Reuven Jhirad, Dirk Huyer, Victoria Snowdon, and Navindra Persaud. "Drug Toxicity Deaths After Release from Incarceration in Ontario, 2006-2013: Review of Coroner's Cases." *PLOS ONE* 11.7 (2016): e0157512. Web.

Janssen, Patricia A., Mo Korchinski, Sarah L. Desmarais, Arianne Y. K, Albert, Lara-Lisa Condello, Marla Buchanan, Alison Granger-Brown, Vivian R. Ramsden, Lynn Fels, Jane A. Buxton, Carl Leggo, and Ruth Elwood Martin. "Factors that Support Successful Transition to the Community Among Women Leaving Prison in British Columbia: A Prospective Cohort Study Using Participatory Action Research." *CMAJ Open* 5.3 (2017): E717–E723. Web.

Kinner, Stuart A. and Emily A. Wang. "The Case for Improving the Health of Ex-Prisoners." *American Journal of Public Health* 104.8 (2014): 1352-1355. Web.

Peer Mental Health Program[1]

MO KORCHINSKI

I START OFF AS A RESEARCH LEAD with Unlocking the Gates peer health mentor program. I meet the women at the bus loop. I don't have a driver's licence, so I have to get around on the bus. It isn't the best way to get around, but I make it work to help women get to their appointments. It takes me hours sometimes, but all that I can offer is my support. I take women to get clothes, set up welfare, and help find a safe place for them to go.

The peer health mentor program has given me chances to help women who are being released from prison. I get to connect with them before they are released, so I can get an idea of what services they will need to have the best chance of beating the revolving door. The saddest thing is that most women are mentally loaded[2] before they even pick up drugs. They are grinding their teeth and losing everything over and over again.

As a peer health mentor, I ask the women to rate, on a scale of one to ten, how much they want to use or drink. The desire just takes over your thoughts. It's the weirdest thing when you have no control over your own thoughts. The best plans go out the window and the cycle starts all over again. I remember, while I was serving time, women would always say that they were done with using and that they were never going to come back to jail. Being able to share my experience with women, I can help them stay focused on just getting through these feelings one second at a time.

> Unfortunately, once we reached the Downtown East Side, A's mood changed and all her plans to go to treatment went out the window! She no longer wanted to be mentored and returned to her addiction. This could have been avoided had we not had to go downtown to pick up her cheque—this was a huge trigger!
>
> —Peer Health Mentor

NOTES

[1] Quotes are from field notes written by peer health mentors about their experiences of mentoring women just released.

[2] "Mentally loaded" is a term used by women to describe someone who is about to be released from prison and whose mind is overwhelmed with thoughts about using drugs. The thoughts get stronger the closer she gets to her release date, until she begins to act as though she has used, exhibiting all the characteristics of an active user.

Being a Peer Health Mentor

PAM YOUNG

I HEARD ABOUT THE TRAINING to become a peer health mentor through Mo on Facebook. I wasn't sure whether I was worthy to become a mentor. How could anyone learn from me? I had only been clean and sober for three years, and I hadn't exactly done anything meaningful with my life so far. But I decided that I would go and do the training.

It wasn't long after that I got a call from Kelly, who was the project co-ordinator at the time. "Pam, I finally have the perfect client for you," she said.

"Where's she going?"

"She's going to Vancouver Island."

"Do I just bring her to the ferry terminal?"

"I need you to take her all the way to Nanaimo, and then jump back on the ferry and come home."

I felt instantly overwhelmed. But I told her I would do it.

Over the next couple days, I planned the bus route and ferry schedule and anything else I could think of. And on the day the woman was being released, I was an hour and a half early because I wanted to be prepared. While idly sitting on the bus, I started to doubt myself. What do I have to offer this woman? How do I help give her hope? But I pushed through my doubts and made it to the bus loop to meet her.

As I sat at the bus stop, I started having the same feeling in my gut that I used to have when I got out. Sitting at that bus stop triggered those feelings in me. I started remembering the last time I was released and dropped off at the bus loop. All I had were the clothes on my back (which were filthy, I might add) and a bus ticket to Vancouver. At that point in time, I never tried to convince myself I could get clean or change my life. I just wanted to get on that bus and get to Vancouver to get high as fast as possible. I never had anyone waiting for me. I never set up any support because I thought it was a waste of my time because I'd only screw it up. These are the kinds of thoughts that go through women's heads when getting out of jail, especially women with addictions: low self-confidence, no self-esteem, and no self-worth.

But on that day, as I sat at the bus stop and waited for this woman to arrive, I began to feel good that I wasn't in those shoes anymore. I felt empowered because I was clean and sober and about to start my journey helping women. I knew that if nothing else I could share my journey of recovery and success at being clean for three years. I had so much knowledge to offer. This day turned out to be a pivotal day. It was when I discovered my passion for helping women leaving prison.

When she arrived, I could see that she was full of anxiety. Her hands were shaking, and she was stuttering, which she told me she does when she has anxiety. She was very concerned about the details of the trip to the island. I reassured her that everything would be okay, that I'd planned everything well, and that I would stay with her all the way to the island. We started our journey, chatting away as we headed to the ferry. As we travelled along, her anxiety slowly went away. And so did mine. I started feeling really good about myself and what I was doing. Once on the ferry, we grabbed a window seat. It was a clear day so we had an amazing view. We spent most of the trip on the deck so we could smoke and enjoy the beautiful scenery.

Eventually, we made it to the island, and I helped her find the bus to get her the rest of the way home. I felt hopeful when we said goodbye that she would go home and do well. As we were saying our good byes, she said, "Thank you for inspiring me to do something different this time. Your stories of recovery have me wondering if I'm ready for recovery too."

"You can do it if you just try and give it a chance."

"I'm feeling butterflies about being back home on the island and wondering what the future holds for me."

"You can do anything you put your mind to. And besides, if I can do it so can you!"

She gave me a big smile and a big hug, and we said goodbye. As I hurried back to get on the ferry, I felt so good about myself. No more self-doubt, no more second guessing myself.

I had a quiet ride home on the ferry that day. There were hardly any people aboard. I grabbed a coffee and put my feet up and enjoyed the ride. I reflected on the day and how I felt about being a mentor. I felt so empowered sharing my stories and experiences with her. I loved being a mentor and I couldn't wait until I could do it again.

When I got home that night after a very long day, I told my husband about my day. I said, "I really enjoyed doing this! I'm excited to do it again."

"You have a lot to offer," he replied.

And for once, I honestly did believe I had a lot to offer these women. Twenty years of experience with addiction and I had been in and out of prison most of my life.

I told my husband, "It feels so good to actually believe my experience with addiction and history of incarceration is valuable knowledge that I can use to help others."

I started mentoring more often. And with each time, I felt better about myself and grateful to be a part of something so meaningful. The one thing I never expected was how beneficial the peer mentor program was to the mentors as well as to the women getting out.

Peer health mentoring empowered me to get involved in other projects and better myself. For instance, I worked for SFU last summer on a research project studying my community. I went out and did surveys and invited people to come to focus groups to determine what kind of support was most needed in the neighbourhood. In this project, I sometimes challenged myself because I had to talk to and work with people I normally wouldn't talk to. I had lots of doors slammed in my face. But when I did connect with people who sincerely cared about the community, it made it all worthwhile. And it was another research project under my belt!

> R. was very relieved to have an escort to the island since she didn't know her way around the city and didn't want to end up stuck in downtown Vancouver using again.
>
> —Peer Health Mentor

Unlocking the Gates—What We Do

MO KORCHINSKI

EVERY WEEK, WE REVIEW THE WEEK'S online court registry and record the names of all women who appear as "in custody." We mail a letter to every newly incarcerated woman, and we make sure to include a description of the Unlocking the Gates (UTG) peer mentor program, our office toll-free number, the UTG staff cell number for weekends and evenings, and an invitation to phone us and enrol in the program.

Our Unlocking the Gates program is accessible to incarcerated women seven days a week, and we don't exclude anyone. Our staff were all incarcerated themselves: we have first-hand knowledge about the challenges women face when they leave prison. Most incarcerated women have had a hard time trusting others, and we come alongside them with compassion, empathy, and a caring heart. We have been there. We listen to their fears and hopes for release, we help connect them to the right resources, and we help them to create a safe release plan.

The UTG peer health mentor program helps women who leave prison feel safe and supported. Women are also supported to achieve their own health and social goals. Being able to connect women with a peer health mentor who has prison experience gives women hope that they too can beat the cycle of incarceration and addiction. Also, women tell us that they take the UTG invitation letter that they received from us, and they use the letter as a lifeline if they get in trouble or need support in the community. Women can contact us if they have been out in the community for a while and need support.

Many women coming out of prison need help with food, shelter, medication, and clothing the day they get released, not a month down the road. Incarcerated women have a higher chance of going back to substance use—and overdosing and dying—if they have no support or resources upon leaving prison. Going back to the streets is the easiest option for someone who has nowhere else to go.

Our program is assisting women to connect with the health and community resources they have identified that they need. This can give them their best chance of ending the cycle of abuse. Generations of families are being affected by addiction, trauma, and crime, and Unlocking the Gates program gives women the hope, purpose, and the support they need to end the revolving door.

Job Interview

PAM YOUNG

I HAD BEEN A PEER HEALTH MENTOR for about a year when a position as a resource lead/tech came up at the Unlocking the Gates peer health mentor program. With some encouragement from Mo and a lot of help with my resume, I applied for the position. I felt overwhelmed at the idea of having a job. I hadn't really done any work that was legal before. One day I was sitting with my husband, and he could tell my brain was in overdrive.

"Honey, why are you stressing yourself out so much? I honestly think you are the perfect fit for the job. You know all about being a peer mentor."

"But I'm not computer savvy and I don't have a clue about working in an office."

"Don't overthink it. Just go to the interview and give it your best, and in the meantime look up some job interview questions online."

"That's a great idea!"

So I went online and started practising my answers to interview questions. I was a nervous wreck the day of the job interview. I looked at my hands when I was on the bus, and they were just shaking. But once I arrived, everyone made me feel more comfortable. I made it through the interview, and shortly afterwards they told me I got the job!

The way I felt that day was a lot like how I felt the day I picked up my first client. I felt empowered. And I was excited about continuing my journey with such meaningful work. I was also feeling excited about the future.

> S. has called me many times before and after her release. I've tried to encourage her to go to recovery, but she's not interested at this time
>
> —Peer Health Mentor

In Loving Memory of Jen (1983-2009)
Excerpt, Women in2 Healing Newsletter, Issue 5

RENEE BANNER

pain   confusion

overwhelming guilt
the soul of a woman wilted

tragic ending
to a burning desire

in her mind there
must have been
terror   fire

we'll miss her
smile   warmth
compassion

wish we didn't have
to say goodbye

her pain was
unbearable yet hidden

well from those close to her
not even they could tell

another life lost
to the disease of drug addiction

never forgotten
R.I.P. Jen Churchill

Milestones In Our Lives[1]

When we started off inside prison
we would not have thought that this would be possible.

Who would?

The other day
all of a sudden, I looked at you

and I realized that I have been present
for three of your birthdays.

And it made me start thinking
how this relationship from inside prison
has moved to the outside,
and we're celebrating life together.

It's like we're best friends.

We don't talk on the phone every day, right—you aren't my best friend
in that sense—but it's a heart connection.
I know that if I needed you, I could pick up the phone
and you would be there in a minute.

Common ground—
prison, research work, being a mother, a spiritual connection.
Intimate moments,
heart connection and trust.
Trust and integrity

I now get to walk with you in your life outside prison.

NOTE

[1]Created from Kelly Murphy's writing in a book chapter that was co-authored with Ruth Elwood Martin (Martin, Murphy, Buchanan).

REFERENCES

Martin Ruth Elwood, Kelly Murphy and Marla J. Buchanan. "Inside and Outside of the Gates: Transforming Relationships through Research." *Feminist Community Research: Case Studies and Methodologies.* Eds. Gillian Creese and Wendy Frisby. Vancouver: UBC Press, 2011. 168-188.

Working with Women

MO KORCHINSKI

WORKING WITH WOMEN with whom I have done time or with whom I have used drugs is not as easy as I thought it would be. After years of doing time together, it is great to see so many women who I consider my family, but it seems like we had more respect for one another behind the walls of prison than we do on this side of the wire fence. There are lots of strong personalities butting heads and forgetting to have respect and compassion for each other! We are more sensitive about our feelings than we were when we hid behind street life and drugs.

I sometimes feel like a referee in a hockey game that is out of control.

In-house fighting breaks out when others feel they deserve the same as someone who has worked hard for what they have. Going to school and applying for a job is not the same thing as being handed something for free. Working hard pays off. I wish everyone could have an education and a great job when they leave prison, and they can if they work hard for it. That life is so much better than living in addiction.

Significant Person in My Life

PAM YOUNG

MO IS THAT SIGNIFICANT PERSON in my life. She's given me ongoing support ever since I first connected with her in 2010 through Facebook. I always liked Mo when we did time together at BCCW and ACCW, but it wasn't until I saw how well she was doing and how many good things she was doing with her life that I really began to admire her. She always makes time for me if I'm having trouble with something at work or if I just need to vent about personal stuff. I consider her a close friend and always appreciate her advice and suggestions.

She's especially been a huge support since I took custody of my grandkids. I don't know if I could have made the decision to take them without her advice. She was right that it would be hard when we first took the kids, but we ended up falling into a routine just like she said we would. Then everything fell into place from there.

One time, I was working on something and I needed Mo's help, so I said, "Mo, can you help me?"

She said, "Sure." So she looked at my computer screen, and she said, "Right click." I clicked left by mistake, and Mo smacked me in the back of the head and said loudly, "I said right click!" We laughed and laughed.

Mo is dedicated to what she does and works hard at it. But she's also a lot of fun, too. Mo is not going to like that I shared this story, but we always get a laugh out of it. I love you, Mo!

Life and Death

MO KORCHINSKI

THE FENTANYL EPIDEMIC raging across British Columbia has caused increased fear among the incarcerated about their release. Women know that they are at risk because of their diminished opiate tolerance, which is due to their enforced abstinence while incarcerated. The number of people overdosing in BC is frightening for all addicts, but even more so for incarcerated women when they are being released with nowhere to go. Women don't want to come out of prison just to go back to using substances and living on the streets. Some, but not all, incarcerated women are released with the Take Home Naloxone (THN) kit after receiving the THN training inside prison. All the Unlocking the Gates peer health mentors have received the THN training and carry a THN kit.

> J. calls the office on a regular basis. Her son just passed away from an overdose, so she's been having a really hard time, especially since her sister overdosed this year too. I hope with some more encouraging I can convince her to give recovery a try. She is almost there.
> —Peer Health Mentor

In Celebration of Mo

COLBY

I FEEL EMPOWERED BY THE WOMEN I have in my life today, and it all started when I walked out of those cement walls.

I was blessed to have three amazing women greet me outside the door. One of them was Mo, and the other two were women I had met in recovery years before. They had always stayed in my heart, even when my heart had slipped away during the chaos of my life.

They brought me to the recovery house where I would reside for the next several months. Before I left, Pastor Mark advised me to continue asking questions. He told me that the truth would come to me. I use that advice in every aspect of my life today, something I never did before for fear of sounding stupid or inferior.

Today I am full of questions, and having women like Mo in my life who are willing to answer those questions has helped me considerably on my journey. Today I am coming up on one year clean, and it has been ten months since my release from ACCW. Today my life has purpose and direction. I started my post-secondary education in 2016, and I am following in Mo's footsteps. My story will turn out differently, even though it started the same way, with just a lost little girl stuck behind the gates of ACCW.

> Since B. is transgendered, she stressed to me how important women's clothing was to her. She said she needed to be able to pass as a woman. She also connected with a wig store, and they donated some good wigs to her.
>
> —Peer Health Mentor

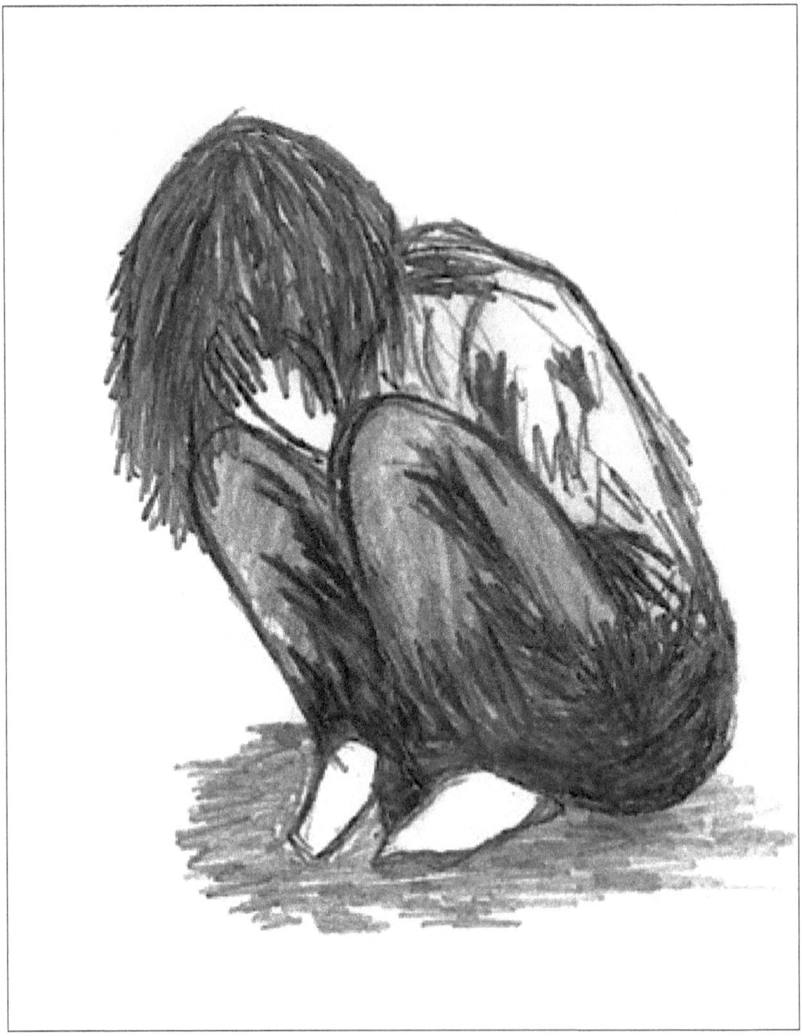

Driving Down the Windy Road

MO KORCHINSKI

Driving down the windy road, the sun is peeking brightly over the snowy tips of the Golden Ears mountain on this fine April morning. I first drove down this road fifteen years ago. Wow! Fifteen years. A lot has changed since then. If you had asked me fifteen years ago where I saw my life going in the future, I never would have imagined what my life is today. I think of all the blessings that I have in my life today, and I am filled with gratitude.

It doesn't seem to take that long to drive when you're not handcuffed and sliding around in the back of the sheriff's van. Knowing that I get to leave after picking up my client is a great feeling.

Today I am picking up a woman who is getting released after being inside for over a year. I got to meet Colby through a staff member at ACCW who wanted us to meet so I could mentor her while she was serving her time. This young lady was so ready for a change and to start her new journey in life. She wanted to get away from drugs, crime, and the lifestyle that goes hand-in-hand with addiction. Colby was given our book *Arresting Hope* to read, and we found out that we had a lot in common.

Today, I get to take her to treatment and watch her grow into the person that she is meant to be. Colby has the biggest, most caring heart I have seen in a person, and she loves her daughter, family, and partner so much. This is going to be one of the hardest things she has done in her life. It's not easy to move away from addiction, but she has some great support behind her. I am so grateful that I get the chance to walk alongside women who are being released from prison.

Today, I can say that I have the most rewarding job I could ever have thought to have. It also can be heartbreaking. Women who I met fifteen years ago are still struggling with addiction and are still going in and out of the revolving door of prison. I have learned over the years that I have to take a step back and not take it to heart that someone that I care about is not ready to change. I can tell them how great life can be away from the drugs, the crime, and the street life, but I know that a person has to be ready for that change. All I can do is be there for them. I will never give up on a woman who is still lost, hurting, and alone on the streets or behind the walls of prison.

> Although L. said she didn't need a mentor, we've been in touch quite often. She was doing extremely well for about three months, but she recently relapsed and I've been working with her mother who lives in the Interior to get her into a recovery house.
> —Peer Health Mentor

Numbers

RUTH ELWOOD MARTIN

AS OF MARCH 2018, a total of 346 women have phoned the Unlocking the Gates peer health mentor office from inside the correctional facility, seeking advice, support, guidance, and practical help. Of these 346 women, 174 women requested the support of a peer health mentor and met with a mentor at a mutually agreed upon location immediately upon their release.

One hundred and five women reported on their experience of three days of mentorship. Here is a breakdown of how they responded to the experience:

- 93 percent stated that their mentor assisted them in accessing community resources.
- 85 percent connected with a community resource during the first seventy-two hours after release.
- 47 percent accessed a family doctor during the first seventy-two hours.
- 30 percent received information from their mentor about how to access a family doctor.
- 83 percent required income assistance, and were accompanied by their mentor to obtain it.
- 90 percent stated that their mentor assisted them in achieving the goals that they had identified prior to their release.

We are keen to assess whether peer health mentoring leads to decreased future involvement with the criminal justice system. As we listen to women's voices, we know this to be true. However, we want to collaborate with the provincial government Corrections Branch so that we might accurately measure recidivism. We are grateful for the ongoing partnership and support from First Nations Health Authority, which recognizes the direct connection between women's experiences of the health system and the justice system, as illustrated by the vast disparities that Indigenous women experience within both systems.

What was it like having a mentor the day you were released?

Mentors: A Love Note

       awesome
my peer mentor gave me confidence
       comforting
inspiring to have someone who has shared my struggles
       great
she can relate to who I am and what I have gone through
       happy
great to have someone help me adjust to being free
       helpful
helpful to know someone who understands the difficulties of getting out
       understood
happy to have someone help me along the way
       hopeful
she knows what I am going through
       gratifying
awesome to be with somebody who doesn't judge you
       pleasant
there is support for us to stay focused and to reach our goals
       exciting
great having someone there to help me get home to the island
       inspiring
she makes me feel like I matter
       relieved
she gave me strength to stay sober
       perfect
I'm relieved that someone can help me
       blessing

she gave me a feeling of confidence that I can be a productive member of society
> positive

she gives me better chances for staying clean and not relapsing
> caring

comforting to have someone who knows what you're capable of
> supportive

she really inspired me to do my best
> friendly

perfect to get out and have someone there and not just be alone
> excellent

I feel like a normal person, not a caged wild animal, not a government number.

V. Preventive Health

I think people forget or don't know how vulnerable women who have faced childhood trauma react to being rejected. I know for me, being rejected just confirmed that I was worthless and that I didn't matter as a person.
—Mo Korchinski

There are so many progressive little pieces in the puzzle that makes up a healthy person. Some of us are missing more of those pieces than others.
—Kelly Murphy

It's easier to hear advice from a peer, from someone who's actually really experienced it and not somebody who's read it in the textbook.... So it touches me when one of my peers talks about stuff.
—Preventive Health Project participant

That was the day I decided with my whole heart that I was going to put everything I could into life again.
—Amber Christie

Doctor's Journey

RUTH ELWOOD MARTIN

WE MET TODAY FOR A PREVENTIVE HEALTH team meeting. The previous few months have been really difficult, with one community-based peer team member needing to be let go by UBC and another one who had relapsed into substance use. I am wondering, as one tends to do at New Year's, about life, and about what I am doing with my research activities. The question at the root of all this is, "Is it really worthwhile, this participatory health research? It is so much work, so emotionally draining—how can I keep this up?"

Today's team meeting was quite a turning point for the project, and for me personally. Community-based peer team members, Marnie, Wendy, and Larry were there. Together, we debriefed about what we'd learned during the difficult times we'd faced over the last year, and we brainstormed our research project goals for the coming year. We talked about health goals for the research participants, and about how we would assist participants to set their own health goals.

It dawned on me that we couldn't ask participants to set their own preventive health goals if we, as a research team, weren't also doing so ourselves. As a family physician seeking to live with integrity, I felt I could not invite patients not to smoke or to change their diets if I wasn't also doing the same. I saw this as analogous to our work with the women. During the meeting, the reality of my own breast cancer diagnosis last May overwhelmed me. I realized, as I sat with the reality of my cancer experience, that I hadn't embraced and integrated "regular exercise" into my life, which is the one evidence-based preventive health intervention that is most highly correlated with cancer prevention. Exercising for the sake of my own health always lands at the bottom of my list of priorities, because there is always some more urgent and pressing matter for me to attend to.

So, during our team meeting today, we went around the circle and *each set our own preventive health goal. I resolved to use my son's old rowing machine to row five kilometres when I roll out of bed in the morning, before breakfast, at which time I would be too sleepy and befuddled to rationalize myself out of this decision.*

—*Journal entry*

Imprisonment itself negatively impacts health for several reasons, including the shock and trauma of incarcertion, separation from families, enforced living with others suffering from serious mental health problems, unhygienic facilities, and poor self-care as a reaction to imprisonment (Douglas, Plugge, and Fitzpatrick).

In addition, people who were previously incarcerated have poorer health outcomes compared with other people who have never gone to prison, for three reasons. First, when people revolve in and out of prisons, they have disrupted access to continuous health care. Second, people with incarceration experience tend to live a life of social exclusion, stigma, and shame, which means that they don't access health care providers and preventive healthcare. Third, people with incarceration experience tend to not incorporate preventive health practices into their daily routines because they have reduced access to preventive healthcare. The longer an individual's incarceration, the more self-reported health problems tend to increase (Lindquist and Lindquist).

When Lora "Koala" Kwandibens and several other formerly incarcerated women were diagnosed with breast cancer, she wondered why the diagnosis was so common for women in prison. She resolved to do something about it, so we secured funding to do participatory preventive projects: a cancer preventive project[1] and a preventive health project.[2] The projects collaboratively adapted, piloted, and evaluated preventive health workshops, tools, and resources, and dealt with topics such as HIV, hepatitis C, mental health, addiction, as well as breast, cervical, and colon cancer, with formerly incarcerated men and women in Metro Vancouver and Nanaimo (Fels et al.). We hoped that the preventive health tools and resources might, one day, be incorporated into preventive health programs inside prisons.

NOTES

[1] A Participatory Approach to Improving Cancer Screening and Early Detection Among Individuals with Incarceration Experience, 2012–2014, funded by the Public Health Agency of Canada.
[2] A Participatory Approach to Developing Preventative Health Tools

for BC Individuals with Lived Incarceration Experience, 2011–2014, funded by the Vancouver Foundation.

REFERENCES

Douglas, Nicholas, Emma Plugge, and Ray Fitzpatrick. "The Impact of Imprisonment on Health: What Do Women Prisoners Say?" *Journal of Epidemiology & Community Health* 63 (2009): 749-754.

Lindquist, Christine H. and Charles A. Lindquist. "Health Behind Bars: Utilization and Evaluation of Medical Care Among Jail Inmates." *Community Health* 24.4 (1999): 285-303.

Fels, Lynn, Debra Hanberg, Larry Howett, Ruth Elwood Martin, Alex Nunn, Wendy Sproule and Renee Turner. "Arresting Cancer: Using Community-Based Participatory Approaches to Improve Cancer Screening and Awareness with Formerly Incarcerated Men and Women." The Collaborative Centre for Prison Health and Education, University of British Columbia, 2014. Web.

Amber's Story
"Walking Around Outside All Free"

AMBER CHRISTIE

IN MY SECOND YEAR DOWN THERE in Vancouver's Downtown East Side, there were bad nights when I'd get arrested. The East Van jail is horrible. There, I go through the worst pain of my life in a cell with two beds for six women. Within six hours I'm in full withdrawal. I'm puking. Then I seize. I wake up with urine all over me. I can't keep anything down. The pain in my legs is atrocious. I am in hell, and I am willing to do anything to get out. The first few times in jail they gave me a day or two, then a week, then two; then I was in there all the time, constantly sick.

In 2005, I was charged with assault with a weapon. I was released on bail, but I was charged with the same offence just two days later. This time the judge said I wasn't getting out, and I was remanded until my trial, almost a year away. My lawyer told me I would get out if I stayed on remand.

That time was my worst detox ever. Normally when you are put on remand you are transferred to Surrey Pretrial, where you get a shower and your own bed. But this time Surrey Pretrial was at full capacity, so I was stuck in city cells for nine days. Nine days of sharing a bed with three women, all drug sick, everybody puking and seizing and some screaming in pain. And it is cold; it's so cold that you sleep with your knees up in your shirt because they took your jacket. You get a blanket from ten p.m. to five a.m. I was finally transferred to Surrey after nine days. By the time I got to Surrey, I was in the next stage of detox and hungry. When I was arrested, I weighed eighty-nine pounds. I was starving.

I was in Surrey Pre-Trial for one day before I was transferred to Alouette Correctional Centre for Women. When we pulled in, I was in shock. There were girls walking around outside all free. The units were very different than the ones in Surrey. They were not cells; they were rooms and they didn't lock. There were beds, real beds. And we weren't confined to our cells. We could walk around in the unit, the bathrooms and showers were all shared, we had a kitchen, and we had TVs.

We were also allowed to smoke, and I smoked the best cigarette in my life. I had gone from absolutely horrid conditions in city cells to what seemed like a resort—well, at least for my first week. You had to work at ACCW. My body hurt every day for the first three months, but I pushed through. Since I had been homeless in the Downtown East Side for so many years, I was in bad shape. I had used too many used needles. In the Downtown East Side, you did ANYTHING to get that next fix.

Dr. Martin was very kind. She helped me get all my bloodwork in order. I was a very sick girl, sicker than I knew. And I was pregnant. I lost the baby. I was just too sick. Dr. Martin encouraged me to reach out to my family. I wasn't sure how I felt about that. Reuniting with my family made me fearful because I didn't want to give them false hope that I was going to stay clean when I got out.

A few weeks later, I had some more conversations with Dr. Martin and I decided I would see my family. My sisters were all grown up now, and they came almost every weekend to see me. My mother had also stayed clean the whole time I was down there and came on a regular basis to see me. I considered staying clean, but that meant having to deal with some really horrible hurt. My daughter. She was never far from my mind. That pain was torture. When I was using, it was easier; it numbed the pain. Now I had been clean for six months and I still had a few months to go, but I still struggled. My body ached for months, but eventually I felt better.

Iceberg

RUTH ELWOOD MARTIN

A GRADUATE PRACTICUM STUDENT, Claire O'Gorman, led focus groups and interviews with men and women with previous incarceration experience. Her goal was to explore what health priorities we might focus on in the preventive health projects. Twelve men with federal corrections experience and six women with provincial corrections experience participated. The men and women talked not only about disease health priorities, such as cancer, but also about the underlying causes of disease.

As Claire immersed herself in the transcript data, an iceberg image emerged for her: the diseases are what can be seen above the water, but many factors that impact health lie beneath the surface, with trauma sitting at the lowest tip (O'Gorman et al.).When Claire shared her iceberg illustration during a preventive health project team meeting, Suzanne, a community-based peer project assistant with incarceration experience, said, with tears running down her cheeks, "I see my life in that iceberg. You've captured my life."

REFERENCES

O'Gorman, Claire M., Megan Smith Martin, John L. Oliffe, Carl Leggo, Mo Korchinski, and Ruth Elwood Martin. "Community Voices in Program Development: The Wisdom of Individuals with Incarceration Experience." *Canadian Journal for Public Health* 103.5 (2012): 379-383.

PREVENTIVE HEALTH

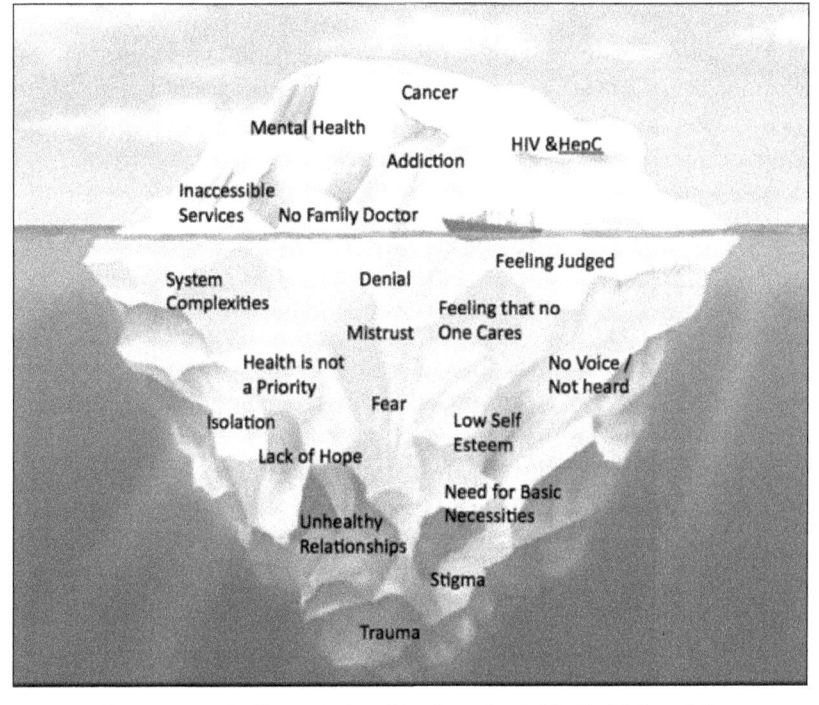

Figure reprinted with permission of the Canadian Public Health Association from O'Gorman et al.

Amber's Story
"We Were Somebody Still"

AMBER CHRISTIE

AFTER I WAS RELEASED I had a few hard weeks, but I decided that I was going to be clean. I was scared; I hadn't done anything without drugs since I was a young teen, and now I was twenty-three years old. I had lost my beautiful daughter. And I was dealing with an incurable disease, which took so much of my self-confidence. But I needed to do something. My family started taking me to NA meetings. I was going occasionally, and I felt like I could relate to some of the people. One night I was heading into a meeting when I remembered I had to turn the car lights off. My aunt gave me her keys and I went to turn off the lights. When I turned around, I saw this gorgeous man looking at me. He was smiling. I turned around to see if there was someone behind me, but there wasn't. He smiled and he just kept staring at me during the meeting. My confidence at this time was so low. I really didn't believe that anyone would ever want to be with me—not with all the stuff I had going on. I just turned away. After the meeting, he introduced himself as Ryan and asked for a ride back to his treatment centre. My family could see what was going on and they were quick to say, "Yes, of course, that's just down the road from us!! Hop in!"

I was nervous. I hadn't been with anyone in so many years. I honestly didn't know what to do. I was an adult now, and I was still learning how to be just me. Me with all my baggage. This man asked to come hang out at my house until his curfew. We talked. I was nervous. When it was time to drive him home, he kissed me. I didn't know what to do. I thought that if he knew about me he'd just run for the hills. He started calling me and we spent time together, but one friend told me I needed to tell him about myself. He said there was no way a guy like that was going to want me once he knew about me. Those were his exact words. I felt crushed, and I started to believe him. I invited Ryan over, and I told him I had health problems. He asked me if I had the big one (HIV) or the small one (Hep C).

I was terrified, but I told him I had both. I waited for him to ask for a ride home, but he didn't. His exact words were, "Okay, we're going to see a doctor and make sure you are going to be okay and healthy." My heart dropped. That was the day I decided with my whole heart that I was going to put everything I could into life again. It was scary, but a month later I had been clean for thirty days. And if you saw where I came from, that was a miracle. All the street workers told my family there was no hope for me. They said that they've been doing this a long time and that girls like me, they don't come out of there. But I took that thirty days—followed by sixty, then ninety—and I kept going. Ryan finished treatment and moved in with me.

Marnie's Health Tips

MARNIE SCOW

I WAS A COMMUNITY-BASED PROJECT ASSISTANT with the preventive health project. I did a lot of research on how I could become healthy after leaving prison, so I created and presented a PowerPoint presentation for preventive health workshops that contained practical, simplified nutrition tips that I had found helpful. For example, you can use your thumb, palm, and fist to estimate portion sizes. I told the participants about the dramatic health improvements that I had experienced since leaving prison by changing my eating habits. I framed the nutrition tips as essential components of my personal success story. I tried to make my presentation personable and relatable, and I also wanted to provide both knowledge and inspiration to participants. During focus groups following the workshops, participants shared that my presentation was their preferred component of the workshop!

Health Workshops and Peer-Teaching

LYNN FELS

"HOW CAN I HELP?" I've come to volunteer for one of the health workshops being organized for the preventive health research grants. They have been designed to reach out to formerly incarcerated men and women, to improve health.

There's an energy, a bustle that draws me into the group where the leaders are giving last-minute instructions to the peer mentors and volunteers. "Over here," calls someone, "we're doing a quick briefing on interview skills." I scoot over and listen intently as we are prepped for the workshop. The workshop leader instructs us on how to ask open-ended questions and how to run the tape recorder, and then assigns interview teams—two per table.

"No leading questions. Just listen," we are told.

This time around, the workshop is on health with guest speakers from the BC Cancer Agency and QuitNow BC. One of the peer mentors, who has several years of incarceration experience, speaks as well. She is nervous, but prepared.

The folks from the BC Cancer Agency overwhelm us with statistics, while the other speaker has us laying down pieces of paper on the floor and hopping from paper to paper like stepping stones in a river. On each piece of paper, we had scrawled ideas about staying healthy during a brainstorming activity she had led us through earlier. In teams, we now have to help each other navigate the stepping stones. "Be careful. Take my hand. Don't fall in the river," encourages one of my team members.

Along with the others, I write down two health goals, addressing the envelope to my home address. The letter to myself arrives two weeks later, reminding me of the promises I had made to myself to drink less coffee. And to swim every day.

Marnie grabs our attention right out of the gate with her presentation.

"I didn't used to look like this," she says, and we gasp when we learn the amount of weight she has lost through exercise and healthy eating. I take notes.

Creating spaces for those with experience and expertise in their own lives is exhilarating, and those of us listening lean into Marnie's advice. Those with incarceration experience recognize which presenters are travelling a similar journey. I am a witness. I am not isolated from their pain. Rather, I am complicit: I am part of the society that has decided that prison bars are a solution.

I listen to the insights, wisdom, and heartache of those sitting at the table as they share their experience, make suggestions, and tell troubling stories about their lives, the difficulties in affording dental care, and health challenges from years of drug abuse and neglect. We are in pairs, one assigned to ask the questions, the other to commandeer the tape recorder.

Listening is hard work.

Later, our research is transcribed, coded into thematic categories, culled for learning. Peer-teaching is hands-down the favourite activity of the workshop, followed by interactive activities. Mine is asking questions and listening to the generous responses that are offered in return.

I learn to listen to the pauses between responses and wonder what is left unsaid.

Anger and Fear

RUTH ELWOOD MARTIN

I AM SITTING IN A DOCTOR'S CHAIR. A man is standing over me, pointing a gun at my head.

I am frozen. Neither he nor I move. There is no sound in the room.

I sense his anger, his rage. Earlier, I had seen frustration and hatred in his eyes.

I am terrified. I want to curl into a ball, but I also want to run far, far away.

I must not let him read my eyes. I must try to appear professional, detached, cool. He must not see how frightened I am.

We have gathered together for a workshop entitled Navigating the Health Care System. It is part of a Rainbows of Desire theatre activity, facilitated by David Diamond. The audience includes project participants (men and women with incarceration experience), academic faculty, health care providers, and students. We selected the story that we are now exploring from among the narratives shared by preventive health project participants about their experiences in seeking health care. David had invited volunteers from the audience to come to the stage to make a shape with their bodies that depicts a desire that is felt by a character in the story. "You're not re-enacting someone's story. You are putting yourself into the situation—a doctor listening to a patient, a patient frustrated because he feels that the doctor is not listening to him." I am re-enacting the professional prison doctor; he is re-enacting the incarcerated patient.

David now encourages us to move into new shapes—our postures embodying the shape of our desires and feelings in response to the previous tableau we had created. "What are you feeling?" he asks. "Make the shape of that feeling." I lie on the floor, curling into a fetal position. The man who had pointed the gun at my head now crouches, head in hands, aghast at what he has done. Our shapes, in tableau, express his deep anger and shame, and my own suppressed fear, not visible when I am sitting in the doctor's chair, but present in the room nonetheless.

Later, when we all debrief with the audience, the man who had spent years behind bars shares that he was surprised to learn that a prison physician could be afraid of him. I share my new appreciation for the anger that incarcerated people feel when they do not receive the health care that they need.

Project participants in earlier focus groups had helped to develop the topics for the preventive health workshops: Navigating the Health Care System; Finding our Voices, Self Advocacy, and Support; Hepatitis C; HIV/AIDS; Mental Health; Addiction; Cancer Prevention and Screening; Cancer Prevention, Nutrition, and Exercise. I anticipated that these workshops would be excellent opportunities for peer-teaching and the sharing of experiences. I had not imagined that I would be front and centre, on stage, a gun at my head, my heart pounding, wondering, "How did we ever arrive at this place of such misunderstanding, anger, and fear in our relationships with one another?"

REFERENCES

Diamond, David and Fritjof Capra. *Theatre for Living: The Art and Science of Community-Based Dialogue.* Bloomington: Trafford, 2007.

Letter to Myself

MO KORCHINSKI

YOU HAVE SUFFERED DEPRESSION and anxiety because I blamed you for never being good enough for anyone, especially me. These thoughts came from experiences I had as a child, and I never learned how to process them. I believed my worth depended on the love I received from others. I didn't feel like I was good enough to be loved. How wrong I was! The truth is that I am an amazing, loving, compassionate, caring person. All the things I view as imperfections are what make me the beautiful person I truly am. I see now the thoughts you had regarding trust issues, fearing abandonment, and the need to be loved even in unhealthy ways came from experiences that were not your fault. I have learned from these circumstances, and they no longer need to define who I am. They no longer need to reflect negatively on you.

I was wrong to make you believe that anyone who didn't see you for who you are mattered. They don't. I know you spent so much energy trying to get the approval of others because I never gave it to you. This only put you in situations over and over again where you felt destroyed inside. You felt broken when someone you loved hurt or betrayed you, because you believed your worth depended on the love you received from them.

I am sorry for not loving you all these years, but I am learning how to now.

Love deeply the ones who see you for you and love you unconditionally. Let go of those who do not. The ones who choose to hurt instead of love are battling their own self-worth issues, and they should not have a single effect on how you view yourself. I realize now the importance of telling you to let go of whatever no longer serves you. Only the ones who understand this are worthy of the love you have to give. Love supports one another.

From this day forward, I promise to make choices each day to be more supportive, more encouraging, and more loving to you than the day before. Everyone will see you as even more amazing than they already do!

Amber's Story
"We Were Somebody Still"

AMBER CHRISTIE

MY LIFE WAS GOOD, but it was hard to connect with other women. So one day I searched ACCW on Facebook, and I found a group of alumni. They were all meeting up to connect and support each other. I decided to jump in. At our first group meeting, we ate great food and we gave our selves a name: Women in2 Healing. And with us in support were Linnea Groom from the W2 workers in ACCW and Ruth Elwood Martin, the gentle doctor, who convinced me to give myself a chance.

These women made us all feel like we were somebody still. We came together from the gutters, and then our journey began. We would meet and make Christmas cards for all the inmates. We made a whole lot of cards. Then around Christmas we decided to get donations of clothes, scarves, makeup, blankets, and money. We went to the Downtown Eastside to hand them out. When we ran out of clothes, Joy Happyheart and I used the money we had raised to clean out every pizza parlour down there and feed everyone we could see. We then went for a Christmas celebration. That day I felt like we became a real team.

I continued to stay clean, and after six months, I felt like I was becoming myself. My new self. Ryan and I moved into another family member's house that was bigger. He began working, and I stayed with NA and stuck tight with Women in2 Healing. I really felt that if these girls could do this, so could I. We all stuck together, and we found that we really wanted to make a difference for women coming out of prison. We wanted to bridge the gaps that have held back so many women when they are released. We were going to help others the way we were helped. That journey got us started on our research. We all came together and brainstormed some of the questions that we wanted to understand. We knew that if we wanted to change things, we needed proof that there was a problem. It took a while to get it all together, but eventually we did it. We applied for funding, and pretty soon after that we were employees of the Department of Family Medicine at the University of British Columbia. We had real titles. We were researchers. When women were released from prison, we invited them to complete a survey. We were hired because we were ex-inmates, and we understood what it was like to spend time in jail.

Wendy's Health Messages

WENDY SPROULE

I FEEL EMPOWERED WORKING on the preventive health project. The realization that I have thoughts and opinions that are a valued component of such meaningful work has allowed me to reclaim my individuality, something that was lost in prison, and very hard to find upon release. Another unexpected but welcome effect has been the interest in my work from peers and family members. Involvement in this project provides community-based project assistants with the capacity to recognize the positive potential of sharing what was seen as a negative experience (incarceration). Self-awareness is another key area that was improved during my participation. This required me to reflect regularly on how I was feeling, and to develop strategies to keep

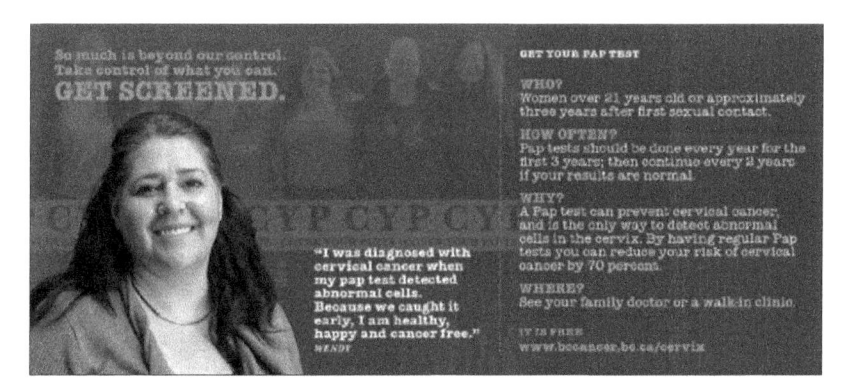

myself positive and confident. As I met goals and overcame obstacles, my confidence in my abilities grew, and I developed an increased ability to set more challenging personal goals (specifically in my career choices) and to actively pursue them. I now have a full-time position in a well-respected social service agency that I had previously felt unqualified to pursue.

We produced posters and reminder cards that feature messages by people with incarceration experience in real language encouraging others to get screened for possible health issues. They don't use generic models, and they focus instead on real people and identifiable situations. The pictures are large and the words are minimal. Overall, they deliver a message succinctly, in a format that could easily be displayed inside prisons to reach those who are incarcerated— a fundamental long-term goal of the project.

Preventive Health Workshops

PAM YOUNG

I CONNECTED WITH THE PREVENTIVE HEALTH Workshops through the Women in2 Healing alumni Facebook page. I went with some friends to see what it was all about. There were representatives from outside organizations who came to talk with us and help us better understand the importance of self-care and cancer screening. We learned about many different health concerns, such as Hep C, HIV, smoking, peer support, weight gain, cancer screening, and so on. I'm sure there are even more I can't think of right now.

The workshops were always very interactive, which helped me retain the information that was presented. And one thing I noticed was that I couldn't wait till the next workshop, mainly because they were helpful and informative and touched on issues we just don't discuss every day. Soon we started talking about these issues more and more as we began learning and the conversations began flowing. And I was able to meet new people and reconnect with old friends.

I love connecting with other people whose histories are similar to my own. It helps me feel like I'm not alone. At that point in my recovery, I needed that feeling of connection. Being around like-minded people helps me find the courage and strength to keep moving forward. Men or women, their struggles are like mine; it's easy to tell we share a connection.

Each time we went to a workshop, we would fill out a paper with our personal health goals, and then they would mail them to us a few weeks later to remind us of our goals. This activity helped me get my ass in gear. When I received my first letter in the mail, it was a reminder to book my pap smear and mammogram, and I was like, "Oh yeah! I was supposed to book my appointments." So I picked up the phone and did that right away before I started procrastinating. I booked my first mammogram and pap smear in two decades. I was in active addiction for most of those years, so looking after my health was pretty low on my list of priorities.

What stood out to me in particular was the workshop led by my peers. They did a presentation on eating healthier. They talked about what worked for them, and they shared lots of little tricks to help keep you focused on making better choices when it comes to eating. I think this workshop stood out to me because I could relate and the topic was of interest to me, and probably to others as well. Everyone seemed more attentive when our peers were doing their presentation than during other presentations; we can relate to one another because of our histories.

I also know that a lot of the other people who attended the cancer-screening workshop went out and got screened. I hope that everyone is still following up on their cancer screening. I know I am!

Doctors

MO KORCHINSKI

FINDING OUT A FRIEND OF MINE had stage four breast cancer opens my eyes to how important it is to get screened. I face my fear and check out a family doctor. Ever since I was sexually assaulted by a family member, I have hated doctors. The doctor I had as a child thought I was sexually active and didn't believe that I had been assaulted. I never told anyone who sexually assaulted me. I made up a story about a stranger.

A friend tells me about a female doctor who is taking new patients. All I have to do is go to the walk-in clinic and see her. My friend goes with me. As the doctor fills in the questionnaire, she asks, "Do you drink?"

I respond, "No."

She asks, "Do you use drugs?"

I again respond, "No," and then tell her that I have been clean for four years.

She puts down her pen and says, "If you relapse, you will have to follow my treatment plan or I will drop you as a patient." I want to get up and walk out. I feel judged, and all those negative feelings about doctors come back. My friend looks at me and smiles and I get through the appointment.

I go for my first pap test and survive, but my second pap test doesn't go as well. They find a lump. I have to go for a biopsy, and I am told I will have to wait a week to get the results. I call my family doctor a week later and make an appointment. I bring a friend with me so I won't miss anything, especially if the news is bad. I am diagnosed with cancer. I ask if I will die, and I am told no. I know I can get through it with the help of family and friends.

Cancer Walks Free

MO KORCHINSKI

MAKING A FILM[1] ABOUT CANCER awareness and prevention among people with incarceration experience is important to me because I have incarceration experience and I am a cancer survivor. For people with prison experience, going to a doctor can be overwhelming. The fear of judgement keeps me from going to a health-care provider even when I know that something is not right. Then a friend of mine was diagnosed with stage four cancer. She knew something was wrong, but it was too late to save her life. I learned from her experience that it is important to get tested early and that testing can save your life. My friend passed away, and today I want to make sure that no one else with incarceration experience has to go through what she and her family did.

As I was filming this documentary, I changed my opinion towards those who work with people with cancer. It taught me that I was being judgemental towards doctors and not even giving them a chance. I found while interviewing doctors that they were caring and had fears of their own. The unknown is scary for both the person with prison experience and the health care provider. My hope is that people who watch this film learn that we need to give others a chance.

Making documentaries is important to me, even telling my own story, because I want the people who are watching these films to see others as humans. As someone's daughter, son, mother, father or someone's sister or brother. I want to humanize the addict who is still suffering on the streets or sitting in prison My hope is that when someone sees a person on the street, they might have more understanding and compassion after watching the films.

NOTE

[1] See "Cancer Walks Free," in Appendix, Documentary Films

Shoplifting

PAM YOUNG

MY BIGGEST CHALLENGE in changing my life to become a normal functioning person in the community was correcting my addict behaviours. I spent more than twenty years as a shoplifter. I never paid for anything other than drugs my entire addiction. When I cleaned up, I never had enough money to survive on. I always went back to what I knew—shoplifting. Nobody is waiting to hire us when we clean up. I used all the money I had to rent a place to live and pay the bills, and there was nothing left for groceries. I felt I had no choice but to shoplift to put food on the table. And that's exactly how I would justify it to myself—I would tell myself I had no choice.

But I saw other women I knew who were working and doing well, and I wanted the freedom they had. I wanted to be able to survive without ever looking over my shoulder again. It's extremely hard for women leaving the criminal lifestyle to move past their addict ways of thinking and addict behaviours. Luckily for me, I had a lot of support from other women in my life and from my partner who encouraged me to let go and find another way.

After two years of sobriety, I let go of that way of thinking. Now I feel a huge sense of freedom. I don't have to look over my shoulder anymore.

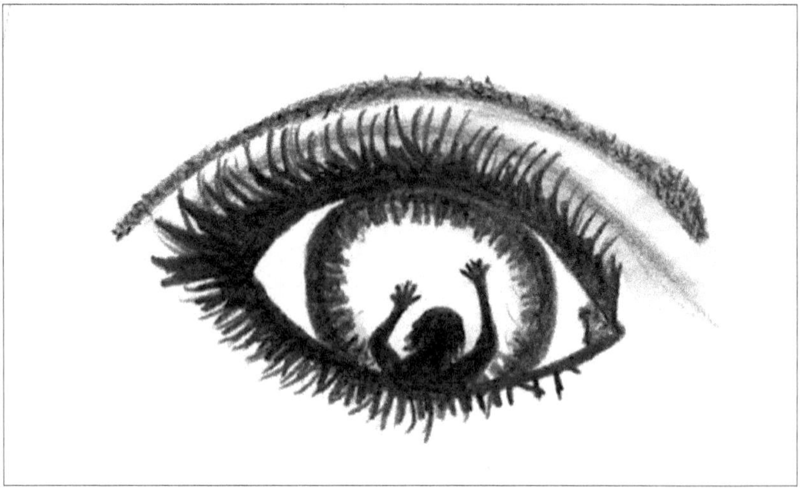

Passport Angst

MO KORCHINSKY

I HAVE A CHANCE TO GO to a world prison conference in Barbados to give a presentation about our research[1] and I am super excited but also scared, especially since I am going by myself and I have never travelled outside Canada before. I have watched so many movies where single women get targeted as soon as they get off a plane in foreign countries. I am freaked out that as soon as I arrive in Barbados they will run my name and see that I have prison experience and stop me from entering their country.

I arrive in Barbados. I am scared, and I look around for people who might be watching me. I have no idea how to get to my hotel. Some guys ask if I need a taxi and I say yes. I arrive at my hotel, and the cab driver helps me carry my bags into the lobby. He stands there as I check in. This makes me nervous. It reminds me of a movie I saw where guys would watch for your room number and then target you later. The front desk person hands me a key with my room number facing up. I think, the taxi driver now knows what room I'm in. I get to my room, and I am freaked out. I need to hide my passport so I am not stuck here forever in case the driver comes in to steal it. I take the garbage bag out, put my passport at the bottom of the garbage can, and then put the bag back in.

I change into my bathing suit and go to the beach. Wow! It is more beautiful than on TV. The water is blue and clear. The beach goes on forever, miles and miles of paradise. I go back to my room and sleep. The conference starts first thing in the morning. I find out that I can walk along the beach to get to the hotel where the conference is being held.

I know a few people from Canada who are going to be here, so I'm not that nervous about going, and I'm not presenting for two more days. My presentation is a photo presentation on Post-Incarceration Syndrome.

I still hate public speaking, but I know my experience will help others working with people in prisons to gain a better understanding of what someone goes through when they leave prison.

The first day at the conference is good—people from all over the world were presenting on their prison systems. Super cool to be here! I get back late and plan to go for a quick swim. I walk into my room and realize that the maid has cleaned it. I remember my passport hidden under the garbage bag. I run over to check and it's gone! Why would it be gone when there was no garbage in the can? Why would the maid touch an empty garbage can?

Oh my god, what am I going to do!? I walk down to the front desk and ask if they have my passport. I explain what happened. They call and talk to the maid and she says she hasn't seen it. I am thinking, Yeah, right, how would you not see it? We look in the garbage outside. No passport! It's gone! I'm freaking out that I will never be able to leave Barbados. The manager tells me I will have to go to the police and report it missing. Then I can get it replaced.

First thing in the morning, I go to the police station. Wow! It's nothing like the police stations in Canada. I walk in and explain what happened, and then the cop starts to yell at me, "What? Are you on drugs? How can you be so stupid?" It is not the smartest thing I have done in my life, but I explain that I have watched too many shows about single women being targets in foreign countries.

I end up walking out in tears. They will not help me, but the hotel manager helps me get a new passport from the Canadian embassy. I cannot wait to leave. My presentation goes well and I leave Barbados, relieved to be going home.

NOTE

[1] In 2009, Women in2 Healing received designated funding donations from academic friends and supporters to fund five members' travel to

present their research findings at national and international academic conferences in Montreal, Barbados, Spain, and Montreal. See Appendix, Funding Support.

Full Circle

AMANDA STALLER

WOKE UP FEELING EMOTIONAL, grateful, and humble that I can write my story when so many have died with theirs still untold. I survived things that kill most people, and I have a new lease on life. I've journeyed with many women, and their stories of pain and heartbreak are endless. Yet these women are so strong, so courageous.

I'm so privileged to be in their company, which brings me to Dr. Martin, who I call Ruth. She was once my medical doctor in prison, a woman I'd watch from afar. Her interest in us made me curious about her—Ruth, the researcher, the prison doctor. She is passionate about incarcerated women, about who they are, what happened to them, and where they go....

Most die, fall back into violence, addiction, abuse, the revolving door of the prison system.

And then there are the miracles, perhaps not fairy tale endings, but significant miracles: a woman who stays clean, seeks an education, and becomes self-supporting, who gives back, lives a life beyond her wildest dreams, and ARRESTS the disease of addiction, is given the greatest gift—FREEDOM, freedom from, freedom to....

I keep coming full circle. Think of it. How lonely I was for three and half years—getting my diploma, running a few races, holding onto affirmation. I was grinding against all odds. I had all these barriers. And, you know what, I'm not finished yet. I don't have anything more to write. The best is yet to come. It's here and it's now and I have new beginnings; the story is really just beginning.

I'm excited about falling in love. We want to be loved and we want to love. For me to have that man, I need to be that woman—independent, self-supporting, with a voice, with self-esteem, with freedom. I want to run with somebody, to go to hockey games, to share recovery, to be involved in people's lives. I want to help people, and enjoy life. I'm just renting a room, a bedroom. I have an old car. I don't have everything, but I have the best. I've had it all—the big house, the sports car. I had it all, but now it's like I'm in the right place in the world; I'm right where I am, and God's not finished with me yet.

What are you most looking forward to now that you have been released from prison?

Get

get my children back
        get off drugs
get into a day program
        get resources
get away from the jailhouse mentality
        get a life
get more education
        get a pardon
get a job
        get a place to call home
get back to the community
        get resources
get good food
        get counselling
get the help I need
        get treatment
get well

In Order To

achieve my goals
        be free
create healthy relationships
        deal with medical issues
enjoy freedom
        focus on the future
go home
        help others
improve my life
        join a program
keep a positive outlook
        live independently
maintain sobriety
        name my fears
open my mind
        pay debts
question why
        reunite with family
start fresh
        take care of myself
understand my past
        voice my stories
work on my new life
        x the negativity
yearn for success
        zero in on what really counts

VI. Indigenous Healing

We've got to research why women in prison are getting breast cancer. We have to stop this and figure it out.
—Lora "Koala" Kwandibens

I found that when the women start to learn about spirituality and ceremonies, they are like sponges—they are happy to reconnect with some spiritual context. It helps them to be grounded no matter where they are.
—Elder Mary "Holy Cow" Fayant

I recently got my daughter back. My children are the reasons that I'm doing what I'm doing now, and the reasons that I am doing so well.
—Odessa Marchand

Doctor's Journey

RUTH ELWOOD MARTIN

*I*AM THINKING ABOUT LORA—*lots of memories come back to me. I think of Lora, with her toddler son in her arms, talking at Collaborating Centre for Prison Health and Education Conference in the UBC Longhouse's Sty-Wet-Tan Great Hall about the need for health in prisons. I think about Lora at a Women in2 Healing meeting, at Nicola Valley Institute of Technology, putting her sticky notes on the board and talking so vivaciously about the research work that she's done for Women in2 Healing.*

I think of her in her townhouse in Mission, where she and Stewart lived. I think of her on Galiano, creating a papoose for baby Stewart to carry him close to her body. And baby Stewart sleeping in a hammock that she devised, strung between two trees. I remember her playing with him, sanding chairs on the deck, her long black hair swaying with her movement, and also pretending to sand Stewart, him giggling and hugging her.

And, a few years later, the kayak. She was riddled with cancer, and she was determined to take him out on the sea. I remember Lora in the kayak, Stewart asleep in the front seat with her, paddling them both back to shore, her face lit up by a gentle smile.

I think of Lora being videotaped on Galiano when she'd lost her hair to chemotherapy. She talked about food and nutrition and what it takes to be healthy. She told me about her childhood in an Objibwe community in the bush where she had lived with her grandparents—hanging the bedding out to dry in the morning.

She was such a strong, passionate person—her laugh, her sense of humour. She suffered so much at the end. I mourn her death. And memories of Lora inspire me to continue in this work. She would say to me, "We need to learn more and to make it better for all these women."

—Journal entry

Indigenous people face extremely high rates of incarceration, as well as of involvement and interaction with the justice system. Indigenous people—meaning First Nations, Inuit, and Métis (FNIM)—in Canada face additional discrimination because of the long-term multigenerational effects of colonization, intergenerational trauma, attempted cultural genocide, and ongoing racism. Canada's colonial history, including intergenerational experiences of residential school abuses and/or dispossession, and ongoing discriminatory practices have a devastating impact on Indigenous peoples' involvement with the criminal justice system, which results in expressions of trauma, pain, anger, and grief.

In addition, the social determinants of health for Indigenous peoples result in health inequities (Reading; CEDAW; Reitmanova). Social adversities and health disparities within the general Indigenous population are well documented and relate to substance use, intergenerational abuse, low levels of education, employment and income, poor housing, and inadequate health care (Adelson).

High rates of incarceration of Indigenous people occur in Canada, with 33.1 percent of all incarcerated women and 19.1 percent of incarcerated men in Canada being Indigenous, despite the fact that Indigenous people comprise only three to five percent of the Canadian population (Department of Justice). In British Columbia, approximately 40 percent of provincially incarcerated women are Indigenous.

In *Arresting Hope*, we described ways in which the prison participatory health research was shaped by Indigenous women who were members of the research team and by Mary Fayant, the prison Aboriginal Elder known as Holy Cow. From the start of the prison participatory health research project, spiritual health was included in the research and was considered to be as important as physical, emotional, and mental health. Conversations in the research room were conducted in a circular manner, with everyone taking turns, so that everyone's voice could be listened to and heard. Indigenous women identified that they needed to research and learn about their cultural practices and their languages, because this was important for their health and healing. Indigenous women on the prison health research team passionately wanted to be reconciled with their children and with their families.

When the participatory health research moved outside of the prison walls, Lora "Koala" Kwandibens and Amber Christie's leadership, passion, and resilience inspired us. Lora became one of Women in2 Healing's most active and passionate members. She urged us to apply for seed funding with the Network for Aboriginal Mental Health Research (NAMHR) in order to explore reasons why formerly incarcerated

Indigenous women in her own neighbourhood (Mission, BC) were not accessing local community health and social services. Amber arranged weekly meetings in a room at Union Gospel Mission, and pairs of community-based project assistants walked around the town, inviting women who were living on the street to participate in semi-structured interviews. Those who remained in the room transcribed the interviews and discussed the emerging findings. Our aim was to understand women's experiences of facilitators of and barriers to spiritual, physical, mental, and emotional health.

In 2015, ninety-four calls to action were published by the Truth and Reconciliation Commission of Canada. Thirteen calls relate to action for justice that directly impacts First Peoples of Canada's experience with the criminal justice system. Other calls are for action in health, education, and culture, each of which have a potential impact on Indigenous people's involvement with criminal justice system. The women we meet in the pages of *Releasing Hope* call each of us to a journey of action, towards a deeper understanding, and towards justice and meaningful reconciliation.

REFERENCES

Adelson, Naomi. "The Embodiment of Inequity: Health Disparities in Aboriginal Canada." *Canadian Journal of Public Health* 45 (2005): 61.

Department of Justice. *Aboriginal Justice Strategy Evaluation: Final Report*. Ottawa: Government of Canada, 2011. Web.

Reading, Charlotte Loppi and Fred Wien. *Health Inequalities and Social Determinants of Aboriginal Peoples' Health*. Prince George, BC: National Collaborating Centre for Aboriginal Health, 2009. Web.

Reitmanova, Sylvia and Robyn Henderson. "Aboriginal Women and the Canadian Criminal Justice System: Examining the Aboriginal Justice Strategy Through the Lens of Structural Social Work." *Critical Social Work* 17.2 (2016): 7-13. Web.

The Convention on the Elimination of all forms of Discrimination Against Women (CEDAW). United Nations Treaty Collection, New York, 18 December 1979. Web.

Truth and Reconciliation Commission of Canada: Calls to Action. Winnipeg: Truth and Reconciliation Commission of Canada, 2015. Web.

They're Going to Be Living in Your Community When They Get Out

ELDER MARY "HOLY COW" FAYANT

Presentation to the Canadian House of Commons' Standing Committee on the Status of Women, Indigenous women in the federal justice and correctional systems[1]

WE ACKNOWLEDGE that we are meeting on the ancestral, traditional, and unceded Coast Salish territory of the S<u>k</u>w<u>x</u>wú7mesh Úxwumixw (Squamish), Tsleil-Waututh, and xʷməθkʷyəm (Musqueam) First Nations. We thank you for the opportunity to share our words with your committee today.

My name is Mary Fayant, born in Saskatoon, Saskatchewan, Métis Cree nation. My teachings are Lakota. I worked at BCCW-ACCW-Surrey Pre-Trial provincial and federal. I have worked with federal women inside for ten years, and now I've been working with men inside for seven years, and also in the community once they're released. I speak for myself, and for my teachings. I always tell the women, "You don't have to take on my teachings; you can borrow them until you can go back home, and then you can pick your own teachings from your own Nation."

Many of the women come into institutions (or live in the community) without knowing their own teachings. They don't have their own identity; they're lost, and they're disconnected. When the women start to learn about spirituality and ceremonies, they are like sponges—they are happy to reconnect with some spiritual context that feels good for them, and they don't have to hurry to learn it. It's not a religion; it's spirituality. It helps them to be grounded no matter where they are.

NOTE

[1] Elder Mary Fayant, Chas Coutlee, Odessa Marchant, Mo Korchinski,

and Ruth Elwood Martin presented to the Canadian House of Commons' Standing Committee on the Status of Women, Indigenous women in the federal justice and correctional systems, on 6th February, 2018. Web.

Notes for Aboriginal Healing Outside the Gates – 1

LORA "KOALA" KANDIBENS

ANOTHER PARTICIPATORY HEALTH PROJECT we're doing is called Aboriginal Healing Outside the Gates.[1] It started when Aboriginal women on the street in Mission started telling me their stories. There were some places they couldn't go anymore (e.g., the Mission community centre, friendship centre, care office, women's resource centres). They were banned because they used them so much and overstayed their welcome. They felt workers had lost faith in them. But they were homeless with nowhere else to go. They were looking for a place without any conditions—unconditional support.

NOTE

[1] Those involved in the Aboriginal Healing Outside the Gates research project came together for a writing retreat on Galiano Island, to discuss and brainstorm ways of writing about the project. We transcribed the audio tapes of our discussion and selected excerpts for *Releasing Hope*.

Notes for Aboriginal Healing Outside the Gates – 2

MO KORCHINSKI

WE WERE RECORDING INTERVIEWEES on the streets with a tape recorder. But we'd go to Tim Horton's and there was music on, so it didn't record very well. We ended up losing quite a few interviews. If we conducted the interviews on the street, the traffic sound interfered. I found audio recording hard. Eventually, we brought the participants back to the Union Gospel Mission to do the interviews there if they wanted.

They weren't short interviews. Even the quick ones were thirty minutes. A lot of Aboriginal women didn't know what mental, spiritual, and emotional health was. We all knew about the medicine wheel because we'd learned it from Elder Mary "Holy Cow" Fayant inside ACCW. We were really shocked that a lot of the interviewees didn't know about it. So they didn't even know what we meant when we asked, "How do you rate your mental health?"

Next time we do it, we will have to explain or give examples. For example, for mental health, we can ask, "What is going on in your head?" and for emotional health, we can ask, "What is going on in your heart?"

Aboriginal Healing Outside the Gates Interview

If you try to push me, then see ya,
wouldn't wanna fuckin be ya.
And then if I decide to
I will come to you.

My daughter was a permanent ward of the custody court, and I got her back.

To just stay clean. If I stay clean, sober, I will do great.
Yeah, and having lots of support out here really helps too.

Emotional, you mean like, being stable and like, um, not all over the place.
I know at some points I get anxiety, and I ... I feel like I'm
all over the place.

Accomplishing something, being able to accomplish everything I want

Working on the problems from all the way back in my childhood,
from childhood all the way up.
The drugs
       and stuff   from childhood.

Just staying clean right now is bringing my emotions out....
I just cover them up.

And having my kids keeps me sane.

Talking to the right people,
changing the old crowd to a new crowd.
When I do go through detox I usually relapse....
I gotta get a grip on what's going on right now inside me.

You're just so isolated and everything,
and you don't know what's happening.

No goals, not yet.
To love myself

I don't understand some of these questions.

Aboriginal Healing Outside the Gates
Theme Analysis

THEME 1: SELF-EMPOWERMENT, CHOICE[1]

"I don't want to be forced to do something. If someone pushes me, I am just going to say fuck it, and when I say fuck it, I mean fuck it. So if you try to push me, then see ya, wouldn't wanna fuckin' be ya."

THEME 2: NEED TO STOP REVOLVING PRISON DOOR

"The best thing for keeping mental health in good shape is staying out of prison."

THEME 3: ANGER/LONELINESS/GRIEF (DEATH)/NO CONNECTION/ DESPAIR

"'Spiritual' doesn't mean anything to me right now 'cause you know what I've been through—so much death in the past few months. I don't believe in anything right now. I'm just choked! My family's gone; my sisters are all gone. It pissed me off. It screwed me around."

NOTE

[1] The quotes and the themes under which they are placed emerged from interpretative description analysis of data from the Aboriginal Healing Outside the Gates research project. Semi-structured interviews were conducted and audio-recorded with Indigenous women who had formerly been incarcerated. Audio-recordings were transcribed verbatim, with identifiers removed, and then transcripts were analyzed.

They're Going to Be Living in Your Community When They Get Out – 2

ELDER MARY "HOLY COW" FAYANT

Presentation to the Canadian House of Commons' Standing Committee on the Status of Women, Indigenous women in the federal justice and correctional systems

IN THE FEDERAL SYSTEM, men and women need to have partnerships with our communities, because they want to learn about the communities that they left behind—the languages, the songs, and the food. They want to speak with their Elders; so bringing Elders from the communities into the correctional institutions would be very good. This would mean having a vehicle available with a citizen's escort to pick up the Elder and drive him or her into the correctional institution. I'm very grateful that this happens in the Pre-Pathways.[1]

Also, I teach the women to share the teachings, so the teachings don't have to come from the teachers and elders only; they can come from each other—the women teaching about each other's nations and each other's ways. The women all come from different nations. I've seen women come together for ceremony. They work together, helping each other; they get the food together, get the wood for the fire together, and prepare the food for the feast together.

NOTE

[1] "As part of the Continuum of Care ...Pathways Initiative provides a path of healing within institutions for offenders who demonstrate a commitment to follow traditional healing as a way of life, twenty-four hours a day. Pathways is first and foremost an Elder-driven intensive healing initiative, that reinforces a traditional Aboriginal way of life through more intensive one-to-one counselling, increased ceremonial access, and an increased ability to follow a more traditional Aboriginal

healing path consistent with Aboriginal traditional values and beliefs" (Canada Correctional Service).

REFERENCES

Canada Correctional Service (CSC). "Establishment and Operation of Pathways Initiatives." Government of Canada. Web.

Aboriginal Healing

AMBER CHRISTIE

Presentation to the Canadian House of Commons' Standing Committee[1]

I AM A CREE FIRST NATIONS WOMAN. I was first incarcerated at the age of twenty, and I returned to prison thirty times over the next five years. I suffered from a severe heroin addiction for many years and lived on the streets of Vancouver's East Side. I have been free of drugs, alcohol, and prisons for four and a half years. I am a mother and a contributing member of society.

We have just gotten to the halfway point of our grant-funded community-based participatory health research project Aboriginal Healing Outside The Gates.

In this project, we are doing in-depth interviews with Aboriginal women who have been in a provincial or federal correctional centre. The goal of this project is to see which challenges Aboriginal women are facing after they have been in the community for a while, what kind of impact incarceration has had on their journey into re-integrating, and what the barriers are. We're also looking at what percentage of women have been accessing health care and community resources after their release.

What we have heard from women so far is that a big percentage of women have reverted to drugs and alcohol due to an inability to properly access resources and gain employment. But women still have hope that they will be able to change things.

They have also told us that they need to be treated with dignity and respect. That's not always the case after being incarcerated. They don't want to be pushed into anything after they've been incarcerated. The biggest positives in my life today are stable employment, a supportive network of safe people, and having someone who listens to me.

NOTE

[1] Amber Christie, Brenda Tole, and Ruth Elwood Martin presented to the Standing Committee on Public Safety and National Security, Federal Corrections: Mental Health and Addictions, Ottawa, March 2010.

Aboriginal Healing Outside the Gates
Theme Analysis

THEME 4: STEP BY STEP/PRAYER/NEED FOR TREATMENT/CREATOR/ SOBRIETY/PEOPLE LEFT/FEAR/REACHING OUT FOR SUPPORT/A POSITIVE STATE OF MIND—INTERRELATED

"Real crucial, like I'm really in need of praying, a dire need to get help. Like a crisis type of deal. Like, I'm trying to get into treatment right now, so my prayers are all ongoing. I'm just constantly praying for, like, a miracle or some frickin' thing. But I know I gotta make it. Like, one day at a time. So, yeah, like it's really important for me, like I'm really relying, trying to rely on the Creator to help me get back on the wagon. I've been clean like two days and its frickin' hard. Like, I'm off pot, right, and I gotta keep it real, right. I gotta stay balanced, like, yeah! I'm living in fear, I think, and I have to pray."

THEME 5: CONCENTRIC CIRCLES/VOLITION

"I think a lot of things in my life are screwed up—mentally and fucking physically! Everything needs to be better and things need to get better in my life—my family, my friends, and everything. But I am not even trying because I am not ready yet."

THEME 6: ACCESS TO FOOD AND NO DRUGS IN PRISON/ISOLATION IN PRISON/DEPRESSION

"I was using for, like, two weeks, three. And then, like, when I was in court, I couldn't even talk, that's how messed up I was on cocaine. Like, the judge was like, Miss, why can't you talk to me? And I was like, *guh, guh, guh,* like I can't."

THEME 7: POOR RELATIONSHIP WITH DOCTOR

"I got a new one, and I don't like him."

They're Going to Be Living in Your Community When They Get Out – 3

ELDER MARY "HOLY COW" FAYANT

Presentation to the Canadian House of Commons' Standing Committee on the Status of Women, Indigenous women in the federal justice and correctional systems

IT IS VERY IMPORTANT for our people to do art therapy—beading, sewing, making drums. This is our way of life and it helps the spirit. It is very important for people to work with their hands; it connects their whole being—mental, spiritual, physical, and emotional.

Many people have wondered why Indigenous women want to have ceremonies and medicines inside prison when they haven't done it outside prison. For some women, they were born with the spirituality and raised with it, but then they got away from it and got into drugs and alcohol, gangs, street life, residential schools, foster care. So when they hear the beating of the drums—which is the heartbeat of the people—they get sad and they cry and they don't know why. It's because they heard it when they were in their mother's tummy or when they were babies, and that connection is there, even if they don't think it is. They don't understand why they are so comfortable with it.

Notes for Aboriginal Healing Outside the Gates – 3

MO KORCHINSKI

LORA WAS DIAGNOSED WITH BREAST CANCER.
Lora kept fighting, so we kept fighting for Lora's passion. We wanted to make it our passion because we weren't sure she would make it through the summer. Lora couldn't sit up, keep anything down, or take care of her son. Her passion turned into our passion. She wasn't sure she would make it.

They're Going to Be Living in Your Community When They Get Out – 4

ELDER MARY "HOLY COW" FAYANT

Presentation to the Canadian House of Commons' Standing Committee on the Status of Women, Indigenous women in the federal justice and correctional systems

IT IS IMPORTANT that women bond with their children. I have witnessed women in prison changing when babies are there—not only those who are mothering the children, but also the rest of the women in the population, all trying to be "aunties" to the child. I witnessed staff helping also, watching the little children picking up drums, and dancing and singing with their mothers. I saw them saying their prayers and learning how to smudge with the medicines before going to bed.

Women change when they can bond with their children—they change emotionally, mentally, physically, and spiritually. Women then have dreams, desires for the future, not only for themselves but for their children. They go after their education and their careers; they plan, and they are productive. Women need more parenting courses to be available so they can learn how to take care of their children.

Aboriginal Healing Outside the Gates
Theme Analysis

THEME 8: ISSUES IN COMMUNITY—ANGER/PERSONAL BOUNDARIES

"I got anger problems and depression. I don't consider them problems cause I can get over them. Butttt, welllll, okay, I really got an anger problem, and when you talk to me, I'll listen, but I don't have a compliment for that. Okay? I'll be pissed off if you say something wrong, but I'll say it right back to you. But anyways go on. I TOLD YOU, don't ask me."

THEME 9: BARRIER TO RELEASE/CYCLE OF ADDICTION

"It was good because I was finally released. It was bad because I went straight to drugs. Into my old behaviours."

"I'm not where I want to be yet. I've been working on that."

THEME 10: COMMUNITY IN PRISON/FEAR AND ISOLATION IN AND OUT

"Paid my dues. And I learned that there were a lot of friends, good friends, in there, and I had a lot of fears that I learned were just in my head. I didn't like being isolated, although it helped me look at my life in a different way. I had a hard time listening to people, figures of authority. I had a hard time with the cops. I had an attitude when I went in there. Paid my dues."

Notes for Aboriginal Healing Outside the Gates – 4

AMBER CHRISTIE

WE ORGANIZED A COMMUNITY FORUM in Mission called the Outside the Gates Info Fair. We presented the findings as a work in progress to members of the neighbourhood's community organizations. I developed and distributed the invitations and organized most of the event, which was held in the Union Gospel Mission building in Mission.

Then I was invited to go to Montreal to give a keynote research presentation about our Aboriginal Healing Outside the Gates research.[1]

NOTE

[1] As mentioned earlier, in 2009, Women in2 Healing received designated funding donations from academic friends and supporters to fund five members' travel to present their research findings at national and international academic conferences in Montreal, Barbados, Spain, and Montreal. See Appendix, Funding Support.

Outside the Gates Info Fair
Research that Matters

MO KORCHINSKI

THE DAY IS HERE WHEN WE PRESENT our research findings at Outside the Gates Info Fair in Mission! We invited community organizations who work with women who live on the street and/or who have been incarcerated. Our biggest question is: why do the women feel like they are not getting the support they need? Are they getting discriminated against because they are Aboriginal and/or because they were in prison?

We sent out invitations to all the organizations that we thought would have contacts or resources to help Aboriginal women with prison experience. We had a great response from the invitees, and so many people responded to say that they would come.

I am so nervous that no one will show up—(I think people forget or don't know how vulnerable women who have faced childhood trauma react to being rejected. I know that for me, being rejected just confirmed that I was worthless and that I didn't matter as a person)—but slowly the room fills up. We serve lunch to our guests and ask everyone to take a seat. We introduce the project and explain why we feel the need to explore women's views on services in Mission. We emphasize that we want the women's voices to be heard.

The response we get after we present the research is great. People are really open to making changes and to work more effectively with Aboriginal women.

After our presentation, I really see the value in research—the questions you ask and the findings. Wow! It can be very powerful information, and it needs to be heard. People who don't have a voice need to get their voices heard.

My first research project is a great success, and now I have the research bug!

I want to keep following this journey....

Aboriginal Healing Outside the Gates Theme Analysis

THEME 11: HOUSING/LACK OF SUPPORT AND DIRECTION UPON RELEASE/FEELING OF LONESOMENESS AND ABANDONMENT

"Yeah, housing is a big issue, actually. 'Cause, what happens is, I coulda gone back to the streets, or I coulda gone home, you know. I coulda done a whole lota things right. And I had some money in my pocket right. So yeah, a lot of support—when you're coming from prison, when you're leaving—would be good to have. Like a support system waiting for you, because when you're released it's just like where do you go? Right?"

"Yeah, you get a little bag and away you go with your little envelope and you're gone—right? There was support there but I had to do it myself (laughing) while I was getting (laughing)."

A Piece I Didn't Know Was Missing

CHAS COUTLEE

Presentation to the Canadian House of Commons' Standing Committee on the Status of Women, Indigenous women in the federal justice and correctional systems.

I AM FROM MERRITT, BC, and I am a mixed-race woman of Nlaka'pamux ancestry from my mother and Irish ancestry from my father. I am the mother of a fantastic twenty-two-year-old daughter. I was incarcerated many times, starting in my late twenties, in provincial and federal institutions. I spent a total of four and a half years inside federal corrections. Now I'm a third-year social work student at Nicola Valley Institute of Technology (NVIT).

I have been in long-term recovery since January 2010. I work as a child and youth care worker with Indigenous youth, which means I am a role model and a mentor. For example, I encourage them to pursue education; I help them to get to doctor's appointments. I am currently doing my social work practicum with Indigenous mothers and children. My goal on this educational journey is to become a specialized and culturally competent trauma therapist working with women to overcome their trauma.

When I was incarcerated for the last time, I had an opportunity to start working on my own trauma through ceremony and weekly visits with a psychologist. I intentionally set myself up to do this work—however big and uncomfortable the feelings were, I needed to know how to live without drugs to numb the pain.

Elder Holy Cow did circles with us every day at lunch. We set up a sweat lodge; we helped her prepare the food. She did pipe ceremonies with us. She was always available. She believed in me. I noticed that women who wanted to participate in ceremonies would refrain from drug consumption out of respect. This was the first time I recognized culture as a powerful and effective tool for recovery.

Elder Holy Cow helped me put back a piece I didn't know was missing. I carried shame for being Indigenous. Because I have light skin, not everyone knows I am, in fact, Indigenous. I hear racist judgments and I internalized the racism. I felt shame for being Indigenous.

Elder Holy Cow became a positive role model for me, and she helped me remove the shame. This was a huge part of my healing. My last parole hearing was in a circle, and we held an eagle feather when we talked. I was able to share my truth and talk about my hopes and dreams for my life moving forward. Because this last parole hearing was Elder assisted, it felt so completely different than a non-Indigenous healing circle. Indigenous support is imperative for Indigenous people.

When I was leaving prison to go to a five-week residential treatment program for survivors of trauma and abuse, I felt scared and broken. Elder Holy Cow believed in me. She was an honourable and truthful woman. She told me my spirit is strong—I believed her. Holy Cow always reminded us, "Just because this is where you're at right now, doesn't mean that this is your final destination. You're someone's mother, someone's aunt, and someday you're going to be someone's granny, and one day you need to pass the teachings down." I wanted more than anything to be a good mum, a good role model for my daughter. And today I am.

I choose to live my life today with one foot in ceremony and the other in education. Indigenous culture saves lives, and education creates choices to live well and become productive members of society.

Aboriginal Healing Outside the Gates
Theme Analysis

THEME 12: ACCESS TO TREATMENT AND CHILDREN POST RELEASE

"Daughter? I lost custody of my daughter 'cause they found out I was using and I was arrested. I had to get help and gain back custody of my baby. I kinda messed up my credibility for her. I had to earn back the trust both from the social workers and from my daughter."

THEME 13: BARRIERS—JUDGMENT/CRIMINAL RECORD

"People judge you. They look at you in a different way, right, like you've been in jail!"

Aboriginal Healing Outside the Gates Interview

How important is spirituality to you?

Real crucial, like I'm really, like, like if I, like in need of like, of praying real hard and everything, like a dire need to like, get help.
Like a crisis type of deal.
Like, I'm trying to get into treatment right now,
so my prayer are all ongoing, like I'm just constantly praying for,
like a miracle or some frickin' thing.
But I know I gotta make it. Like, one day at a time.
So yeah, like it's really important for me. Like I'm really relying, trying to rely on the Creator to help me get back on. I've been clean like two days and it's fricken hard.

Like, like, I'm, I'm off of pot right and S** took off right and A**'s gone and I'm like k, I gotta keep it real, right, I gotta stay balanced, like, yeah.

Out in the Community, I Felt Dropped

ODESSA MARCHAND

Presentation to the Canadian House of Commons' Standing Committee on the Status of Women, Indigenous women in the federal justice and correctional systems.

I'M A STATUS ABORIGINAL PERSON. My status is from Vernon. I've been in and out of jail since I was twelve years old. The last sentence was ten years; I did seven years, and I'm now on parole. I was granted day parole under Section 84[1] for Aboriginal people.

I have two children—a daughter who is thirteen years old and a son who is eighteen months. I recently got my daughter back. My children are the reason that I'm doing what I'm doing now, and the reason that I am doing so well.

I recommend that there be more support in the community for Indigenous people who are out on parole. When I had a parole hearing, there were a lot of Indigenous people there to support me. I went to a non-Aboriginal half-way house, and there was very little support for me and my culture there. When I wanted help from the Aboriginal liaison person, I couldn't get a hold of him. Inside the federal correctional facilities, the Aboriginal Elder is always available.

Now that I was out in the community, I felt dropped and didn't know where to go for help. I went to sweats voluntarily on my own. It made me feel like a failure—why was I asking for help and not getting it? I recommend that an Aboriginal Elder meet regularly with Indigenous people in the half-way houses, with a set meeting time each week.

NOTE

[1] Section 84 of the *Corrections and Conditional Release Act,* which is "Aboriginal Parole Supervision."

Aboriginal Healing Outside the Gates Interview

How important is spirituality to you?

spirituality doesn't mean anything to me right now
cause you know what I've been through
so much death in the past few months
I don't believe in anything right now
I'm a little choked and pissed off
it makes me mad cause it just made me lose my sister those motherfuckers
I'm just choked

it's just not wanting to believe, to realize that my family's gone,
my sisters are all gone
cause ugh it pissed me off and it screwed me around
and I was a little bored and
it sucked and it sucked

They're Going to Be Living in Your Community When They Get Out – 5

ELDER MARY "HOLY COW" FAYANT

Presentation to the Canadian House of Commons' Standing Committee on the Status of Women, Indigenous women in the federal justice and correctional systems.

WOMEN ARE INTELLIGENT. Women need more opportunities for education, to get skills in a career that they want to establish themselves in. If they don't have the skills, they're not going to have that job. They're going to be living in your community when they get out. It is imperative that they get trauma treatment in order to be productive in life.

Lora "Koala" Kwandibens
In Memory

WE REMEMBER OUR DEAR FRIEND Lora "Koala" Kwandibens, a member of the Ojibway Nation, who spent many years as an adolescent and young adult inside correctional institutions. Lora was a passionate member of the Women in2 Healing participatory health research projects; she inspired us to apply for funding to improve cancer education and cancer screening for incarcerated people because she knew that cancer prevention and cancer screening is not given priority among prison populations. Lora was diagnosed with breast cancer at the age of forty-one. Lora died of metastatic breast cancer in February 2013, leaving behind her six-year-old son.

Reprinted from Lynn Fels et al., "Arresting Cancer: Using Community-Based Participatory Approaches to Improve Cancer Screening and Awareness with Formerly Incarcerated Men and Women." Collaborating Centre for Prison Health and Education, University of British Columbia, 2014.

What does spiritual health look like to you today?

Listening to the Women

attending the fire pit

    being a good person

being connected to God

    being happy with myself

being mentally healthy

    being on the right path to healing

being well rounded

    believing in God

connecting with Elders

    doing the right thing

doing the twelve steps

    drumming

exercising

    feeling positive about the future

following my heart

        forgiving myself

getting baptised

        getting involved

going to acupuncture

        going to church

going to NA and AA

        healing

hoping

        improving daily

joining a fellowship

        keeping in touch

learning about God's word

        learning about my culture

learning about my emotions

      learning from the past

loving myself

      making time for dreams

meditating

      naming blessings

opening up possibilities

      participating in fellowship

praying

      questioning the past

reading the Bible

      recognizing ambition

seeing my counsellor

      singing

smudging

      thinking positively

understanding myself

      viewing the future

writing poetry

      x-ing out bad stuff

yearning for the good

      zeroing in on what's really important[1]

NOTE

[1] This Found Poem was created from responses provided by Indigenous women in Mission who participated in the study, Aboriginal Healing Outside the Gates.

Hope: Interlude Two

Re-Leasing Hope

ALISON GRANGER-BROWN

We must accept finite disappointment but never lose infinite hope. —Martin Luther King

THIS BOOK WAS INITIALLY TITLED *Sustaining Hope* until the editors settled on *Releasing Hope*. This change caused me to reflect for a long time, as I wrestled with the idea of releasing hope. That sounded to me like letting it go, but perhaps it is about emancipating hope or freeing hope. Eventually, I started to think of it as "re-leasing hope." Of the hundreds of people I have journeyed with in various prisons, I would say that the seemingly hopeless cycle of addiction, crime, and incarceration only changes when individuals discover even a small piece of personal power. From that place they can get a new lease on hope; perhaps they are released with hope.

The Indo-European origin of the word hope is *keu*, which means curve, to go in a different direction. This fits with Charles Snyder's hope theory, that people who are "high" in hope are able to change direction, shift gears, and "re-goal." Hope is present in every moment, in every small action or goal we may set, whereas hopelessness is rooted in blinkered, narrow thinking, and inflexibility. In our work, we tried to release creativity; we tried to think outside the box and to change the brain's habituated pathways to solving problems in personally and socially detrimental ways. We spent much of our time at ACCW dreaming up ways of using donated materials, of making something out of nothing, and trying to solve some of the pressing issues faced by the women in unique ways. Through this we found multiple opportunities to give back to society and volunteer in the local community.

I became interested in transformative or transformational learning; I began to recognize the multiple types of intelligence and to seek opportunities for all the women to find their own unique talents and gifts. Transformation begins in the imagination, in hope, in the ability to visualize what is possible, not fantasy but ... right sized.[1] Quite often women would be challenged by the work or by having to collaborate with others they disliked or distrusted; these and other triggers were all opportunities to reflect and review values, behaviours, attitudes, etc.

One event or a myriad of accumulating triggers may well shift the balance from what is habit, normal, and safe to what is new, open, and often scary. The dissonance in this space becomes intolerable and transformation may occur. And .... we all have the free will to decide to live with dissonance, in disequilibrium, and untransformed for a long time or even forever. Here is the dilemma, what some women call the "done button": what can we learn about the critical point, when the choice is ultimately made? How can we support people to firmly hit this button?

Indigenous Canadians are grossly over incarcerated, serve longer sentences at higher security ratings, and are less likely to apply for or be granted parole. In Cree, the word for hope is *Ihtatihtumown* or *Pukoseyimowin*, which means that "We must look forward to moving toward good things. We need to have a sense that the seeds we are planting will bear fruit for our children, families, and communities" (Elder Mary Lee). Here we see that hope has a communal and interdependent quality, quite different from the North American research (see Snyder) that focuses on personal growth, individual gain, and one's own future. This definition shows us the collective nature of the idea of hope; our work is for the children, families, and community.

I believed that service was a way to feel connected to the community, even when so many people in prison feel disconnected, having felt different from others and excluded for much of their lives. It is the blessing and the blight of prison that after people find community, become attached, and often find a sense of identity through their jobs and routines within the prison's walls, they then have to leave and return to isolation and indifference. Many women over the years have told me their relapse to substance use and crime came because of boredom and loneliness, and that the possibility of changing their destiny seemed hopeless.

The "helping relationship" is one of mutuality... both are helpers creating hope together. The women and men that I have journeyed with inside the fence have done the work themselves; once you see the spark of hope, what follows is an inferno of growth and development that has been arrested by violence, neglect, or physical, emotional, or sexual abuse. Each journey is separate and distinct—no responsibility can be taken on either side—but the collaboration is more than the individual journey. This avoids the feeling of dependence, reliance on the other, being less than, and avoids feeding the ego of the helper, such that it takes something from the one needing help.

WHERE DO WE FIND HOPE?

We can only find hope inside ourselves, when we are open to the mystery of who we are; when we can love, honour, and protect that spirit; and when we can be transparent and clear about who we are. It can only be held as a possibility by others.

This journey to re-lease hope is one of emptying our hearts and minds of the negative, self-defeating beliefs about our failures implanted by people earlier in our lives. It is about the future, about moving towards our goals rather than away from our ghosts. I always tried to help the women envision what they would gain in recovery rather than focusing on what they must give up. Viktor Frankl shares,

> Those who know how close the connection is between the state of mind of a man (sic), his courage and hope, or lack of them, and the state of immunity of his body will understand that the sudden loss of hope and courage can have a deadly effect. (96)

WHEN WILL WE FIND HOPE?

After all these years, after getting to know hundreds of people in prison, I believe that every person can live drug and crime free in the community so long as they are supported to the degree necessitated by their mental health or functional capabilities. I am not trained in the science of actuarial calculations, and so I have no business in probability or predicting who will or will not be successful re-entering the community, but nearly two decades of this work have proven to me that there is always possibility. Even those thought by many to be lost causes can thrive and become valuable members of society. People beaten down by trauma, grief, anger, and the endless struggle for basic survival in addiction can escape that nightmare, re-awaken their dreams, and take a new lease on hope. Optimism is about probability; hope is about possibility.

NOTE

[1] See "Becoming Right Sized."

REFERENCES

"Becoming Right Sized." The Miracle Is Around the Corner. 4 October, 2012. Web.

Frankl, Viktor E. *Man's Search for Meaning.* Boston, MA: Washington Square Press, 1984.

Lee, Mary. Elder. *Cree (Nehiyawak) Teaching.* Four Directions Teachings.com. 2006-2012. Web.

Snyder, Charles R. "Hope Theory: Rainbows in the Mind." *Psychological Inquiry* 13 (2002): 249-275.

VII. Mothers, Babies, and Children

The claim that children should not be with their mothers is not evidence based. It is a mean-spirited perspective that robs incarcerated mothers of their self-identity and hope, and robs their children of the best chance for flourishing lives.
—Chaplain Henk Smidstra

The biggest gift to me is having my children back in my life, forgiving me and being proud of me…. There's no drug out there that can replace the feelings I get when I rock my granddaughter to sleep and kiss my daughter goodnight.
—Mo Korchinski

The majority of us are mothers, mothers that have distanced ourselves from our children. This separation, the perpetual feelings of guilt, and the despair of not being able to mend relationships blinded me to the possibility of hope.
—Kelly Murphy

Doctor's Journey

RUTH ELWOOD MARTIN

I AM WRITING THIS FOLLOWING yet another media interview, this time at seven in the morning, and I wonder wearily, "How many more years will I be doing this?" The answer I always come back to is, "Until I die!" This morning, I was interviewed by Rick Cluff on CBC Radio AM, about the guidelines that we officially launched last week, on September 10, 2015. The interview didn't go as smoothly as I had hoped—I'm not a morning person and a seven a.m. interview is not what I would wish upon myself, since I usually haven't really woken up or had enough coffee by then. In fact, I don't feel that my strengths lie in being a "media person" at all, but I agree to interviews like this one because I know that people everywhere need to hear about this issue.

Whenever I spend time with my eighteen-month-old granddaughter, Lucy, I feel the poignancy of my health advocacy role regarding the best interests of infants born to incarcerated women. I am totally in love with Lucy—she lights up my world—and she knows that she is surrounded by love.

For incarcerated mothers, having their babies taken from them immediately following birth has to be one of the most devastating events that ever occurs in their lives. How can a woman ever recover from the despair and grief caused by such an event? And, the impact on the baby, to be separated from their mother at birth, is immeasurable. The baby has lost forever the opportunity to breastfeed and to establish maternal-infant bonding, a loss which current medical epigenetic evidence says will have a direct consequence on that infant's long-term health outcomes.

—Journal entry

It is in the best interests of the child to remain with her/his mother, to breastfeed, and to be allowed to develop a healthy attachment (UN).

The wide range of psychological, physiologic, and developmental harm caused by separation of a child from her/his mother is well documented (See Howard, Martin, Berlin, and Brooks-Gunn). Recent epigenetic evidence demonstrates that a newborn's attachment to her/his mother is critical to her/his long-term healthy development (Murgatroyd and Spengler). However, the majority of incarcerated women are of child-bearing age and, tragically, all are separated from their children, due either to the logistics incarceration or to the fact that their children are in foster care due to their prior substance use issues.

We are also becoming increasingly aware of the impact of adverse childhood events (ACE) on long-term health outcomes for men and women (Edwards, Anda, Dube, Dong, Chapman, and Felitti). A high ACE score predicts worse health outcomes. The ten items in the ACE scale enquire about conditions experienced by individuals when they were young children: neglect and abuse (emotional, verbal, physical, and sexual). This compelling data demands a paradigm shift in the way that society perceives and supports incarcerated mothers, as well as their infants and young children, both inside prison and following their release. All programs and policy directives must be guided by the best interests of the child.

During the participatory health research (PHR) project in ACCW, incarcerated women told us that one of their health goals was to improve their relationships with their children and families. Women told us that they wished to learn how to become better parents. For many women, the hope that they would one day be reunited with their children was a major motivating factor in their lives. Of the forty-six PowerPoint educational presentations that the PHR participants developed, which represented topics that women thought prison PHR should focus on in order to improve the health of women in prison, seven focused on improving parenting skills.

During 2004 to 2008, the warden developed a collaborative arrangement with BC Women's Hospital and the Ministry of Children Family Development, and piloted a mother-child unit in ACCW. Nine babies born to incarcerated women returned from the hospital delivery suite to ACCW with their mothers (Martin, Lau and Salmon).

We are now compiling some follow-up evaluation data on those nine babies (who are now children, ten years later) living in the community with their families. A recurring emergent theme is how difficult it is for women with incarceration experience to find affordable places to live and to secure basic needs for survival for themselves and their children.

Women with incarceration experience tell us that they want to become the best mothers they can be, but that they need support. They want to learn parenting skills, such as how to become trauma-informed parents,[1] and they desperately want community and health support for themselves and their children. Society must listen!

NOTE

[1]See: http://traumainformedparent.com.

REFERENCES

Child, Family, and Community Service Act. Chapter 46. "Canada: Queen's Printer."Victoria, British Columbia. 1996. Web.

Howard, Kimberly, Anne Martin, Lisa J. Berlin, and Jean Brooks-Gunn. "Early Mother-Child Separation, Parenting, and Child Well-Being in Early Head Start Families." *Attachment & Human Development* 13.1 (2011): 5-26. Web.

Ip, Stanley, Mei Chung, Gowri Raman, Priscilla Chew, N. P. Magula, Dina DeVine, Thomas Trikalinos, and Joseph Lau. "Breastfeeding and Maternal and Infant Health Outcomes in Developed Countries." *Evidence Report Technology Assessment* 153.153 (2007): 1-186.

Martin Ruth Elwood, Joshua Lau and Amy Salmon. "Incarcerating Mothers: The Effect on the Health and Social Well-Being of Infants and their Mothers." *Incarcerated Mothers: Oppression and Resistance.* Eds. Gordana Eljupovic and Rebecca Jaremko Bromwich. Bradford: Demeter Press, 2013. 197-209.

Murgatroyd, Chris and Dietmar Spengler. "Epigenetics of Early Child Development." *Frontiers in Psychiatry* 2 (2011): 1-15. Web.

United Nations (UN). *United Nations Rules for the Treatment of Women Prisoners and Non-Custodial Measures for Women Offenders with their Commentary ("the Bangkok Rules").* General Assembly, 16 March 2011. Web.

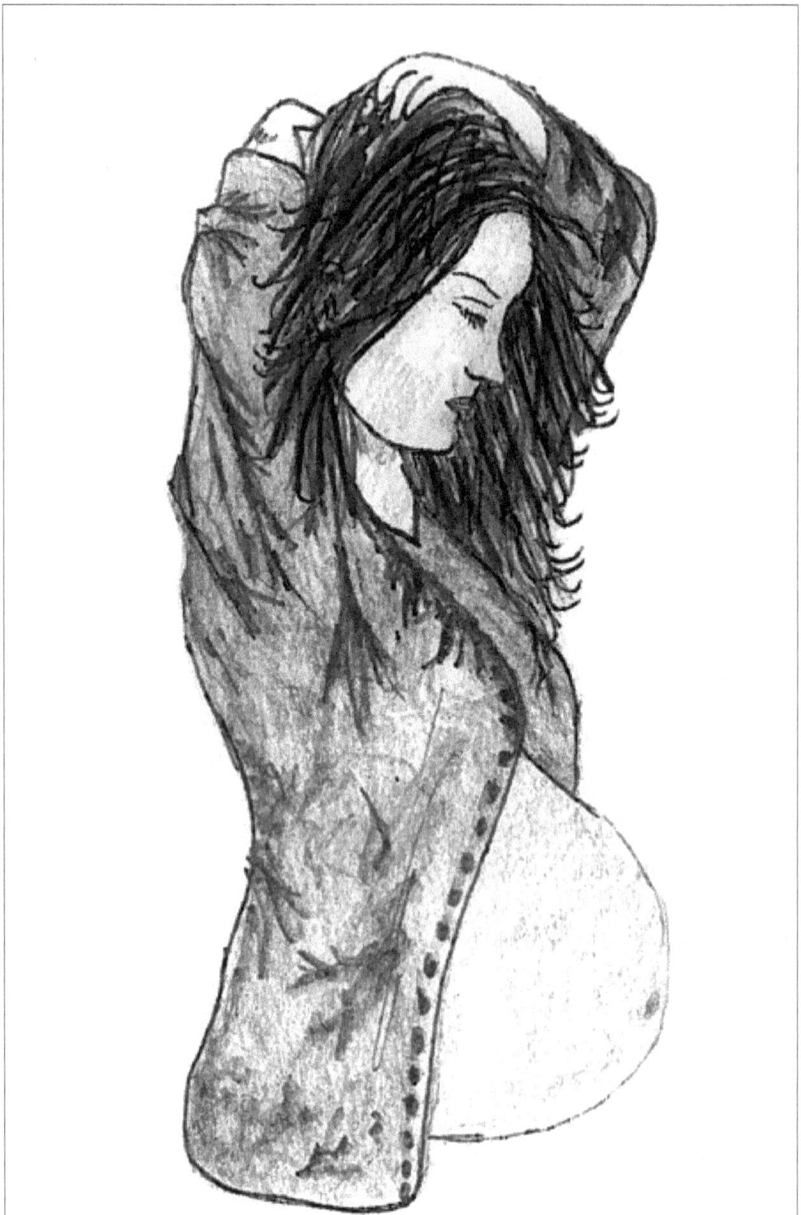

Mothers Separated from their Children

CHAPLAIN HENK SMIDSTRA

A GOOD NUMBER OF THE MOST DEPRESSING and painful life situations that I witnessed inducing hopelessness were the forced separations of incarcerated mothers from their children. As prison chaplain, I was privileged and therefore free to leave the prison every evening to be with my family—not so for the prisoners I would leave behind the walls. At ACCW, many of the incarcerated women had been suddenly separated from their families and children, and had to face this gut-wrenching pain of separation. They craved to be with their sorrowing children with every fibre of their bodies and souls; they could no longer see any hope for the future. I couldn't imagine going through what they or their children were experiencing. Where would they get the strength, the hope, to continue on?

Often, I would sit with the women, one on one, and they would pour out their souls to me. They didn't only talk about their regrets regarding the mess they got themselves into, or about the injustice that overwhelmed them. They would often explain that they certainly deserved to be punished for their crimes, but that their children did not deserve to be punished by their absence. This situation caused extreme anguish, as did the fact that they were powerless to address their children's misery.

Often, after some time, they would lose all hope. They would be lost in a pit of despair, or fall into a disassociative state, denying the reality of the situation. Some, of course, with religious faith, found comfort in the belief that God or a higher power could mystically be there with their children, to somehow protect and empower them. Some were thankful that their parents could be caregivers, preventing their children from being taken by social services. But there was a bittersweetness in this. In their feelings of failure as mothers, of guilt and shame before God and parents, they often felt as if God had abandoned them and that their parents or children might never speak to them again. They saw themselves as incompetent and worthless human beings, defined by their failures in relationships and in parental competency. This self-definition left them feeling hopeless.

Obviously, it is important for a sentenced mother to have her child with her during incarceration or during her time of judicial sanction. It would not only be restorative and empowering for the mother's spirit, but it would also rebuild the brokenness in her life and family. The child too would not be forced to suffer the sudden loss of his or her mother. Being in the mother's presence—particularly during her or his developmental stage before six years of age—is critical for the child's long-term health and wellbeing. Though legally the mothers have been labelled criminals, relationally they were good, loving mothers.

Over the years, in many appropriate cases, and under appropriate supervision in a safe and empowering environment, children could bond with their mothers at BCCW and ACCW. For society to simply insist that criminals don't deserve goodness, that they should receive nothing but the evil of retributive punishment, is morally deficient.

The claim that children should not be with their mothers is not evidence based. It is a mean-spirited perspective that robs incarcerated mothers of their self-identity and hope, and robs their children of the best chance for flourishing lives. Treated retributively, the incarcerated mother has no choice but to identify with society's demeaning labels—"yes, I am no good, a bad person, and a bad mother"—and then, robbed of hope, to continue to live up to the ascribed negative self-image.

Best Interests of the Child

BRENDA TOLE

BRITISH COLUMBIA CORRECTIONS has a history of allowing babies born in custody to return to the correctional centre with their mothers, and we, in collaboration with the BC Women's Hospital and other ministries and agencies that were stakeholders, planned a mother-child unit at ACCW. The primary focus was the best interests of the child. We focused on health outcomes for the children, as well as their right to have this very important early relationship with their mothers. Instead of an application process, whereby the mother's petition would have to be approved, there was an assumption that the visits would occur unless there were very significant reasons that it would not be the best arrangement for the child.

Lost Time With My Son

CHRISTINE HEMINGWAY

AFTER SEVENTEEN MONTHS OF BEING LOCKED UP in prison, the day is finally here! I get to go home. It will be so great to see my only child, but I am also scared about how Sheldon will respond to me after all the time I have been away. While doing my time, a piece of my heart has been missing. And I know I will never get back the lost time with my son.

As I was walking through the gates, Alison Granger-Brown, the recreation therapist, told me, "It's not the same out there. It will be difficult after spending all this time here at ACCW."

I replied, "It's a piece of cake. I can handle it."

I now wish I could eat those words. It was hard to leave ACCW. I had made a lot of friends, both good and bad. I was afraid of how things were going to be, especially after being locked up for so long.

My ex came to pick me up. The drive home was quiet, and we were distant with one another. We didn't talk much—only about Sheldon, who was twelve years old. While I was in jail, my ex and I had terrible fights on the phone. He would only bring my son to see me when he felt like it. And he tried to sell my house. Luckily for me, the offer on the house was low and he was greedy and didn't accept it. Otherwise, I would be homeless.

I looked out the window, not really seeing anything. I was crying quietly, turned away from my ex so he couldn't see me. I didn't want him to think I was weak. I knew there would be a battle over the house. I could not wait to get home. A friend was staying at the house. She was recently released from jail, and I had invited her to stay at the house until she got on her feet.

It was strange going into my house. It didn't seem like my home anymore. It felt weird! What a horrible feeling! My house had changed. I had become so familiar with my little square unit in jail with everything in one room—bed, sitting area, and toilet. I hated that small space, but I was comfortable in it.

I could not wait to see my son. He was happy to see me. We hugged. It was hard to talk to him. Sheldon was seventeen months older. He was only eleven when I went in. I didn't see him for three months when I first spent time in Surrey pre-trial until I arranged a visit in an open room. I didn't want my son to see me through glass while we talked on the phone. I had to explain to him what had happened, and that I would not be coming home for a while. Sheldon was staying at the house with my ex. I told him Mummy did something that she shouldn't have, that she made a mistake.

I didn't know what to say. I felt so guilty. I didn't really know how my son felt. I didn't want to ask him things. I didn't want to upset him. I would only talk about happy things. I knew I would have to deal with it, but I didn't know how I was going to deal with it. I felt so guilty about being away from him and not being able to talk to him.

Living on Alder
Excerpt, Women in2 Healing Newsletter, Issue 1

KELLY MURPHY

I THINK THAT A VERY LARGE PIECE of the despair is the guilt and shame that possesses women when they are finally incarcerated, when they can no longer resort to crime and substance misuse. As they are forced to withdraw from their sources of numbness, the consequences of their actions begin to reveal themselves. The majority of us are mothers, mothers that have distanced ourselves from our children. This separation, the perpetual feelings of guilt, and the despair of not being able to mend relationships blinded me to the possibility of hope.

I had the unique opportunity of being incarcerated at Alouette Correctional Centre for Women in 2007. I was housed on the mother and baby unit. At the time, I didn't realize that living alongside the mothers and their children would be a catalyst for one of the most profound transformations in my life. The pregnant women, the mother with her newborn, and even a little toddler were to be my teachers.

When I arrived on Alder living unit, the babies were crying and toys were strewn in what appeared to be a daycare. I was second-guessing my decision to move onto the "quiet unit." As with any unit change within the prison setting, I had to navigate the hierarchy of unit residents and undergo their scrutiny as they decided whether or not I was "solid" enough to fit in. Even though I was welcomed to settle, I vowed to myself that I wasn't going to get close to the mothers and definitely not to their children. I was carrying my own bitterness about my broken relationship with my daughter. So what was I going to do with this pain? I understood that it was a wound that kept me "out there"—clouded in an opiate haze and re-offending to maintain the euphoria.

The problem was, as the years moved forward, the pain intensified, the drugs stopped working, and my daughter became more damaged by her mother's abandonment. Time to get a grip, pull myself out of my own selfishness, and mend the hurt between my daughter and myself. I saw the babies as an opportunity to confront my failures as a mother and to open my heart. I had a desire to change.

Finding My Children

MO KORCHINSKI

MY DREAM OF RECONNECTING with my children grows stronger and stronger the longer I stay with my treatment program. I need to know if my children are alive and healthy and what they look like. I could walk down the street and not even recognize my own children. It has been eleven years since I walked out on them. They were only babies, and I must learn to live with the guilt and shame of abandoning my children. I still think it was the best thing for them not to have me in their lives as I was not a healthy person when I was living in my addiction. I am so glad I did not drag them into my lifestyle. I always hoped that their fathers were raising them well. I hope they are happy.

This is not the first time I tried to find my children. While I was in prison, I looked for them with a social worker. I didn't have any luck tracking them down, but the good news was that my children were not in the child welfare system. We checked 411 phone directories to see if we could find a phone number for their fathers, but we had no luck. It's like they don't want me to find my children, so they don't have phone numbers in their own names.

I feel lost about what to do to find my children. There has to be a way for me to find them. My friend Tina asks if I have tried Facebook. I say, "What is Facebook?" She pulls up her Facebook account and shows me the social media site.

"What are your children's names? We can see if they pop up on the list of people on Facebook."

I get butterflies in my stomach thinking I am going to see a picture of my daughter. I give her my oldest child's name, Cassandra. No luck. A little piece of me dies inside. I think this is going to be a dead end; I will never find my children.

"What is your other daughter's name?"

I say, "Michelle."

I sit there waiting for her to type in her name, and it feels like it is taking forever. Then all of a sudden her name shows up. Tina clicks on my daughter's name, and a picture comes up of my little girl who is not so little anymore. She is now sixteen years old. There on the computer screen is a part of me that has been lost for so long. I never thought I would ever see her again. She is perfect. Staring back at me are my green eyes. I look through her Facebook photos and find a picture of her with her little brother. I am so happy but still a little sad that there are no pictures of Cassandra. Where is she? Where is my firstborn child? I have no idea what to do next. Tina says, "Why don't you send Michelle a message? It looks like her last post was five weeks old."

I ask, "What does that mean?" Tina tells me that when you post stuff, there is a time and a date and that the last activity on Michelle's Facebook is from five weeks ago.

I struggle to decide what to do. I don't want to hurt my children any more than I have already. I have no idea what their fathers have told them happened to me. Do they think I'm dead? What if all of a sudden they get a message from me when they think I'm dead? What will that do to them? I have so many questions and uncertainty about what to do. I ask my drug and alcohol counsellor how I should handle reaching out to my daughter. She says she will help me write a message that I could send to Michelle. I send the message to Michelle, and every day for weeks I log in to Facebook to see if there is a message back from my little girl. Every day there is no word from Michelle, a little piece of my heart breaks. All I ever wanted my whole life was for my mom to love me. I hope Michelle might read my message and know she is loved by her mother.

Okay, let's do this!

Dear Michelle,

Hi, this is your mom. I got together with your auntie Shauna, and she gave me some pictures of you. I am so proud to know that you are doing well and growing up so beautifully. I am really hoping that we can one day get together and share some time. I miss you and love you. Hope to hear from you.

(daughter replies)

Hi, Michelle,

Wow! You made my day today. I was so happy that you wrote me back. You don't know how much that means to me.

There hasn't been a day that has gone by that I haven't thought of you and Corey and Cassie. The day I phoned your grandma and found out that you guys were doing well was such a relief for me. It was so hard not knowing if you guys were okay or not. I'm doing well now. I'm in school. I'm taking a carpentry course. I've got four weeks left. I work at a treatment centre for women with drug and alcohol problems. I love working there. School's awesome. I'm top of my class and the only woman in the course. I can't wait to come and see you and Corey. I wanted to come today when I got your letter. I miss you so much and I want to get to know you so much. I have a lot to tell you about my life, but today I'm in AA. And I've been clean for twenty months. I've come to terms with so much of my past, and I am truly happy today. I cried so much when I got your letter, and I had a client walk in the office and see me crying and she took my picture because I don't cry. You sure changed that for me today. I haven't been this happy in so long. I'm so proud of you. And I love you so much and I can't wait to see you and your brother. I can't believe how much Corey looks like your dad. And everyone says you look like me. Well, I've got to go study. I've got a big test tomorrow morning. I can't wait to hear from you again. I LOVE YOU SOOOOOOOOOOOO MUCH. MOM

(daughter responds again)

(son responds)

(eldest daughter responds)

(mother-in-law responds)

I know it's going to take time for Cassie, but I'm just happy to see a picture of her and know that she's alive. I don't expect her to understand what my life was like. It goes back to my early childhood. I've had a drug and alcohol problem since I was twelve. I've learned lots about my disease in the past two years, and I found out who I really am for the first time. I now know what happiness is, and I have learned to let go of my past. I never really thought that I deserved to be a mom, and I never knew how to be one. I didn't have a great role model in that department. I know that staying clean and sober is the best amends I can make to my children, and that it will take time for them to realize that I'm not the same person I was. Thanks for writing me. You don't know how much it means to hear from you. The last thing I want to do is hurt my daughter, but I had to try and find her and give her the choice this time—if she chooses not to forgive me, I'll still love her and she will always be in my heart. Take care and I do miss you and love you.

(mother-in-law responds)

Grandma! Wow! Maybe I can do a better job at that then I did as a mother? I wish I could take all her pain away, but I know I can't. I would love to be able to start over. Yes, I will call you soon. Thanks for caring and giving me a chance and not judging me. I've worked so hard on not judging myself and feeling guilty. It's something I've done a lot, and I'm still working on it. I went through this with Michelle and Corey. I chat to them a couple times a week. I pray every night for my children, and I think that is why my higher power has given them back to me. I've worked hard to change; I love who I am today, and I have faith that Cassie will too, in time.

(son replies)

Well, it's great to see you on Facebook. I can finally get to know you. So, how does it feel to be an uncle? Have you talked to Cassie yet? She is having a little girl on April 19. I just found her two weeks ago, and I have talked to her on the phone a couple of times. I've been doing really well for the last couple of years. I've taken a lot of chances in my life. I now work at a treatment centre that helps women with drug problems. So, it's a really cool job. I love it. So, what do you like?

1. *What sports do you play?*
2. *What are your grades like?*
3. *Do you like school?*
4. *Do you stay out of trouble?*
5. *Are you happy?*
6. *What's your favourite colour?*
7. *Do you and Michelle get along?*

Well, I could go on and on, but I'll wait to hear from you again. I'm so happy that we can chat all the time now. Saying sorry that I haven't been around for the past ten years sounds shitty, but you wouldn't have wanted to know that mom. But today I'm an awesome person, clean for two years, and I'm happy, a lot happier now that I have found all my babies. I hope life has been good to you. There wasn't a day that went by that I didn't think of you, and you have always been in my heart. I love you so much. Well, I don't want to going on too much the first time I write you. Welcome to Facebook. Love you, Mom

(son replies)

Well I just talked to Cassie for an hour. She's doing great. She says to say hi. It was great to come home and find a message from you. You asked me where I've been, and the answer is going to take me a couple of days to write. Please, give me the time. It's going to be a hard letter to write. So, I hope you have a great day at school and I'll try to write the answer tomorrow. Goodnight. I love you so much and miss you more than words can say.

(son replies)

Dear Corey,

So where have I been for the last eleven years? Where do I begin? I guess at the beginning. When you were born, Cassie and Michelle were home with your grandma. I was at the hospital by myself. When you were born I was so happy that I finally got a son. Back then, they didn't tell you what you were having, so you were a happy surprise. The girls were so happy to have a brother to play with. We spent a lot of time camping on the beach, the four of us. We were really close. Six weeks before you turned two, I got a call that my mom was dying and they needed me in Nanaimo. You went to stay with your dad, and I flew home. It wasn't much of a home since I was kicked out when I was twelve years old. My life with my family was very cold and involved a lot of pain. My mom only had three days to live, but she survived for six weeks before she died on your second birthday. My life fell apart that night. I thought the best place for you and your sister was with your dad, since I've always struggled with a drinking problem. In the last two years I've gotten help for my addiction, and now I've been clean for two years. I'm working at a treatment centre helping others with the same problem. During these two years I've been trying to find you and your sisters. A friend suggested Facebook, and I looked up all three of you. I found Michelle in September 2007, then Cassie three weeks ago, and then you. So, in these last five months, I've been able to find you all. I know that I can't replace the last eleven years, but we do have so much time left in our lives to have a relationship. My leaving had nothing to do with anything bad on your part. All I ever wanted was the best for you guys. I've never gone a day without thinking of all three of you. You've always been with me in spirit and in my heart. If you have anything else you need to know, please, ask. Love, Mom

(ex-husband responds)

Wow! Not sure how to feel about this message. I have never denied that drugs and alcohol was the reason I left, but I feel it is important for my children to know why drugs and alcohol took over my life. I have lived with shame and guilt for so many years, and I am not going to live my life that way anymore. I can own that I was not there for my children, and I know that I was not healthy enough, emotionally or mentally, to be raising children. I was a wounded soul that needed to find healing, but I found a way to escape those feelings by not feeling my feelings. Drugs.... It is so easy for others to judge me, but I judge myself more than anyone else can. I still feel that my children were better off without me in their lives. I would have hurt them more if I had stayed. I didn't know how to love another person. I couldn't even love myself. I hope one day my children realize that my leaving them was my way of loving them.

Mo's Story
Excerpt, Women in2 Healing Newsletter, Issue 3

MO KORCHINSKI

ALL THROUGH MY ADDICTION, after my children were not in my life, I missed them but never worried about them because I knew they were being taken care of. I never thought that my children would blame themselves for me not being in their lives. I was out there getting high, and after a while I stopped telling people I even had children. It was easier than answering questions as to where they were. My selfishness almost cost my daughter her life.

I used to tell myself that I would wait until my children were older to find them so I wouldn't hurt them by coming back into their lives. I never thought what having her mom walk out of her life would do to my little girl. Here is this child who grew inside me for nine months, who was a part of me, who I loved more than life. I didn't just give up on myself, I gave up on my children. The biggest gift to me is having my children back in my life, forgiving me and being proud of me. Today I've been out of jail for over two years and have been clean and sober for thirty-three months. I have a strong relationship with my children, and it's getting stronger every day. There's no drug out there that can replace the feelings I get when I rock my granddaughter to sleep and kiss my daughter goodnight.

Seeking to Forget

MO KORCHINSKI

I NEVER HAD A CLOSE RELATIONSHIP with my family when I was growing up, so when my children wanted to have a relationship with them, I had mixed feelings. If my family want nothing to do with me, why would they want to know my children? But it meant a lot to my children, so a visit was arranged. It was over before it even started.

My children were upset that my family wouldn't tell them where my father's care home is; they wanted to visit their grandpa. They told my children that they had to keep me away from my father because I was dangerous, and that because of this my children couldn't see him either.

Today my children are proud of who I am, but my family didn't care to see or understand that I was no longer that broken person I was years ago. Sometimes time doesn't always heal wounds, and people don't forgive or forget.

It's taken me many years to find myself, and I will not have people in my life who don't respect me. I lived my whole life without having my family in my life, and I am better off without them in it today. Bringing my family back into my life is not worth my losing my recovery or losing myself.

Today I am proud of the person I am, and I no longer need others' approval to find self-worth. I am just starting to like who I am as a person. I am working on loving myself, and all of who I am.

Amber's Story
"He Is Loved by All"

AMBER CHRISTIE

BEING IN THIS PRISON is so different from being anywhere else. There are babies in this prison. One day, when we are all in our units for count, the SCO (supervising corrections officer) comes in and sits us down and tells us an inmate is bringing her child back from the hospital. They are trying a new program.

I am in shock. People seem to think that because we are in prison our nature changes. That is so far from the truth. When the baby arrives, everybody is eager to see him. Like any other mother, the woman has a stroller and takes her baby for walks. The baby unit has cribs and toys—probably a lot more than many people could afford.

Being in prison doesn't change who you are.

At least eighty percent of the women here are mothers.

The baby is like gold.

He is loved by all.

Closing of the ACCW Mother-Baby Unit

BRENDA TOLE

AFTER I LEFT ACCW as the warden, many initiatives at ACCW were cancelled. The most devastating to all involved, particularly the women in custody, was the closing of the mother-baby unit and the change in policy that stopped babies from returning to ACCW at all.

It is impossible to describe the horrible impact of these changes on women expecting to give birth while in custody. They had to find out that they would have the babies removed from them after birth. This decision was very hard to accept or to understand, since all the research available supported the positive short- and long-term impact of the program for the child and emphasized the problems created by denying the child access to breastfeeding, bonding, and attachment.

Accommodating women and their babies born while incarcerated is considered normal practice in most countries of the world, including England, New Zealand, Wales, Spain, Sweden, Germany, Netherlands, Russia, Brazil, Austria, Italy, Greece, Denmark, Kyrgyzstan, Ghana, Egypt, India, Chile, and some U.S. states. It is considered the right of the child to have this very important early relationship with the mother.

There is so much compelling research that pregnancy and children bring positive change in the lives of incarcerated women. From a health perspective, it is widely accepted that if babies remain with their mothers after birth in order to foster breastfeeding, attachment, and nurturing, there will be significant positive differences in the long-range mental and physical health of the children. Although our focus is on the best interests of the child, the research also informs us that pregnancy and children are the most significant factors that influence women to make positive changes in their lives.

There had been no negative events at ACCW to create concerns about the program, or about the nine babies who had returned to ACCW with their mothers and remained with them until release into the community.

Several individuals, agencies, and ministries, including BC Women's Hospital, the Ministry of Children and Family, and the Ministry of Health, requested that BC Corrections reconsider the closure of the mother-baby unit at ACCW, but BC Corrections would not change their position.

Babies

RUTH ELWOOD MARTIN

IN 2008, WHEN THE MINISTRY OF JUSTICE announced that the mother-baby unit was closing, we were absolutely devastated. I phoned and wrote a lengthy letter to the Assistant Deputy Minister in order to express my concern about the impact of the closure on the health of the currently incarcerated pregnant women and their unborn children. I wanted to know what the reasons were for the closure—what was the decision based on? I received no reply to my letter. The Medical Director of Corrections phoned to explain that the decision to close the unit was because of liability and legal concerns, that Corrections did not feel that they should be responsible for babies. They had not considered the success of the ACCW mother-baby unit, nor the fact that mother-child units had proven to be successful in most countries in the world!

My personal dilemma at that time was how much I should or could do to advocate for the situation as a contracted prison physician with BC Corrections Branch. All health care staff were told not to refer any future pregnant women to BC Women's Hospital, despite the fact that this hospital was the leading centre for treating mothers (and their newborn infants) with substance-use disorders. I had to explain to distraught pregnant women, whose babies were to be born during their sentences, that because the mother-baby unit was now closed, their baby would be apprehended at the hospital.

As a medical staff member of BC Women's Hospital, I asked the hospital leaders to assist in advocating for the situation. Together, we wrote a memo to the Assistant Deputy Minister, in which we reviewed the international published evidence. That effort resulted in nothing. I also worked with Fir Square to compile a sub-set evaluation on the eight women (three of whom were Indigenous) who had delivered at Fir Square, and who had subsequently returned to ACCW with their babies. (The ninth baby was not delivered at Fir Square because the mother did not have a history of substance use.) All of the babies except one breastfed for the duration of their prison sentences, and all of the babies stayed with their mothers for the mother's entire prison sentence. Eight of the nine babies breastfed "on demand." We had observed the mothers and babies playing, singing, learning to live together, and taking parenting classes. All babies had normal developmental check-ups. We presented this evaluation data at international and national conferences.

But these initiatives resulted in no changes to the situation! Babies born to incarcerated women continued to not be given the opportunity to remain with their mothers. This seemed to me to be a Canadian Charter issue: babies were being denied the opportunity to breastfeed and to develop infant-mother bonding because their mothers were incarcerated. I wondered if any of the mothers, who were devastated because their babies had been taken from them, would be interested in pursuing this injustice as a court case. I anticipated that this situation—babies being discriminated against—would be a major Canadian Charter case and that some lawyer(s) might take it on pro bono in order to ensure that justice be done.

I hate to suggest that lawyers are saints, but each of the lawyers who took on this case earned a special halo in my book of sainthood. No one was in this for personal gain—especially not the women themselves, because they had had their babies taken from them. I think we all got involved because of a deep conviction that we needed to stop a cruel injustice from happening to future babies born to incarcerated women, not only in British Columbia, but also across Canada.

Five women initiated the legal action in 2008; only two women, Amanda Inglis and Patricia Bock, were able to stay with the case, which resulted in a four-week BC Supreme Court hearing, in May 2013. Amanda and Patricia testified for several days, each relating their story of having been separated from their baby because they were incarcerated. I can only imagine how difficult it was for them to re-live in a courtroom the trauma of those experiences. For myself, I felt humiliated and powerless in court when the opposing lawyer continuously undermined my "expert" opinion.

New Mother-Baby House in Maple Ridge

MO KORCHINSKI

I STORM INTO THE MAYOR'S OFFICE in Maple Ridge to see him about the closing of the mother-baby program. "What are pregnant women in jail going to do now? What the hell is going to happen to them?" In the first ten minutes of our conversation, the mayor, Gordon Robson, asks us if we want a house for the mother-baby program. It turns out the mayor lives in a seven-bedroom house and has been looking to provide space for an initiative. The mayor's wife, Mary, is devoted to caring for women in addiction who have babies. As we are talking, the mayor calls into his office a councillor who had visited the jail when the mother-baby program was operating. He says he isn't happy that the program is no longer at the jail, and he tells us that he and the council will support us in any way we need.

We set up a time later that day to see the house.

As we pull up to the white gates, our mouths fall open. The house is huge and gorgeous and right on a golf course. We buzz to get in the gates and park our cars. Mary comes outside to meet us.

We start our tour downstairs. The floor consists of a laundry room, four bedrooms, one bathroom with a sink and toilet, and another with a bath tub and sink. One bedroom has an en-suite. Then we go upstairs to a large kitchen, two living rooms, a dining room, and a large balcony. On still another floor is a nursery, a den, and the master bedroom with an en-suite. Each floor is fifteen hundred square feet.

After the tour, we sit down and talk about the mother-baby program with Mary and her middle son Gordon Jr. for about a half hour. It is a very exciting day for Women in2 Healing—we are overjoyed to receive such a great gift, to be given the opportunity to help women and their children have a fighting chance to make the changes they need to make and to create healthy bonds.

Planning the Mother-Baby Proposal

MO KORCHINSKI

IT IS TIME FOR THE TEAM to step up, to act without the help of Alison, who is sick and can't make it to the planning meeting. Before the meeting, I begin to think about how we are going to put a proposal together, but then I realize I don't have a ride Linnea's house in Mission, since Alison was going to pick me up. It's still hard for me to ask for help, and this stops me from phoning up Linnea or her husband Don for a ride. I still struggle with the humility part of my recovery, and the fact that I screwed up my driver's licence so bad in my addiction and owe a lot of money doesn't help. Damn fines!

Linnea calls me to find out what is going on, and I tell her Alison is sick and I'm stuck in Maple Ridge. So she jumps into her car and drives to Maple Ridge to pick me up. On the way to her house we have a good talk, which we do most of the time, about life and the challenges around being parents and our powerlessness over our children. When we get to her house, Jenn, Sandy, and Yvonne are there already having coffee. Linnea serves us all a lunch of smoked salmon, cheese crackers, a veggie plate, and a fruit platter. We all sit down to eat before we start to work.

We pick Jenn to do the typing as we all sit around the kitchen table brainstorming about how to write a proposal and what to include. I am the only person who has ever written a proposal, but that was in jail and it wasn't going to the mayor for something as important as a housing for so many women and children. First, we write about who we are in Women in2 Healing, and how we came together, and we just keep going from there. Jenn is great and very patient as we keep changing our minds, adding more in or taking sentences out. After a while, it is time for a break with homemade lemon meringue pie and coffee. As time goes on, we have lots of laughs, and after about an hour and a half, we come up with a rough draft of a proposal. Then we email it to the rest of the team for feedback and suggestions.

Mother-Baby House Update

MO KORCHINSKI

WITH A LOT OF HARD WORK and a lot of patience on the part of Jenn, who spent lots of time adding everyone's suggestions, we come up with a proposal for the mother-baby house to take to the mayor's office. We are told that the mayor won't be in the office that week. We ask to make an appointment, and the clerk at the desk says that we have to make it through the mayor's secretary. She then asks for our names. Yvonne and I both introduce ourselves, and the clerk says, "Oh, you're here about the mother-baby house."

We say, "Yes."

She gives us his cell number. We thank the clerk at the desk and go outside to make the call, only to get his answering machine. Yvonne leaves him a message with her phone number for him to call us back.

We decide to go have something to eat. We go to the minimart and order steak, egg, and cheese breakfast sandwiches. Yvonne has a two for one coupon, so breakfast is a great price. We sit outside in her truck and eat and talk while we wait to see if the mayor will call us back. After we finish eating, the mayor still has not called. So Yvonne drops me off at home. We decide that if we don't hear back from him today, we will go over to the house the next night to see his wife and give the proposal to her. About two hours after getting home, Yvonne calls and says the mayor has phoned and wants us to drop off the proposal at his office so he can read it first thing on Wednesday morning.

Second Visit with the Mayor

MO KORCHINSKI

YVONNE PICKS ME UP to go to the meeting at city hall at 1:35 p.m. We arrive twenty minutes early, so Yvonne goes to the library and I go to the drugstore across the street to pass a little time. Yvonne is finished first and goes into city hall to let them know we are here, but she is told that our meeting is at the coffee shop next door. I meet Yvonne outside at 1:55 p.m., and she informs me that Mary and Gordon are in the coffee shop. We go into the coffee shop, spot them, and join them at the table. Gordon is just finishing another meeting. We chat with everyone and then go back over to city hall to Gordon's office. As we are waiting for Gordon to finish his phone call, three police officers come in and walk towards me.

As it turns out, I am just standing in front of the front desk. There's still a part of me that jumps when I see the cops, but then I remember, *Oh, yeah, I've got nothing to worry about.* Yvonne loves the look on my face. After Gordon helps them, we go upstairs to the mayor's office to go over our proposal. It takes a while for Gordon to find it—I guess the mail service in city hall is worse than Canada Post—but eventually he locates the two copies that Yvonne dropped off on Tuesday. In the future, we will remember to bring copies with us in case that happens again.

Mary's first question is about the budget—how much is it going to cost to run the house, for transportation, insurance, and the staff? Throughout the conversation, Mary and Gordon are very helpful, pointing us in the right direction and giving us ideas for where to go next.

These are the points we need to address and highlight:

1. Who is going to support this project?
2. That we need to write a letter of request to the Rotary Club

3. Lease the house from Heather Hill Farms Society
4. Ministry's position
5. Time frame on a start date
6. Cost overall
7. Highlight positive integrations back into their community of choice.

Mother-Baby House Postcript

MO KORCHINSKI

POINTING US IN THE RIGHT DIRECTION is great, but there is one big element that we are missing, having the support of the courts and BC Corrections. At this time, the mother-baby lawsuit is still waiting to be heard in British Columbia Supreme Court and the mother baby program is therefore on hold. What does that mean for women who are having babies in prison? No one knows how long it will take for the case to be heard in court, so at this point it is a waiting game. I'm not sure how long Mary and Mayor Gordy Robson will hold the house for us, but without all the players at the table, the house is only a dream. In my opinion, it is the best solution for mothers and babies.

Bonding Beyond Bars

MO KORCHINSKI

> *Your baby, your child, is your heart on the outside, you can't beat without it.*——Planning Circle mother[1]

I GET AN EMAIL FROM A WOMAN named Samantha who is looking for women with prison experience to join a planning committee to help organize an international roundtable on incarcerated mothers and their children. She is looking for ten mothers and their children to participate, and I am happy to help—it will allow me to work and to see women from ACCW. I love it when all of us women get together and share our stories in order to help make a difference for women coming after us.

I am super excited for the first planning meeting next week. We're planning to meet once a month to offer direction and set priorities for the upcoming roundtable. We'll work with delegates during the roundtable to protect the health of and bond between incarcerated mothers and their children. I am excited to see what other countries do in regard to women who have babies in prison. Do they treat women better than we do, or is this a way of the world, to take newborn babies from their moms right after birth? With the mother-baby court case starting next month, this is the perfect time to see how other countries deal with women having babies in prison.

> *I have friends who have had their babies ripped away from them at birth. They leave the unit to give birth and when they come back four hours later, it's not the guards who cuddle and comfort them—it's the women.*
>
> —Planning Circle mother

The goal of the Bonding Through Bars roundtable is to advance equity-centered approaches to protect the health and bond of mothers with lived prison experience and their children. It is an unprecedented opportunity to bring a diverse group of experts and women with lived experience together to explore a research agenda and then take action. The conference invited twenty delegates from six countries—Nepal, Kenya, Australia, Demark, the United States, and Canada—to collaborate and explore how equity-focused approaches can help protect the health and bond of incarcerated mothers and their children. It also provided the delegates with the opportunity to speak to what works in their country and what doesn't.

> *We know the system as we have it today isn't working and will never work. Every time a child is not able to be with its mother, they are losing something. It's hard when you see what is going on—separation and criminalization. For every woman in prison, we have thousands more that have been damaged. We've been working for a long time to get a better story.*
> —Sharon McIvor, Aboriginal lawyer and activist

Many of us were coming from different positions, so we didn't agree on everything—abolition, jail as an opportunity for healing and new beginnings, whether mothers and children should be behind bars together, etc. But we sat in circle, passed the talking stick, and listened, navigating our way through the waters of tension, emotion, experience, each individual brought to the circle through mutual understanding and willingness to work together.

Bonding Through Bars conference was a great opportunity for many of us women from prison to speak up about being mothers. We may not be full-time moms, we may not have been part of children's live, but we are still moms.

> *My son is an angel to me. That is my reason for being here, because of how much trauma he has from me being in prison and in addiction. He is ten years old, and I been incarcerated for seven years of his life.*
> —Nicole Birch

That bond that is created when you make a baby inside of you for nine months is like no other bond. I know that, for me, the guilt and shame I live with now that I am clean and sober is something I will live with the rest of my life. No amount of time or healing will change the regret that I feel every time I look at my children. The time I lost during their childhood is something that I will never get back.

I'm sad that my children had to grow up thinking that I didn't love them. I did love them, and I thought that not being in their lives was the best thing I could do as a mom. I was not in a healthy place to be raising children, and my children's fathers are good men who are way better at being a parent than I am. I still believe that I did the right thing leaving and not dragging my children through a life of an addict. But the scars and mistrust I see in my children's eyes when they look at me breaks my heart.

> *What do we do to heal our children's hearts? For my daughter to make it through the times apart from me, she had to harden up because I wasn't there to heal or nurture her. How do I heal that little heart?*
>
> —Planning Circle mother

I'm hoping that this conference helps us women find some healing and acceptance of our pasts, and that we can help make change for other women and children who are trapped in the prison system. No child should be taken from their mother, and a mother shouldn't have to give birth, and three hours later, go back to jail with no idea what is happening to their baby. The system is missing out on a great opportunity to support a new mom to be a better parent, to give them the skills to be able to raise their children. A baby can give a woman hope that she never had before, and everyone needs hope in their life.

> *Well, I am much more cognizant of the issues, and I am already on the path to doing something different. As a warden of a federal women's site, I have hired a contractor to support the mothers of children, and I am currently working with some community agencies to look at how we might start up some support groups for both the mothers and the children/young adults.*
>
> —Warden, institution unnamed

I think most of us are bringing our children or our moms to speak with us. My oldest daughter and granddaughter are coming with me. It will be interesting to hear how my being absent from her life has affected her. We don't really talk about how she felt and how it affected her growing up. I'm really nervous about what she is going to say.

I know telling your story is very healing, and I am hoping that all the women and children who are part of the roundtable find peace with their pasts. I am hopeful that by telling our stories people will realize that we need to help other women get the help they need to heal from whatever it is that is keeping them in addiction.

> *My son and I had a great talk all the way home about me being in prison and how he was affected. It was the first time we actually opened up to each other, and I learned a lot from him about how he was feeling about me being away. The Planning Circle brought us closer together."*
>
> —Christine Hemingway

I don't have to speak until the third day of the conference, but I am up for day one of filming my story.[2] I am still a wreck when speaking in public, and I know there will be people watching while we film. But I know my story will help others and hopefully help change the policies for women in prison.

NOTES

[1] Quotes re-printed with permission from the manuscript, *Bonding Through Bars: Equity-Focused Knowledge Translation* (EqKT) *and Collaborative Research Approaches with Mothers with Lived Prison Experience,* by Samantha Sarra, Kirsten Hargreaves, Mo Korchinski, Pam Young, Ruth Elwood Martin, Tara Zupancic, Jane Buxton. Unpublished manuscript.

[2] See *Bonding Through Bars,* Appendix, Documentary Films.

Visiting Mom When I Was Thirteen

MATTIE CAMPBELL

I REMEMBER EVERYTHING from sitting in the back of Gramma's car, reading a book, to what the exact inside of the building looked like. Driving to Maple Ridge was a bit of a blur, but the minute we turned onto the dirt backroad, I remember everything so vividly.

Driving up, all you could see was forest, a green field with a fence, and some little buildings spread out. The closer we got, there was the big grey-blue building with more fences and security. The fences weren't nice—they were pretty much what they look like on TV. You had to go up to the stairs and press a buzzer to be allowed in. Inside there was one more flight of stairs, and then you came into the waiting room.

The office area had plastic wall protection, and you could slide things underneath to the security officers. We had to take off anything metal and leave it inside a locker. They gave us keys for the lockers, and we also had to remember a code. After everyone showed ID and was "checked in," we waited for the other families that were coming to visit that day.

Once everyone was good to go, we went one at a time through a metal detector that was hyper sensitive. I remember Grandpa had some change or a zipper or something, and he had to go through about five times. After everyone was clear, we went through heavy locked doors to a little room. Then through another set of doors into a long hallway. The hallway had rooms on each side, and each one held maybe two people, but my Grandma, Grandpa, and I all fit. The hallway was a lot darker than the rest of the place, with navy blue carpeted floors.

Sitting in the room was the hardest part because we had to wait. There was a plastic wall so there was no way for us to touch you, but there weren't any phones. Just some holes in the plastic so we could hear you. Of course, your nerves were acting up so we had to wait a little longer for you. When you sat down for the first time, I tried to act so strong for you.

I tried to make sure you thought I was okay, because I didn't want you knowing how upset I actually was. However, seeing you and not being able to touch you was too much. It hurt so bad, and I couldn't contain it anymore. I remember losing it when the time was up. I know I didn't have a choice, but I hadn't seen you in weeks. Christmas was coming up, and all I wanted was to hug you and bring you back home.

I walked down that hallway sobbing. I couldn't contain it because I didn't know when I was going to see you again, and hearing your voice and seeing you in person just made it seem so much more real and scary. I didn't care that all the guards and the other families were watching me. No one else seemed that sad, and I seemed to be the only one crying like a baby. But you're my mom. You're not supposed to be in there—you're supposed to be out here with me.

I couldn't begin to wrap my head around the fact that it had gotten this far. "Mommies need their babies and babies need their mommies." It was something I always said to you, because it's true. Without you, I wouldn't be who I am. I couldn't imagine losing you, and I don't want to think about the fact that one day I will have to. I'm just glad that I haven't yet.

You're the best thing in my life, even if for a good chunk it was pretty shit. It's only made our bond stronger. Yes, we do fight like sisters, but I'd rather fight with you like a sister than like a mom. You're still my mom, but you're so much more than that. You're my best friend. You're the one thing that keeps me going, and you know me better than I know myself.

I'm glad you went to jail just because it gave you the chance to get better that you never would have had otherwise. I'm glad that I never have to visit that place again, even though the memory still burns in the back of my mind like it was yesterday. I love you so much, and I'm so happy you're better.

Court Decision

RUTH ELWOOD MARTIN

SIX MONTHS LATER, the judgment was released. The Honourable Madam Justice Ross concluded that,

> the decision to cancel the Mother Baby Program was arbitrary, overbroad, and grossly disproportionate and therefore contrary to the principles of fundamental justice.... [It] violated s. 7 and s. 15 of the Charter in that it deprived provincially incarcerated mothers who wish to have their baby remain with them while they serve their sentence, and the babies of those mothers, of security of the person equal protection, and equal benefit of the law without discrimination, in a manner not in accordance with the principles of fundamental justice. (189-190)

The judge told BC Corrections that they had six months to remedy the situation. A mother-baby unit had to be opened in the provincial women's correctional centre by July 2014. The BC government had one month to decide whether to appeal the decision to the Supreme Court of Canada; to their credit, they decided not to.

REFERENCES

Ross, Honourable Madam Justice. *Inglis v. British Columbia* (Minister of Public Safety). Vancouver; 2013.

Creating Guidelines for Mother-Baby Units in Correctional Facilities

RUTH ELWOOD MARTIN

I REALIZED THAT THE COURT ORDER to re-open the mother-baby unit was a unique opportunity for the Collaborating Centre for Prison Health and Education to demonstrate international "best practices" and to try to influence the development of policy regarding infants born to incarcerated mothers in British Columbia. First Nations Health Authority gave us funding to support a meeting to bring experts together to develop guidelines for the implementation of mother-baby units in Canada. We invited representatives of community organizations, health and correctional experts, and mothers with incarceration experience (international, national, and provincial) to come together for one and a half days in March 2014 at UBC. We opened the event with an evening public forum, at which lawyers told their story of the court case and a mother told her story of being incarcerated with her child.

We had anticipated thirty attendees for this meeting, but fifty people came! Due to travel delays and illness, two participants joined us over Skype: Dr. Mary Byrne, a leading academic, and Elaine Lord, a retired warden from the Bedford Hills Correctional Facility for Women in New York. Two people came from New Zealand, where mother-baby units have operated within correctional centres for many years. Despite having just engaged in a five-year court case, the warden, deputy warden, and two senior correctional officers of the BC provincial correctional centre attended the meeting. Also, a representative came from the women's sector of the federal correctional services.

We structured the meeting around an appreciative enquiry framework: women with incarceration experience presented in panels alongside correctional and health experts, and all panel presentations were followed by small group discussion. All discussions were audio-recorded and transcribed, and the transcriptions were then subjected to thematic anaylsis. Throughout the meeting, I sensed that everyone wanted to be there. Correctional officials, health practitioners, academics, NGO organizations, formerly incarcerated women—we were united in our diversity; we all wanted to put the best interests of the child first.

The ensuing guidelines evolved over many months of careful and collaborative editing and revisions; they were sent and re-sent to the delegates who attended the working meeting. Then, I very systematically approached each organization that was represented at the meeting in order to invite them to endorse the guidelines. Twenty-three organizations endorsed the guidelines. The guidelines are available in English and French, and we distributed a copy to every provincial and federal women's correctional centre in Canada (Collaborating Centre).

Although the BC and federal correctional organizations did not endorse the guidelines (which was disappointing to me), these organizations did incorporate the guidelines' principles and language into policies that govern their respective mother-baby units.

REFERENCE

Collaborating Centre for Prison Health and Education. *Guidelines for the Implementation of Mother-Child Units in Canadian Correctional Centres*. Vancouver: Collaborating Centre for Prison Health and Education, University of British Columbia, 2015. Web.

Fifteen Guiding Principles for Mother-Baby Units in Canadian Correctional Facilities

1. The best interests and safety of the child are a primary concern in addition to the rights of the mother.
2. Protection of the family unit is at the core of our societal value system and is entitled to protection by the state. The woman defines who are members of her family unit.
3. Preserving the integrity of the mother-child relationship should be a priority at all times and is the responsibility of all service providers. Any practice that separates a child from her/his mother (for any reason other than the safety or wellbeing of the child or the wellbeing of the mother), and does not provide for the maintenance of the mother-child relationship, harms the family unit.
4. Canadian correctional gender-based statements of philosophy affirm that correctional practices should be responsive to the needs of women both inside a correctional facility and in the community (Correctional Service Canada).
5. All efforts should be made to seek supportive community alternatives to custody for women giving birth during their sentence (UN).
6. Child safety is the shared responsibility of the child protection authorities and the ministries of health and justice (including correctional staff and hospital staff).
7. Women are incarcerated for many reasons, and only some reasons are associated with child protection concerns. Therefore, correctional mother-child care should be reviewed on a case-by-case basis, with child protection authorities' involvement in cases only where deemed appropriate.
8. Woman-centered care should be implemented in correctional facilities, using the same standards as the community, recognizing that incarcerated women are valued as key informants for all decisions for their care and their future, including defining their own families.

9. Pregnant and parenting incarcerated women should be informed of their choices and rights.

10. Women's religious, cultural, and spiritual customs and beliefs relating to pregnancy, giving birth, and parenting should be respected without compromising safety and security (see Wilson).

11. Respectful and trauma-informed care that is sensitive to the needs of those recovering from past trauma and/or substance use challenges should be offered to all incarcerated women; correctional staff should be responsive to the impacts of physical, psychological, and/or sexual violence in women's lives (see *Gendering the National Framework*).

12. Pregnant or postpartum incarcerated women should receive appropriate individual holistic health care, in the form of an individualized health care plan, which has been developed in collaboration with a qualified health practitioner. Within correctional facilities, pregnant and postpartum women, and their babies and children, should be offered adequate and timely nourishment, a healthy environment, and regular exercise opportunities, similar to that offered in the community (UN).

13. It is important to identify and build on strengths and protective factors of incarcerated women, their families, and their communities. Focusing on protective factors, such as improving housing and nutrition, can improve outcomes for mothers and their children, thereby reducing harm.

14. When planning for release, a continuum of help should be accessible and offered to women and their families in order to support and to respect women's goals for change. In addition, integrated case management, including continuity of medical care, should be actively supported on release to community, in order to nurture and stabilize mother-child relationships.

15. Collaborations should be fostered between correctional facilities/ministries and community health organizations/ministries in order to provide seamless care for mother-child unit participants.

"Fifteen Principles" were reprinted with permission from Guidelines for the Implementation of Mother-Child Units in Canadian Correctional Centres, *Vancouver: Collaborating Centre for Prison Health and Education, University of British Columbia, 2015.*

REFERENCES

Wilson, Don, with Aboriginal Health Initiative Committee. "Health Professional Working with First Nations, Inuit, and Métis Consensus

Guideline." *Journal of Obstetrics and Gynaecology Canada* 13.35 (June 2013): 550-553. Web.

Correctional Service Canada. *Ten-Year Status Report on Women's Corrections, 1996-2006*. Ottawa: Government of Canada, 2006. Web.

Gendering the National Framework Series (Vol 4): Women-Centered Harm Reduction. Vancouver, BC: British Columbia Centre of Excellence for Women's Health, 2010.

Thibodeau, L. M. "Doula Program in a Provincial Jail, the Birthing Well Collective." Presentation, Panel 3, Mother and Baby Prison Health Working Meeting. The Collaborating Centre for Prison Health and Education, University of British Columbia, Vancouver, 2014.

United Nations (UN). *United Nations Rules for the Treatment of Women Prisoners and Non-Custodial Measures for Women Offenders with their Commentary ("the Bangkok Rules")*. General Assembly. 16 March 2011. Web.

After the Trial

BRENDA TOLE

AFTER SO MUCH TIME HAD PASSED and so many negative comments had been made about the program, I began to question my own judgment and beliefs with regards to my tenure at ACCW. It was wonderful to hear the comments of the judge about the program; however, if the government felt they were being forced into reinstating the program, my concern was how committed they would be to the initiative.

The court case had pitted those of us involved in the former program at ACCW against the government during the trial, and although it was good to hear our past work acknowledged, it was important to create a positive relationship with BC Corrections so that all the knowledge and experience of the past could contribute in a helpful way towards the development of the new mother-baby unit at ACCW.

After several discussions with some of the key people involved in the mother-baby unit at ACCW, Dr. Ruth Elwood Martin suggested we work together to organize a two-day working meeting in March 2014 to generate best practice evidence-based guidelines to inform the implementation of mother-baby units across Canada.

The Collaborating Centre for Prison Health and Education hosted this event, and fifty stakeholders, including both BC Corrections and Correction Services Canada, participated, as did some of the mothers who had participated in the unit at ACCW. The process provided a significant forum for presentations and discussions about all aspects of optimal child and maternal health inside a correctional facility.

This was a very positive, even therapeutic, process for me. We had done everything we could to contribute to the kind of mother-baby unit that would allow for a positive experience for all involved. I am ever hopeful that in the future this initiative will be the normal approach to women who give birth in custody, and I am happy that we were able to give several women and their newborns that opportunity.

ACCW Mother-Baby Unit Update

RUTH ELWOOD MARTIN

THE ACCW MOTHER-BABY UNIT re-opened in July 2014. Since that date, only one mother was approved to live with her infant in the unit, even though many more babies have been born to mothers at ACCW. It has been frustrating and distressing for us on the outside, knowing that each pregnant woman inside ACCW is living with uncertainty, anxiety, and grief, not knowing whether or not their newborn baby will be taken away at birth. I assume that any support at the highest ministry levels is not trickling down into practical support for on-the-ground action. I assume that fear and risk-aversion overwhelm the frontline workers (e.g. social workers) who make the decisions regarding whether a woman is able to care for her baby inside prison. Although the BC Supreme Court ruled that separating a baby from her or his mother in prison violated the Canadian Charter, more advocacy and education needs to happen before the paradigm shifts and it becomes the norm, rather than the exception, for mothers with incarceration experience to live with their babies, regardless of which side of the gates they happen to be living.

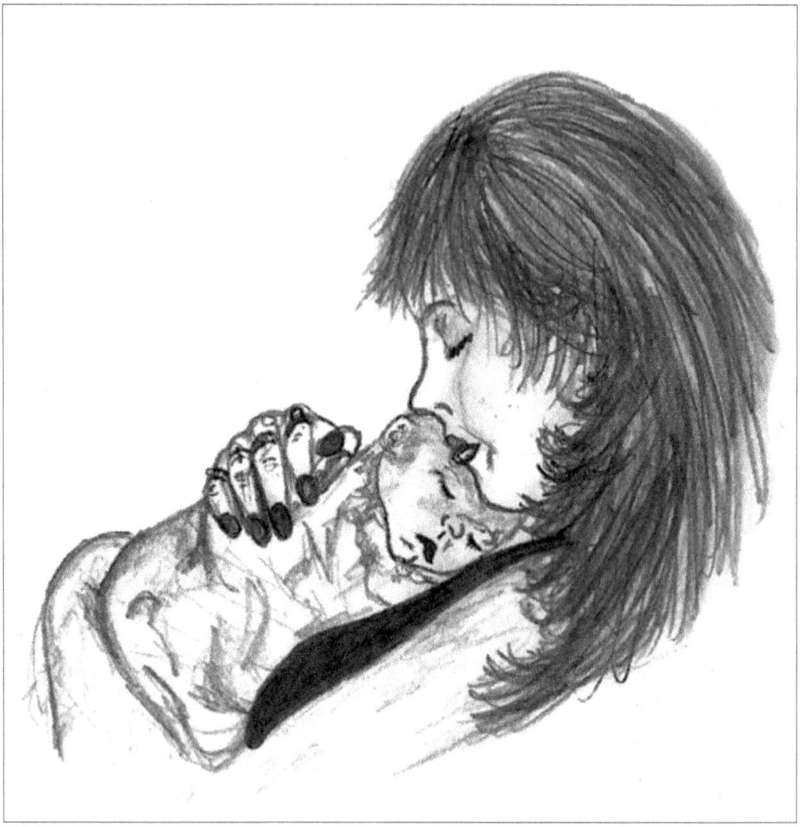

Amber's Story
"To Never Give Up"

AMBER CHRISTIE

MY LIFE CHANGED. By this time I was two years clean. Ryan and I had decided to see a doctor. I had one burning question: could I safely have a child? It was scary to ask, but we were very glad when we did. Throughout the last couple of years, I had done the Hep C treatment. Now I was cured, and I took all the medication I needed to keep me healthy. When we asked about children, I was told that with the medicine they now have, babies are being born negative every day. This gave us such hope. The day I learned I was pregnant was one of the best days of our lives. We both screamed and cried. I never stopped thinking about my first daughter. I searched and searched without success. But for now, my life was amazing! I had the most beautiful partner, I was having a baby, and I had so much support because I took a chance and jumped in. Nine months later, our son Clayton was born. Perfectly healthy and negative of course! I want women who are facing the same obstacles as I was to never give up. I want them to know there are options now.

How many more years will I be doing this?
—Ruth Elwood Martin

Letter to My Granddaughter

MO KORCHINKSI

ONE DAY I WOKE UP and life's energy had changed, somehow forever. It was a subtle change, and at first I didn't realize my old existence had been transformed. I looked in the mirror, and a person looked back with a loving soul. I'm not sure when that happened. I opened my eyes, and I felt peace, exuberance, gentleness, gratitude, and laughter. My eyes were wide open for life. I recognized I could never go back to the "old me."

My vision had expanded. I inhaled and exhaled with the breath of new life in my once-broken soul. I slowly recognized and completely embraced the person who looked back at me. Everything had changed. My heart burst with gratitude. I embraced the new vision; inspiration and energy flowing through me from head to toe. Life had changed forever.

You've been a part of my life for almost eight years now. I want you to know that these eight years have been the happiest in my life. I've enjoyed every moment of it! Even though we've gone through some rough times, I have never thought of trading a single moment of my time spent with you for anything else.

I cannot imagine what it would be like if you were not in my everyday life. I don't think I could stand it. For so many years I questioned what love is, but holding you in my arms for the first time, I felt love. I knew what love was. I hope that there never comes a time when we'll be apart. I hope we will always want to be together. I love you so much that just the mere thought of not being with you breaks my heart. Know that I have made a promise to love, cherish, and be with you for the rest of my life! You can always count on that, my love.

Custody of Grandchildren

PAM YOUNG

As I've been writing here and there the past couple years, my story has evolved. I have had permanent custody of my two granddaughters for just over a year and a half. In the beginning, it was a shock to the system…. I mean we had been alone for so many years, and then suddenly we had two kids. I used to go into my room and cry because I didn't think I could do it. But as time went by, we developed a routine and now I couldn't imagine life without them. Their mother (my daughter) is currently in active addiction, so the best thing for the girls is to be with family. And the girls are happy to have a stable and healthy environment in which to live. The girls have grown so much since we were given custody, and their progress has been remarkable.

It feels like we were given a second chance in life to make up for where we went wrong with our children when they were younger. My husband, as always, has been my rock through all these new changes. He is an amazingly patient man. He dedicates so much of his time to helping the girls with their educational stuff, but he always finds time to have fun with them even while he helps out with a lot of the everyday supervision. I admire him so much, since I know I don't quite have the patience that he does. It's like our relationship has come full circle. We started out as young parents raising three kids, and here we are almost twenty-five years later doing the same thing. Except this time we know so much more and have learned the hard way how important family really is.

Obviously, I'd love to see my daughter get into treatment and work towards getting the girls back, but it doesn't look like that will happen for quite some time. I believe she needs to come to an understanding that in order to get clean, quitting drugs isn't enough; you need to lay a strong foundation to build off by going to treatment and trauma counselling, finding second-stage housing and employment, and learning life skills.

I know that if I hadn't done this, I wouldn't be where I'm at today. I'd probably be out there somewhere on the streets, smoking crack, still stuck in my addict behaviours. I can't dwell on what's going on in her addiction because I have no control over what she does. She knows that when and if she's ready to go to treatment, I will help her in a heartbeat, but I can't allow myself to live in her dysfunction. It was hard for my husband and me to let go and just focus on the kids. As a mother, you want to rescue or save your child. I know we enabled her for way too long before we came to this understanding.

I am so blessed with an amazing partner and two of the most resilient kids I know. There's no obstacle we can't overcome as a family. It's a good feeling knowing you're a good role model, that you've become someone your family can look up to. We also find time to take our three other granddaughters (my son's kids)—but not all at once. We like to rotate as much as possible, but we mostly have the oldest who is two-and-a-half years old. She's such a sweet little girl. We have so much fun with her. I'm sure when the babies get older we will have them more often too.

It is funny how life keeps throwing you curve balls, but it's wonderful that you now know how to catch them.

Gratitude
Excerpt, Women in2 Healing Newsletter, Issue 6

AMBER CHRISTIE

WHAT A DAY! I just left the baby shower held by Women in2 Healing. What a miracle that we could all come together to share such an event. Who would have thought that we would all be there to celebrate such gifts?

A day of pizza, veggies, treats, and Alison learning not to give a one-year-old a whole cupcake—what fun! There is hope out there for women; we can make it if we support each other without judgment and conditions. We have all been subjected to way too much in our lives. We all need the support from other women who have gone through what we have gone through. Thank you Women in2 Healing for being there to support me in my journey!

Little Angel Above

MO KORCHINSKI

You are home in Heaven
My arms are empty
If I could just hold you once
It didn't take long for you to steal my heart
It happened the moment I heard your heart
With tears in my eyes, love filled my heart
Little did I know you wouldn't be with us long
You were such a strong girl but so small
You were our blessing then as you are now
I'm thankful for your short life
Nana will hold you in her heart forever
Even now you're always on my mind
No one will replace you or take your place
You'll always be my granddaughter
And my precious little girl
I miss you more than I can express
Lillyanne, my little angel, above

What would you like people to know that would be helpful for women being released?

We're Human

We're all human
We're only human

We aren't bad people
We just made mistakes

We all make mistakes
We just made bad choices

We are trying to change
We deserve a second chance

We need help getting back on our feet
We deserve a chance to get things right

We are broken, struggling, wounded
We can be fixed with love and support

VIII. Education

My goal is to be an educated woman, not a statistic. I can be a role model for my daughter. Now in recovery, I believe with education plus my history I will be a great helper to others who struggle.
—Recipient of an education funding award

…The number of people we have lost since I got clean. That's why I'm going to Cuba, to Africa—there's so much to see in the world. I am this tiny thing in the universe. I wasted thirty years in addiction. There's so much to see and do. Paths are laid out for us. I can't feel guilty about my past. My life included being an addict and going to prison, as well as my kids' journeys. There's no reason to be angry. My past makes me who I am.
—Mo Korchinski

I plan to work closely with Indigenous communities to promote wellness and healing from trauma and wellness. Education has given me choices and will help me to affect my community in a good way.
—Chas Coutlee

I graduated with honours, and my graduation day was one of the proudest moments in my life. Putting on that gown, walking onto the stage, and being given my certificate was an amazing moment. After I came off the stage, the photographer took my photo, and it was the best photo I've ever seen of myself. I looked so incredibly happy—and I was!
—Pam Young

Doctor's Journey

RUTH ELWOOD MARTIN

I THINK ABOUT MY OWN EDUCATIONAL JOURNEY, which was a simple and relatively easy straight line from elementary to secondary school, from undergraduate university to medical school and residency, with a supportive family and financial assistance along the way.

Today, I went to the graduation ceremony at Nicola Valley Institute of Technology (NVIT). Mo received her social work degree, and Pam and Chas received their diplomas. Mo gave the valedictorian speech. The NVIT Elders spoke about the power of education to bring about change.

I reflect on the educational journey that Mo, Pam, and Chas have each taken. Each woman endured childhood adversity and trauma, and struggled with substance use, self-harm, depression, and self-doubt. Seven years ago, inside prison, these women were fearful about the uncertainty that lay ahead, terribly afraid of the sort of life that they would face on the outside.

I can only imagine how much courage, determination, and vision they needed in order to move forward and to succeed. And I know that each woman struggled to find the financial means to stick with her education.

Today, Mo, Pam, and Chas were surrounded by family—children and grandchildren (Mo and Pam)—proud and celebratory, loved and much-hugged. I feel humbled, inspired, and encouraged to bear witness to today's celebration.

—Journal entry

Population health outcomes are correlated with a population's level of, and access to, education, particularly for girls and young women (Baker, Leon, Smith, Greenaway, and Movit). Some countries, such as Ireland, offer financial assistance to support women in accessing post-secondary education. Such countries recognize that supporting women's education, with its impact on children and communities, is the key to a healthy nation.

A low level of education is a known socioeconomic determinant of poor health (Mikkonen and Raphael), and this determinant is highly prevalent among incarcerated women, worldwide and in Canada (van den Bergh, Gatherer, Fraser, and Moller).

Over time, we recognized that our projects are prison health and education research projects, because health and educational goals are synergistically intertwined. During the Participatory Health Research at ACCW, incarcerated women gave voice to their goals for improving health, as well as to their desire to engage in meaningful education. As one woman in prison stated, "Can you imagine...? What if, instead of going to prison, women were sentenced to education?" (Ann et al. 301).

REFERENCES

Ann, Danita, Devon, Julie, Lynn, and Shelley. "'Can you imagine... What if women were sentenced to education?' Women speaking out inside the gate." *Poetic Inquiry: Vibrant Voices in the Social Sciences.* Eds. C. Leggo, P. Sameshima and M. Prendergast. Rotterdam, The Netherlands: Sense, 2009. 301-306. (Last names withheld due to confidentiality)

Baker, David P., Juan F. C. León, Emily G. Smith Greenaway, J. Maxwell Collins, and Marcela A. Movit. "The Education Effect on Population Health: A Reassessment." *Population and Development Review* 37.2 (2011): 307-332. Web.

Mikkonen, Juha and Dennis Raphael. "Social Determinants of Health: The Canadian Facts." Toronto: York University School of Health Policy and Management, 2010. Web.

Van den Bergh, Brenda J., Alex Gatherer, Andrew Fraser, and Lars Moller. "Imprisonment and Women's Health: Concerns About Gender Sensitivity, Human Rights, and Public Health." *Bulletin of the World Health Organization* 89.9 (2011): 689-694. Web.

Career Builders Program

MO KORCHINSKI

I WENT TO CAREER BUILDERS to figure out what I wanted to be when I grew up! When the teacher found out I was in prison, he told me I could only work in the construction field and that I couldn't do anything else because I have a record. I got funding to go to school to learn how to build houses—something I enjoy doing as a hobby, but not as a career. I'm not sure I want to work outside in the cold rain for eight months of the year, plus I am forty years old and not sure how long I could do the job. I want to help people who are in danger of going down the same path I did. No one was there to help me as a child when I was getting beaten by my mother, and I want to stop other children from going through that. No child should feel like they are alone and have no choice but to hide their feelings with alcohol and drugs. I want to show youth that someone cares and understands. I'm pissed at myself for wrecking my life and not being able to leave my past in the past. The course is eight months long, and I am the only woman in the course. I enjoy the course and everything I am learning, but I feel like I am missing something. I don't feel this is what I cleaned up to do. I feel like God has a bigger plan for me—I have to believe this since it helps me to accept my past. I believe that what we go through in life only helps us to be better people. Life is its own classroom.

Dressing the Part

AMANDA STALLER

WHEN I GO TO BUSINESS MEETINGS, I dress the part of a professional and put a little bit of makeup on. I make sure my hair and my clothes are well kempt (that's the thing about Lululemon—you can dress it up or dress it down). When I'm at work, it's t-shirts and jeans; I wear runners and shorts and my baseball cap because I'm hands on. If I haven't got my hands in the recycling, I'm in the office doing intakes or facilitating groups. I multitask all day long, yard work, making sure the house is operating, etc. It's a recovery house—Talitha Koum means "girl get up." It reminds me of resurrecting from the dead, and I resonate with that). I walk with these women and I have discussions with them....

I'm in a position of authority, and I use my voice. You learn a lot about yourself and others when you're living with, working with, running with them, when you're shoulder to shoulder with them. I'm all about team building and drawing on other women's assets to collaborate. I have this vision about how to help women get back on their feet. It's important to lead from behind. It's important to me to be in this position of authority, to work with all of these professionals—probation officers, nurses, support workers, social workers, and other professionals in the community. Who would have thought I'd be a spoke in that wheel?

Live Your Dreams

CHAS COUTLEE

Presentation to the Canadian House of Commons' Standing Committee on the Status of Women, Indigenous women in the federal justice and correctional systems.

AFTER I LEFT JAIL FOR THE LAST TIME I was offered a job at the recovery house I went through. First, I was an overnight support worker, then I moved into a facilitator's role, and eventually I became the program director. I loved serving the women and children who were seeking recovery. I knew I wanted to go back to school so I could be a more effective helper in my community. At Vancouver Community College, I took the twelve-week basic counselling course, paid for by a religious organization that believed in me. And then I heard about the Chemical Addiction Worker program offered at Nicola Valley Institute of Technology.

It was hard because I was funding myself, and I had no access to family to provide housing or financial help. Whenever I needed to go to the food bank, it would mean taking a day off work or school, and I couldn't afford to do that either. It was hard, but I pushed through. I heard about a group called Soroptimist. They give education awards every year to women like me who are the sole economic support in their families and who are overcoming great challenges and still applying themselves to getting an education. I fit the criteria perfectly. I applied and I was selected as a recipient for a "Live Your Dreams" award.

I graduated with my Chemical Addiction Worker Advanced Diploma in April 2016. I am currently working towards my Bachelor of Social Work. Education has always been a strong family value. My grandmother went back to university in her sixties and used to be an elder at NVIT as well as a language instructor. My mom also received her BSW at NVIT in partnership with the University of Victoria. I know that education brings choices. I am still mindful of being a good role model I am to my daughter, and I am happy to say that my daughter is also in school. My daughter is pursuing a career in pediatric nursing, and I could not be prouder of her. After I complete my degree at NVIT, I plan to take Aboriginal Focused Trauma Therapy at the Justice Institute and then move on to a Master's degree. I plan to work closely with Indigenous communities to promote wellness and healing from trauma. Education has given me choices and will help me to affect my community in a good way.

Presentation at Douglas College

CAT WILSON

A COUPLE OF WEEKS AGO, I heard that Mo and Alison Granger-Brown were going to Douglas College to do a PowerPoint presentation. I asked to go with them. I thought it would be neat to see Mo in action! Well, to my surprise Carrie Smith and I were presenting too. Gulp!! Not funny, Mo.

When we first got there, I was a bit scared and intimidated. I felt totally out of my comfort zone. We were very warmly welcomed by the instructor and started to set up as some of the class came in. We presented to thirty-one Rec Therapy students. Mo and Alison were very well prepared and had put together a great presentation on addiction.

Then came the time to share and answer questions. Carrie, Mo, and I took turns talking about our addictions, where they had taken us and how we were doing now, what was working for us and what had helped. The students were curious about what kind of professional support worked for us.

All three of us were in agreement that unconditional love and support, not being judged, and total acceptance no matter what, were key elements for professionals to keep in mind while working with us.

Overall, it was a great night and I felt really good about doing something productive and giving back by helping others. I still have a fear of speaking in front of others, but I know I can do it with the support of my friends. I look forward to doing more.

Going Back to School

PAM YOUNG

ABOUT A YEAR AFTER I started working with the Unlocking the Gates program, Mo told me about this amazing course at NVIT—the chemical addictions support worker course. Of course, the self-doubting began, and I automatically started coming up with reasons why I couldn't do it. I'm too busy. I can't do it! But Mo challenged me to apply. So I decided to do the entrance math and English exam. When I walked into the room, my confidence was low. I felt very intimidated. I aced the English exam and failed horribly at the math. In that moment, I felt relieved that I was off the hook! But much to my surprise, they accepted me anyway! They told me I wouldn't graduate with my class if I didn't upgrade my math before graduation in the spring. Once I was accepted, my confidence level went up and I began to think: I can do this!

It was tough going back to school. I had poor listening skills, and I struggled to retain the information. But after a couple of months, I started to love it. I loved it because there was such a strong sense of community. NVIT is an Aboriginal school, and all classes have an Aboriginal twist to them. We learned a lot about colonization and intergenerational trauma, which stirred up a lot of feelings for me. I really had no clue exactly how horrific colonization was, and what happened to the First Nations people angered me.

I was a straight A student. And thanks to the computer skills Mo had taught me, I was able to succeed in my presentations and get good grades on my papers. I graduated with honours, and my graduation day was one of the proudest moments in my life. Putting on that gown, walking onto the stage, and being given my certificate was an amazing moment. After I came off the stage, the photographer took my photo, and it was the best photo I've ever seen of myself. I looked so incredibly happy—and I was!

Having my husband, daughter, and granddaughters there to see me walk across the stage and receive my certificate was such a huge accomplishment. My daughter had just come back into my life after nineteen years. I had only begun to get to know her and the girls, so having them there meant so much to me. And of course it was perfect having my husband there! It was a miracle that we made it out of the Downtown East Side alive, and here I was graduating school with him by my side. It's especially hard for families to stay together during addiction. My family fell apart early in my addiction, and we had all been reconnected for only a year or less. So for them to be there for one of my proudest moments was amazing.

Battle Out of Darkness

COLBY

I KNEW IT WAS WRONG, but something in me told me to keep going. I'd been down that road before. It took me to a place of extreme darkness, a place filled with hopeless, unhappy, sad eyes. Something was telling me that this time would be different, and although I wasn't quite convinced, I kept going.

A flash of light startled me. I rubbed my eyes, partly because I was blinded by the light and partly because I couldn't believe what I was seeing. Two angels with wands—one in black, one in white—were floating in the air right in front of me. I watched in wonder as the two angels battled. Then the dark angel dropped his wand and bowed before the light angel. No words were spoken. The dark angel disappeared into thin air.

The white angel was now shining much more brightly. Yet I was not blinded by her light. She turned to me and said, "My child, you are putting yourself in a very dangerous position. You're lucky I was here to help!" I was unable to respond, still completely shocked by the events I've just witnessed. She said, "That dark angel was sent by the devil to steal your conscience. You are his purpose, and he will never give up! You need to stay in the light where you are safe. I will not be able to save you once you have wandered off too far. Now turn around and walk away!!" Terrified, I turned and ran, ran until I couldn't run any more. Strangely, I was not afraid of the dark angel; I was afraid of the light angel. But after that day, I never strayed from the light.

Funding Education

RUTH ELWOOD MARTIN

DURING THE PRISON PARTICIPATORY HEALTH research project, women gave voice to their goals for improving health, including their desire to engage in meaningful education. The idea of establishing an education award fund arose during the PHR retreats on Galiano Island. We launched the education fund in September 2009, with funds raised from the sale of restored wooden chairs. We have now transferred the fund to Vancouver Foundation and re-named it the Arresting Hope Education Fund.

The Arresting Hope Education Fund seeks to empower women to pursue education and to foster opportunities for transformation and hope. All proceeds from book sales of *Arresting Hope* and *Releasing Hope* are being donated to the Arresting Hope Education Fund.

The fund provides financial assistance to currently and previously incarcerated women and their children in order to further their education. The education awards are administered by a selection committee hosted at Nicola Valley Institute Technology, which is British Columbia's Aboriginal public post-secondary institute. The selection committee members have many years of experience in community service, corrections, and education, and donate their time and expertise to the selection committee processes.

As of October 2017, the fund has provided awards to eleven women with incarceration experience, as well as one child who has a mother with incarceration experience. Award recipients' career goals include becoming an addictions support worker, obtaining a Master's degree in Psychology, obtaining a Bachelor's degree in Social Work, and pursuing careers as a healthcare accountant, a journeyman welder, and a veterinary technician. When asked about her financial needs, one woman explained that the award would give her a bit of financial relief because it was difficult to meet the cost of living. Another woman stated that she just wants to earn a living and feel good about what she's doing, not shameful. A single mother shared that she struggles with basic needs such as food for her children.

When award recipients were asked how they think this course of education will impact the wellbeing of their families, communities, and themselves, the women responded:

> *I advocated for a woman in family court, and I saw that it was full of Aboriginal women trying to regain custody of their children. I thought that there was something more I could do to support these women, so I enrolled in school.*

> *My education is important in removing the stereotype of being in prison.*

> *I am by myself, so my family doesn't play a part of my decision making. I want to be part of the wage-earning, law-abiding public and not return to my criminal lifestyle.*

> *I have an infant son, and working in health care will open up more flexible opportunities and give me health benefits, enabling me to save for his education.*

> *I am an addict in recovery. I am also a mentor in the downtown Hastings area, and I always use myself as an example to my fellow peers.*

The kindness of those who donate to the Arresting Hope Education Fund is greatly appreciated by those who receive the support to pursue their education. Thank you for supporting, through your reading, the education of women who are learning new ways of being present and pursuing leadership in the world.

Donations to the Arresting Hope Education Fund may be directed to Vancouver Foundation. Please see https://www.vancouverfoundation. ca/arrestinghope.

Learning and Growth

LARA-LISA CONDELLO

SINCE 2009, ELEVEN FEMALE STUDENTS with incarceration experience living in British Columbia have received awards from the Arresting Hope Educational Fund. Nicola Valley Institute of Technology has become the administrator of the award. Approximately half of the bursaries were awarded to NVIT students.

Supporting my students to succeed, and encouraging their self-determination, fuels my heart. Ultimately, it's the NVIT community that motivates and sustains my work. NVIT encourages learning and growth by offering opportunities for career development and training, and by providing services and supports that honour an Indigenous experience ("Strategic Direction"). NVIT was created in 1983 to provide a learning space for thirteen Indigenous people to study. Today, NVIT enrols approximately fourteen hundred students annually, both on the Merritt and Vancouver campuses and in the community, servicing sixty percent of First Nations communities in British Columbia.

NVIT is an advocate and role model for Indigenous education. I believe one of the core strengths of NVIT programming is our leadership's ability to respond to the educational and training needs of Indigenous communities. At the core of NVIT is the strength of our Elders Council. They remind us that the educational journeys that we forge together are crucial in helping us to embrace our history and identity. NVIT Elders eloquently share that:

> Our identity and culture are the past. It is only when we can unwrap the past that we can also embody our healing and the gift that is NVIT. That is the journey. The doors of our building welcome us every day and remind us, as we enter, of the footprints that we are leaving for the next generation. Just as our Elders taught us, we welcome all nations through

our doors, and in so doing we are building a unity. ("Elders' Message")

I deeply value my work at NVIT; this institution has become my community, my extended family. In my Italian culture, we use the term *fogolar* or fireplace to symbolize the importance of extended family to our personal resiliency. I thank NVIT for welcoming me to their fire, and for offering a warm sit for any learners who desire inclusion and self-transformation.

Last summer I learnt that *Na'tsa'maht* is a Salish word that means "unity, pulling together, and being of one mind." Indigenous scholars remind me that we are from "one origin family of creation" (Absolo). Indigenous scholars, community leaders, and knowledge keepers are beacons of hope; they embody the "resistance, survival, and resurgence" of Indigenous worldviews (Smith). I was inspired by their call for collective action to revolutionize the "academic industrial complex" into communal, relatable, meaningful, and accountable learning circles and, in so doing, to foster sustainable futures for our children (Corntassel).

Lastly, I embrace the teaching of my Dean, John Chenoweth who humbly states that, "the strength of any organization is in the strength of its people" (personal communication). Since writing my entry in *Arresting Hope*, my role with many of the recipients of the Arresting Hope Educational Fund has transformed; I have gone from being an instructor and advocate for them to being in relationship with them as a colleague and community member. This has been one of my most rewarding experiences of the past decade. Awarding a former recipient's daughter with an award is a testament to the strength of women and their ability to promote transformation across generations.

> Women have always been a beacon of hope.... Mothers and grandmothers in the lives of our children, and in the survival of our communities, must be recognized and supported. The justified rage we all feel and share today must be turned into an instrument of transformation of our hearts and our souls, clearing the ground for respect, love, honesty, humility, wisdom, and truth. (George 12)

REFERENCES

Absolo, Kathy. "Keynote." S'tenistolw Conference. Camosun College, Victoria, BC. 23-25 Aug 2017. Web.

Corntassel, Jeff. "Keynote." S'tenistolw Conference. Camosun College, Victoria, BC. 23-25 Aug 2017. Web.

"Elders' Message." Nicola Valley Institute of Technology, Vancouver, BC, 2017. Web.

George, Patsy. "Reconciliation: More than a Symbolic Gesture." YWCA Calgary. June 27, 2017. Web.

Smith, Linda Tuhuwai. "Keynote." S'tenistolw Conference. Camosun College, Victoria, BC, 23-25 August 2017. Web.

"Strategic Direction." Nicola Valley Institute of Technology, Vancouver, BC. 2018. Web.

Filmmaker as Educator Activist

MO KORCHINSKI

THE MOTHER-BABY UNIT IS SHUT DOWN. I'm pissed off for all those mothers and babies who will miss out on a great program. *What is going to happen to these babies now?* This event raises some important questions for me. *How do we change policy? Who can change policies? Doesn't the public, that votes politicians into position of power, make these decisions? How do we get the word out there?* We need to make a video so every person can watch how great and empowering the mother-baby unit was! How beneficial the program was! How important it was, not just the mothers and babies in the program but for all the women at the prison!

I do research, but I can't find anywhere to raise the money to make a documentary. *This really sucks, that this awesome program is not going to be heard about.* A couple days after I give up on the idea of making a film, a friend tells me about a scholarship to a film school in Vancouver. I look it up and call for an interview for next week.

I show up and meet a guy named Steve who sits me down and starts asking me all these questions. I explain why I want to learn how to make documentaries. He keeps saying that he needs to make a film about me and I keep saying, "Yeah, right, that ain't going to happen." Right there on the spot he tells me that I got the scholarship for an eight-week film class.

The film class has eight students plus me, and we will be broken up into three groups of three to make a short documentary over the next eight weeks. We will learn plots, storytelling, cameras, and editing, and we will use our new skills to come up with a finished film to show at an open house. I'm paired with Alex, a man from Mexico who came to Canada just to take this course, and Chris, a woman who does advocacy for environmental issues.

Between the three of us and Steve, we have to come up with a concept to start working on. Steve is pushing for the film to be about me, but I keep trying to sway it in another direction. Over the next eight weeks I lose the fight. The film is called *Revolving Door*.[1] While we are editing, I keep trying to cut myself out of the film, but I lose that battle too. Now the film is based on my story. Don't get me wrong—it's a very powerful film, but I so hate seeing myself on camera.

Later, while we are writing up a grant to disseminate the findings from the Doing Time project, we build the cost of filming a short documentary into the budget. We want people to hear the women's voices and highlight the issues that came out of the research project. That film is called *Unlocking the Gates*.[2] I make sure this time I am not in the film, but I do end up doing two cameo spots! I love using this film, instead of a PowerPoint presentation, to show the research findings. Seeing the real people behind the data telling the stories of their struggles is way more powerful.

NOTES

[1] See *Revolving Door,* Appendix, Documentary Films.
[2] See *Unlocking the Gates,* Appendix, Documentary Films.

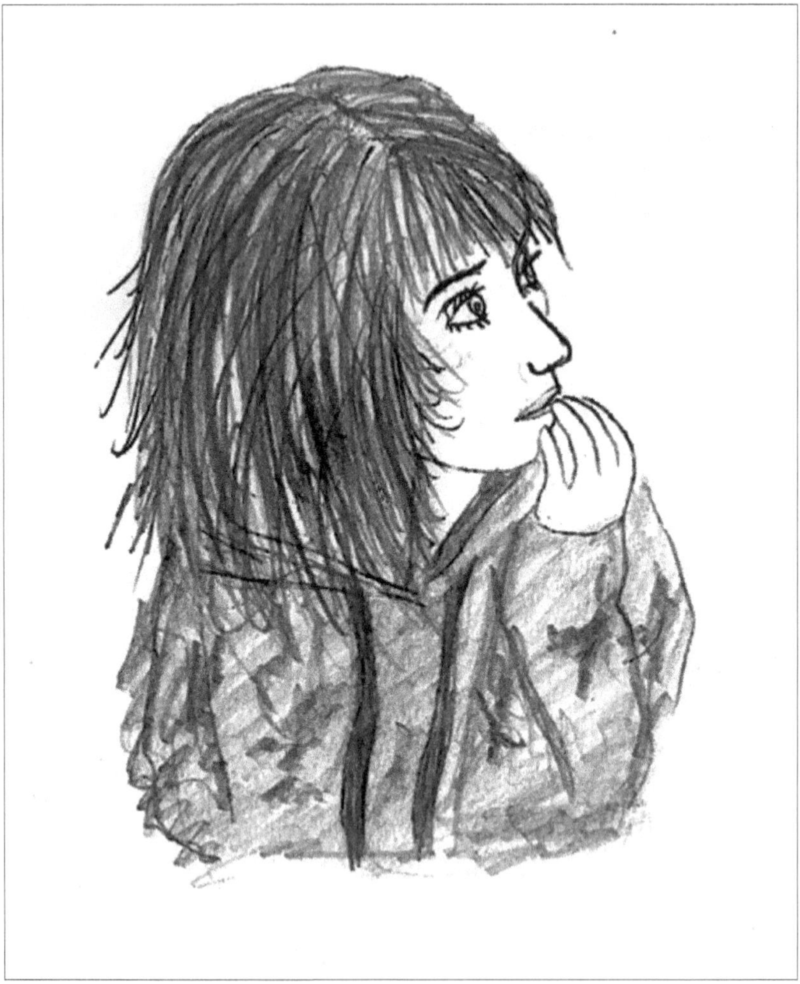

Alumni Speech
NVIT's Vancouver Graduation

MAURA GOWANS

MY NAME IS MAURA GOWANS, and I was born in Yellowknife, Northwest Territories. I was raised in a family that made many sacrifices for me, my brother, and my sister to have the best life possible. This meant that my dad often worked away from home so that my mom was able to stay at home and raise us. This was a huge sacrifice in itself because my mom had to give up her job as an English teacher to do so. The importance of education was instilled in us, and my mom would spend our summers teaching us summer school in a way that was fun. Every birthday and Christmas we would receive new books that we cherished. We were taught to work hard and do our best at everything, that through hard work we could accomplish anything.

I am the mother of five beautiful boys. As a family, we made sacrifices for me to become a registered social worker, which has always been my dream. Growing up, I always wanted to save the world. I would bring home kids who had little parental supervision, and I would bring home stray cats. My dad would always tell me that he would help me to become a social worker when I was older, but that right now I just needed to be a kid. I had so much love in me to share because of all the love I received. I was taught the importance of family and that, above all, your children and family come first. This has allowed me to teach my children that they are loved always and forever.

I dropped out of school at the age of fifteen. I was a great student until this time. I took education and sports very seriously, and I was a competitive runner, skier, and swimmer. My parents attended all of my competitions, and I can still see my parents running with me to the finish line or passing the pool with each lap I swam. We moved from Anchorage, Alaska to Saskatoon, Saskatchewan when I was fourteen years old and in the ninth grade. I experienced racism for the first time, at least the first time that I am aware of. I ended up drinking alcohol to fit in. Then I ran away from home, was fired as a swim coach, and got expelled from school, all within six months. My parents moved to BC, and I followed after attending a residential treatment centre.

I moved to BC at the age of sixteen, and soon I was living in the Downtown Eastside. I was a teenager in 1994, and women were going missing all around me. A close friend's body was found in a dumpster after she was murdered and left there, like garbage. I have witnessed too many violent acts to mention. It was acceptable then, as it is now and has been throughout our history, to be subjected to harm, violence, and abuse. Rather than confront and put an end to the systemic and pervasive racism and resulting violence, society made it acceptable by dehumanizing and labelling us, making it easy to violate and murder individuals with multiple barriers.

I was able to leave many times, only to return. I know without a doubt that what finally saved me, what continues to save me, are the values I was taught growing up. I was taught that love from my family, who loved me for who I was, could break through the walls. My parents believed in me so much. I thought this was wishful thinking at the time, but then I learned to believe in myself. I learned that with hard work, whether it be pursuing an education or overcoming your own personal demons, you can be successful if you persevere.

I was told by broken systems that I was a high school dropout, that I would never be anything, that I would always be incarcerated or in and out of foster homes. I was a file with a meaningless name. Thankfully, I had a family, and although I pushed them away, they never gave up and fought even harder than I was willing to fight in order for me to live. And I can honestly say now, twenty years later, I have lived and lived and lived life to the fullest. I walk with humility, compassion, and empathy for all those who I have lost and all those who still suffer. Because of an education and NVIT, I can now make a difference in many of their lives.

At NVIT I learned how to learn. Slowly, I started to change the script. I was no longer just a high school dropout—I began to believe in myself. The teachers were there to support me and encourage me. There were so many obstacles. I remember that my battery would die at every stop light on my way to school. I would jump out with jumper cables and a battery pack to jump start my vehicle. Other times I would get to school with no idea how I would get home because I didn't have bus fare. Then the Elders would give me a bus ticket. There are so many memories that have taught me how to work in a system with so many barriers and so many things that are broken, and I take those reminders with me every day I get up and go to work.

Education is a privilege. What are you going to do with it? How are you going to work in a system that we know is broken? How are you going to be the change? I ask you to be the one that works in the grey areas and uses your voice to bring about change. I encourage you to accept, respect, and support individuals regardless of where they are at in their lives. To recognize how colonialism, racism, substance use, struggles with mental wellness, and gendered patterns of violence intersect. Understanding these intersecting oppressions can inform our daily work with and alongside the individuals we serve.

Every day over the past fifteen years, I have seen the huge need for vulnerable individuals to receive and access services. Many organizations do not accept those who struggle with barriers such as mental wellness and substance use. Many of them live in unsafe conditions with no supports, a circumstance that increases their risk of being harmed. There are so many young girls being pushed out of care and into the world, with little or no preparation. This also increases their risk.

Living was one of the hardest things I had to do. For a time, I could not figure out how to live when I had lost so many women that I loved. My family held onto me. My mom even took me to work with her because I was scared to be alone. Despite their love, I could not fathom loving myself. Counsellors told me this was "survivor's guilt." I lived and they died, and for a very long time I did not understand why I was still here. In order to live, I chose to live for them—for the women I loved, the women I lost. I chose to raise my voice for so many of the women whose voices were never heard, and to dedicate my life to the work of ending systemic violence.

Return to School

MO KORCHINSKI

THE DOING TIME PROJECT is coming to an end soon, and I have no idea what I am going to do for work. When I got the job at UBC, one of the qualifications was you must have previous incarceration experience. Now that the research project is nearly completed, I need to figure things out. I have learned that I really enjoyed having job security and a steady income. At forty-five years old, I need to get my life together. So after my first experience in college taking a research method class, I realize that I really enjoy school.

> *Good Afternoon to our Elders, honoured guests, ladies and gentlemen, and the graduating class of 2013! On behalf of NVIT's Student Society, I would like to pay tribute to each and every one of you. As you stand on the brink of moving into life beyond NVIT, change will be inevitable! It is inevitable and indeed gratifying to see that our Graduating Class of 2013 have developed and become skilled in their field of education, ready to tackle life beyond school.*

I like that NVIT has small class sizes, and that it was founded on Aboriginal learning. Each course has an Aboriginal component. I book an appointment to check out my options for what degree I should pursue, even though I have no idea what field I want to get into. After going to NVIT, I learn that I need to write a CAAT test to see if I qualify for college. I book my test for two weeks from now, and then I go to a few websites where I can see what kinds of questions they will be asking me. I have to refresh my memory about math—there are many things I don't remember how to do, like subtract, fractions, etc.

> *I would also like to pay tribute to the wonderful Elders,*

teachers, deans, and staff at NVIT, *as well as the families who have guided, moulded, and shaped the ladies and gentlemen standing here today. The hours of studying, writing papers, and attending classes have seemed like an endless journey, but today the payoff is gratifying for you and your families.*

The day of the test is finally here. It can take up to four hours to write. Some parts I whip through, others I struggle with, but I get it done. And now, the waiting game. It takes a week to find out that I passed my CAAT test and I can register for classes. I decide to do my undergrad in general arts and keep my options open so I can figure out what I want to be when I grow up.

I'd like to share a quote with you all from a famous author by the name of T. S. Eliot: "Only those who risk going too far can possibly know how far one can go."

It's my first day of school and I have to get my books. *Holy smoke! School books are expensive!* I apply for the Women in2 Healing education bursary, which I hope I will get—it would help me get through spending all my savings on school fees.

I cannot believe how much I love school. I am taking four classes, and I can still work with Doing Time until the project ends. The only thing is that it takes me two-and-a-half hours each way to get to and from school, but I love reading so this time gives me a chance to catch up on books that I have wanted to read. I can also read the reading assignments on the bus.

So from today on, always remember what you have learned and have accomplished, but also remember to go out and enjoy your new careers.

The first two years go by fast and I get to graduate college and walk across the stage to get my degree. I joined the student society during my second year at NVIT. I was elected vice chair, and I got to be involved in planning student events. It brought back so many great memories of planning events inside ACCW.

The world is waiting for you, and it's time to conquer it!! On behalf of the Student Society, we wish you all the best. Congratulations class of 2013!

The chair of the student society can't make it to the graduation to give the graduation speech from the student society, so as vice-chair, it is up to me to write one and stand up in front of the class of 2013. I have now decided that I am going to get my Bachelor's degree in Social Work. I love helping others, and I love prison health, and I know I can make difference given my own experience with the justice system.

Two years later...

> *Good afternoon, Elders, honoured guests, ladies and gentlemen, and graduating class of 2015! On behalf of NVIT's student society, I would like to congratulate each and every one of you on your graduation. This day marks the end of another chapter in your journey and the start of a new beginning. As you stand ready to move on and explore life beyond NVIT, change will be inevitable!*

It's my last year of college—my fourth year!—and I still can't believe how fast it went by. It's time to plan graduation, and I am still on the student society. Since 2013, I have been elected chair. I enjoy being a part of the student society, but again I have to write a speech and talk in front of all the grads and their guests. I still find it hard talking in front of large groups of people, but it is also a great honour to represent my grad class of 2015.

> *It is clear and indeed gratifying to know that our graduating class is equipped to make a difference. You have developed skills and knowledge in your fields of expertise that can transform lives beyond your own. Remember to hold true to your values and beliefs, your work ethic, and, most importantly, your humanity.*

Today I have these three letters—RSW—behind my name. It feels so good to have earned my degree when I was told so many times that I couldn't become anything with a criminal record.

> *The gowns you wear here today are symbols of your achievement as well as reminders of how fortunate you have been. Not everyone gets a chance to attend university, and very few have access to the calibre of education that you have received here. Most crucially, NVIT has educated each of you to go out into the world and make it the place that you want to*

live in: a more just place, a more equitable place, a fairer place, a more humane place.

I know I have security for my own future, and I get to do what I love most: help women who are still stuck in the revolving door of addiction, crime, and prison.

As Gandhi once said, "Live as if you will die tomorrow, but learn as if you will live forever." So my friends, through your education, you are truly free. Free to choose your paths in life, armed with an education to take you wherever you desire to go. That is the greatest freedom of all. Congratulations class of 2015!

A Moment of Hope

PAM YOUNG

WHEN I FACE A CHALLENGE or am plagued with doubt, I remember how all the things that were missing in my life made their way full circle and came back. I now draw my strength from my family, my friends, my job, my education, and the way I tackled and beat my addiction. I now feel invincible; there's nothing I can't overcome. Being on the Downtown Eastside was a humbling experience, and that's what keeps my life simple.

The opportunities I've had to share my story and help people better understand that there is a life for them after addiction have been so amazing. Who would have ever thought that a hardcore junkie like I was could ever get off the streets and build this wonderful life filled with family, friends, and passion for helping others? I never thought I'd be able to rebuild my relationship with my sisters, my mother, and my children.

It's still a work in progress. It took years to destroy everything good in my life, and it will take years to rebuild. The reality is that nothing will ever be the same, but there's hope now, and that's more than I ever had during my addiction. I draw strength from my grandchildren. If I had not changed my life, I would never have five beautiful granddaughters, two of whom I now have custody of. I can't think of anything that would inspire me more than my granddaughters to become a better person.

Do you have any fears about being released?

Meatloaf Nightmares

when asked if they had fears
about being released

one woman responded:
meatloaf with family

almost half of the more than a hundred
respondents responded:
no, no fears because
everything is up to me

others responded:
yes about learning to live

&

life
goals
health
failure
change
anxiety
finances
addictions
old friends
being alone
re-offending

relationships
not staying sober
not being able to stop using
not being able to work on my priorities
not having any place to live
not having support
reintegration
shoplifting
temptation
working
relapse
triggers
support
public
safety
stress
using
trust

IX. Ways Forward

It is one year tomorrow since I held my father's hand as he passed. Our last conversation was about how proud he was of what I have become—that I've made a career informed by my experiences and struggles—and that he was completely at peace knowing I would continue to support my mom after he was gone. That kind of trust is something that we rebuilt over time, and for me, believing that he was again able to place that kind of faith in me means everything.

—Wendy Sproule

And then there are the miracles, perhaps not fairy tale endings, but significant miracles. To see a woman stay clean, seek an education, and become self-supporting; to see her give back, to live a life beyond her wildest dreams, and to overcome the disease of addiction; to see her be given the greatest gift: FREEDOM...

—Amanda Staller

After all these years and hundreds of inmates, I still believe that every person can live drug and crime free in the community so long as they are supported to the degree necessitated by their mental health or functional capabilities. This will not only save the taxpayer enormous amounts of money, but it will preserve the wellbeing of those dedicated to rehabilitation....

—Alison Granger-Brown

Doctor's Journey

RUTH ELWOOD MARTIN

*T*HIS WAS AN AMAZING DAY, *and I find myself pinching myself because maybe it didn't really happen. It was an exceptional series of events, each dependent on the other, like successive turns in a maze leading to the solution in the centre. I realize that this work is bigger than any one individual—it has a life of its own—and there is a liminal, ethereal aspect to it.*

I was feeling disconsolate about the future of the Unlocking the Gates peer health mentor program because we had exhausted all potential funding avenues and our funds were running out. I had given termination notice to Mo and the peer health mentors.

Vanessa, a journalism student, was taking the UBC *Prison Health 481C course to which I had invited Mo as a guest lecturer. Mo told the students about her incarceration and her mentor work with women who are leaving prison. Vanessa was starting a two-week internship with The Globe and Mail and asked to interview Mo about her work.*

Sarah phoned me at UBC. *She had read the newspaper article in* The Globe and Mail *about Mo and the Unlocking the Gates peer health mentor program. The newspaper article had deeply moved her, and she wanted to help.*

Today, Mo and I met Sarah for coffee. Sarah has read Arresting Hope *and bought five copies for friends. Sarah told us that she wants to give, anonymously and quietly, a donation to cover all the expenses of the peer health mentor program for the next twelve months.*

—Journal entry

When participatory health research started inside ACCW in 2005, I could not have imagined the journey that we were embarking on. I expected, at a cerebral level, that three aspects of PHR would emerge: first, the development of new health knowledge that is relevant to the community being studied; second, mutual learning and capacity building; and, third, social action and change to improve health (Green). But I could not have predicted or imagined the exact nature of these aspects.

Viv Ramsden, my mentor in this work, advised me in October 2005 to "Trust the process." I have been reminded of Viv's wise words many times since that day. If I try to be in control of PHR activities, I feel completely overwhelmed. Instead, I try to relish their serendipity and spontaneity. Another name for PHR is "transformative research" (Ramsden). As a result of this work, lasting changes in the interests of better health will occur, as Barbara Israel et al. describe so well. In addition, all members of the PHR team—academics, participants, collaborators—are transformed by the PHR process:

> Empowerment is promoted by people taking an active, deciding role in all aspects of the research process. In addition to learning and empowerment on the part of those participating in the research, transformations can take place in terms of concrete health indicators or social and political factors impinging on the health of those whose life or work is the subject of the study. These transformations are the result of the actions undertaken during or directly consequent to the research. A quality criterion for PHR is supporting transformation processes which go beyond the span of the research project so as to contribute to lasting change in the interest of better health. (ICPHR 11)

Thus, PHR follows the explicit goal of creating positive social change as a result of the research process for those persons whose lives are the focus of the research. One surprising aspect for me is the continuous and living nature of PHR social action changes—it is as if concentric circles of change are multiplying and moving outwards, like when you throw a pebble into a pond.

In previous chapters, we described some of the stories that resulted from the prison PHR work. In this chapter, we allude to future action, possibilities, and ways forward, because transformative social action work will continue, through the voices of women with incarceration experience and their children, and through students, readers, and listeners who are impacted by their stories.

REFERENCES

Green, Lawrence W. with University of British Columbia, Institute of Health Promotion Research; Royal Society of Canada; BC Consortium for Health Promotion Research. "Study of Participatory Research in Health Promotion: Review and Recommendations for the Development of Participatory Research in Health Promotion in Canada." Ottawa: Royal Society of Canada, 1995.

International Collaboration for Participatory Health Research (ICPHR). "What is Participatory Health Research?" Berlin: International Collaboration for Participatory Health Research, May 2013.

Israel, Barbara A., Chris M. Coombe, Rebecca R. Cheezum, Amy J. Schulz, Robert J. McGranagh, Richard Lichtenstein, Angela G. Reyes, Jaye Clement, and Akosua Burris] "Community-Based Participatory Research: A Capacity-Building Approach for Policy Advocacy Aimed at Eliminating Health Disparities." *American Journal of Public Health* 100.11 (2010): 2094-2102.

Ramsden, Vivian R. and Integrated Primary Health Services Model Research Team. "Learning with the Community: Evolution to Transformative Action Research." *Canadian Family Physician* 49.2 (Feb 2003): 195-197.

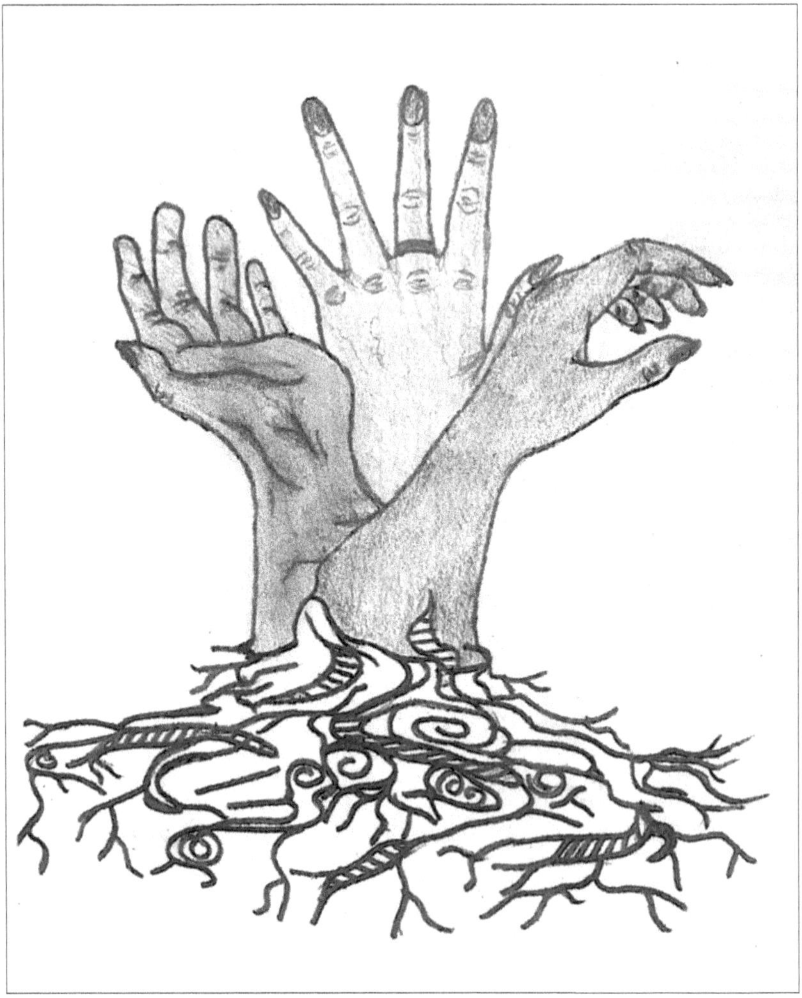

Staying Hopeful

PAM YOUNG

I'VE LEARNED A FEW THINGS about making your way back to the community after you've been incarcerated. I don't always divulge my history. It's up to me who I want to tell. I don't have to tell everyone. Once I build a rapport with someone, then I'll tell them. But since working with the Unlocking the Gates project, I've done quite a bit of speaking to different groups of college and university students and classes. And I've been involved in conferences where my experience in and out of prison was valued.

It really feels great to know that there are people who value your knowledge and experiences in the correctional system and in active addiction. So, I've become more open about my history.

But I'm also aware there are A LOT of people who will judge you, and that's okay because these people don't know you. If they took the time to get to know me, they would find out I'm a good person. I now look at life like my worst day now is better than my best day in my addiction. There's nothing that can happen in my life that would be worse than what I've been through already. I always remain hopeful that everything happens for a reason. So, I stay positive and just keep moving forward.

What Changed?

COLBY

WHEN PEOPLE ASK ME "WHAT CHANGED?" my honest reply is, "everything!" I have been abstinent from drugs for two-and-a-half years, and I'm leading a productive life as a part of the community. Three of the most important things that changed were my perceptions about myself and those around me, and my connection to community.

I'm grateful that when my inner shift—or as I like to think of it, my spiritual awakening—occurred, someone noticed, gave me the benefit of the doubt, and reached out to help. That's when I was first introduced to Mo, when we first met face to face. She had been where I was, and she had taken the necessary steps to change her life around. Now she was sitting across the glass divider that separated us in the visiting room at ACCW, and she was telling me her story. This gave me hope and inspiration that I too could beat this life and be a successful person. I connected with her instantly and started to set goals to achieve some sort of purpose. I began working on my high school diploma while inside the jail, and by the time I was released I had completed two courses with two left. With a new perspective on life, I was willing to ask for help but also now able to accept the help available to me.

The day of my release, I was excited to move on to the next chapter, and as I walked out those heavy steel doors for the last time, I was greeted by three familiar faces. These women, including Mo, were all a huge part of my support system. I had support from these women from the minute I was released into the outside world.

When we arrived at the house where I would reside for the next six months, with a forty-day trip to treatment in between, I was so grateful and willing to do whatever it took to build a strong foundation for a healthy future. I fought hard through my fears and I ventured outside of my comfort zones. My natural instincts have always been to do things alone. But I knew that if I wanted any chance of success, I had to trust and allow others into my life. I learned how to feel my feelings and recognize what those feelings were. I had been so numbed for so long that I had no idea how to recognize what I was feeling, put a name to my feelings, and work through them. I had to reach out to others who understood what I was going through. I struggled deeply with reaching out, but I found the more I did it, the easier it got. The more I felt a sense of belonging, the happier I became, and the loneliness I had felt for so long started to melt away. The more I put myself out there, the more the gifts and opportunities just kept rolling in.

The biggest gift of all was that my daughter had her mom back in her life, and we were able to begin building a relationship. I also began mending my relationships with my family and friends. I have always had amazing love and support from my family, but though all the years of self-destruction, they had to pull away from me. My dad used to say, "I love you but I don't like you." This was hard to hear, but I knew it was true. I didn't like myself either. Today I can be accountable and available for them. I attend family dinners and birthdays, and I phone often just to see how they're doing. Having these relationships back gives me an indescribable feeling of warmth and fulfillment that I hope I never have to lose. I am once again a mother, daughter, granddaughter, and friend.

Once I completed treatment and was ready for the next step, an amazing woman who I had also met in recovery came to me with a job opportunity in a commercial kitchen where she worked. Having worked in the kitchen at ACCW cooking for all the women, I already had experience in this type of setting and caught on very quickly. While continuing with my high school education and working part time, I was beginning to feel a strong sense of my place in the community.

One day, I was getting my nails done in a salon and the nail technician was making small talk as they often do. She was simply asking what I do, where I work, and so forth, and for the first time in a long time, I didn't have to make up some story. These types of normal day-to-day social interactions had always caused me great discomfort because the shame and guilt of what my life had become was so unbearable that it caused me to lie on many occasions. On this day, however, and every day since, I can be proud of myself and what I do. Now I'm able to face these situations with ease. This is a freedom that not everyone can recognize with such gratitude.

I spent a year living in the lower mainland of British Columbia before making a move over to Vancouver Island. I am currently working part time at a restaurant and will be starting some exploratory programs at

Vancouver Island University in the fall. I haven't yet sorted out exactly what I want to do, and I'm okay with that. I don't know how I'll feel tomorrow, but today I'm feeling content with how my life is unfolding. I struggle day to day with the unknown, and I can still get into a state of hopelessness once in a while, but today I have the skills and tools to get me through those tough moments. Being able to give hope to those still struggling by sharing my stories is what I believe this world is all about. Selfless acts of kindness.

Meaningful Work

PAM YOUNG

MEANINGFUL WORK IS SO IMPORTANT to women getting out. If you can do something you love or like to do, you'll be a much happier and more productive person. If you're scrubbing toilets or working construction and you hate every moment, you probably don't go to work excited about the day. And you probably don't go home at night feeling fulfilled. My suggestion to women recently released from incarceration is to go to school and build a new future. This can be challenging for these marginalized women because they often have low self-esteem. Some may have a poor credit rating, and no one to give them a student loan. It's not easy for women getting out to get decent jobs. Most places don't want to hire someone with a criminal record. But once women find something they feel passionate about it, everything changes. They will feel excited about whatever they are pursuing. They will want to know everything about it, and they will begin to soak up information like a sponge. And then they begin evolving into a confident person who has hopes and dreams.

My work with women in prison gives me so much purpose. I love going to work and doing something I love. I really enjoy talking to the women. We get calls from women who just want to chat or who need you to call family or friends to let them know they're in jail. And I also do intakes with women to get a better idea of what resources they will need to connect with the day they get released. I've been told numerous times what a huge relief it is to know that someone will be there to walk with them for the first few days after their release. It gives women hope that they can find their way back to the community. And it gives them hope that they can stay clean and sober, since the majority of the women have issues with addiction. I find it so rewarding that I can be a part of such an amazing program and offer my life experience to women in prison.

Advice

PAM YOUNG

IF I COULD TELL THE WORLD the one thing women getting out need to make their way back to the community successfully, it is support. This can take many forms, from taking time to help women connect with resources in the community to just being there to offer kind words. These women need someone to believe in them until they can believe in themselves.

From my personal experiences, I can testify about how crucial it is to have support people in place when someone leaves prison, especially if they have issues with addiction. How are people expected to be successful at making their way back to the community when the community doesn't welcome them back with dignity? These women don't want to be drug addicts, and with the right support, they can overcome their addictions. They need ongoing encouragement.

For me, personally, one of the women who supported me was Pat, a drug coordinator in the drug court. Some days I would go to Pat's office and tell her, "I don't think I can do this. I'll never be normal."

And she would say, "Normal is a setting on your washing machine. Just keep coming here and going to group even on the days you don't want to and you'll begin to see changes."

And she was right! I'd show up even on the days I just wanted to give up and go get high, and over time those urges to get high started to go away.

I started thinking about graduating from drug court and moving out of the recovery house into my own place. Finally I was dreaming about my future. It didn't happen right away. I kept putting in my hours and moving forward, and my husband started working, and we saved up money to buy a car. And even though some people said couples shouldn't be in the same recovery house, it really seemed to work for us. And all the kind words and moral support kept me from using.

After almost two decades of being in active addiction, I had never had someone believe in me.

If communities actively welcomed and supported women coming from prison, there would be more success. The crime rate would be cut. The money it costs to incarcerate women would be saved. Women would become valuable members of society. Without the community's support, these women are stuck in a relentless cycle of recidivism.

No Threat to Others

ALISON GRANGER-BROWN

I DO NOT HOPE FOR THE PEOPLE HELD PRISONER. I know they all have the possibility for growth, change, and renewal of their life's dreams and aspirations. I do however struggle to hope for the social systems that maintain the notion that punishment and imprisonment is the only answer to the mainly self-destructive behaviours of people who are struggling, both with addiction and with overcoming early life trauma.

Certainly, there is argument for the security of the community in some exceptional cases, but most people I have met over the last eighteen years are no threat to others. The biggest threat to their healing is incarceration.

You Against Them

COLBY

WHEN YOU COME FROM A WORLD where you are a social reject, you can never do anything right, and when you do, it is not significant enough for anyone to notice. In other words, the bad far outweighs the good.

When you make an honest attempt to live by society's rules and regulations, you quickly fall short in the eyes of "the men" before having a chance to fully stand up. Your reality and their reality is so very different and yet so very much the same. We are all on a quest for happiness. The harder you push, the harder they pull, and when you fall, they are not there to catch you.

Who can you trust when no one, even those you are told you can count on, really understands? You feel forced to tiptoe around because there's a personal war going on in your head. For twenty-four hours a day, seven days a week, you're in a state of hyper-awareness, awaiting ambush the moment you drop your guard. Then one day, the evil is lifted, and the light shines through, and you're hit with the reality that it's not them, it's you.

The war is over; in fact, it never began. Your significance diminishes as you realize it's not all about you. All I asked for was an ending; I begged for it to be over. Instead I was blessed with a new beginning that ironically started with "happily ever after."

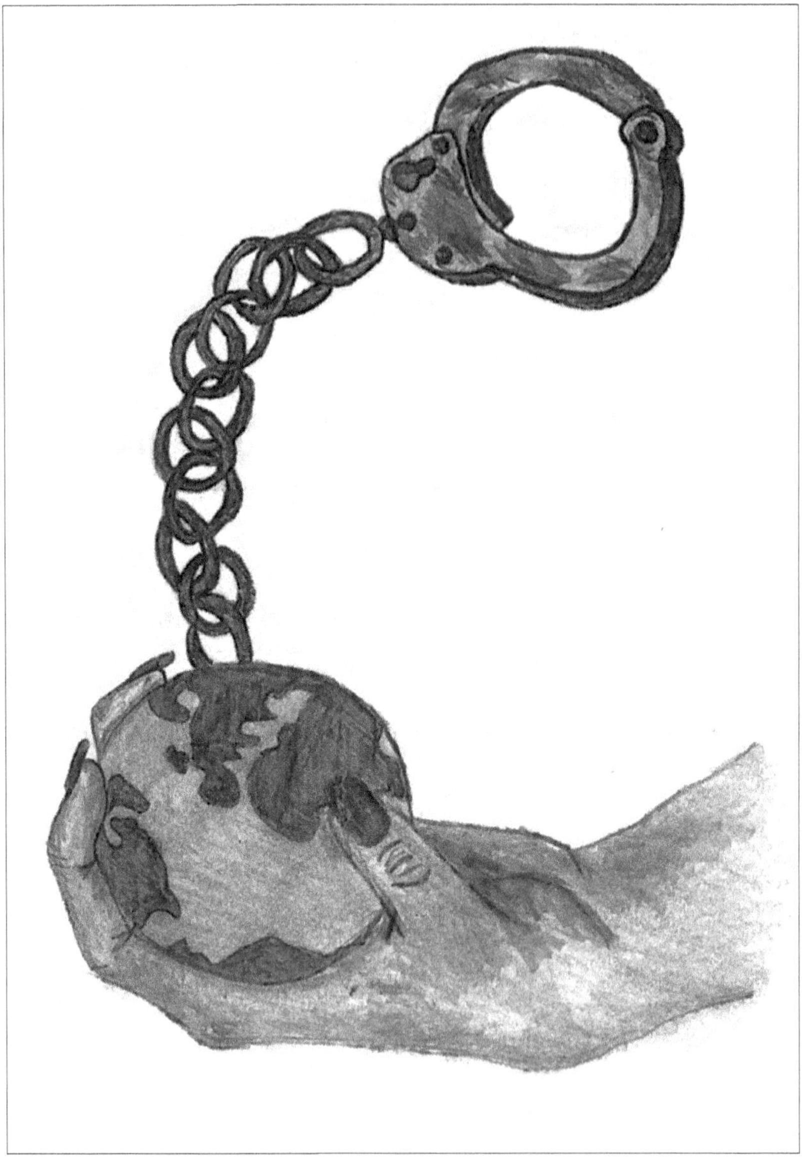

Done Button

MO KORCHINSKI

I get asked a lot what was it that helped me to stop using drugs.
Why am I one of the few
        who has left my old life behind
and become a success in my life?
I now have an education, a job I love, family, and great friends,
all because something happened and I was done.

Did someone push a button and
                      POUFF!

                                      I was done?

I'm not sure there is one answer except I was done.
Like a button was pushed and I was done.

If I could figure it out and put it all together
and make a magic "done button"
Wow! How many people could be saved from addiction!!

I'm not sure if it was age, or if I was just sick of living a life of chaos.
all I know is that I was done.
I just wish others could see how great life can be clean and sober.
I never worry about going to jail or running out of drugs or not having
a home to go to.

Life is amazing....

Amber's Story
"I Never Would Have Believed You"

AMBER CHRISTIE

OUR RESEARCH CONTINUED, and we all started to become the people we never thought we would be....

We flew all over the world to present at conferences about research we were passionate about.

And we also went on retreats to Galiano, sometimes to refinish chairs to sell and put into our bursary fund to help women who are released with funding for school. And in September—when my mom, Ryan, and our son Clayton went over for one of our retreats—Ryan and I went to the beach, and he proposed to me. He is now my husband.

A friend, Lora Kwandibens, and I learned that a big percentage of Aboriginal women were not accessing Western health care and were ending up with cancer and HIV and all sorts of health problems. So, we decided to apply for a grant so we could do our research and help our community. We met in Mission, and we supported each other, and we conducted our research. Unfortunately, Lora passed away from cancer herself. She will always live on in Women in2 Healing.

When the Doing Time results were published, *Macleans* magazine wrote about our research.[1] Then, a journalist called Perrin wrote a story about me and my bad teeth, about how the expense of dental care held me back from being healthy.[2] A dentist read my story and volunteered to fix my teeth for free. He did the same for some other women who have done time.

I was asked to go to Ottawa to testify before the Standing Committee for Public Safety and National Security about what needs to be changed in our prison system. They flew me, Ruth Elwood Martin, and Brenda Tole, the previous warden of ACCW. I got to see all of the Parliament with these two ladies. If you had told me that five years after being released I was going to be testifying with the warden of ACCW and the doctor, I would never have believed you!

But today none of us are the women who left that prison; today we are productive members of society. I actually have gone into ACCW as a guest for information fairs, and it still feels strange to walk back out. I've stayed out of prison for the last ten years. I still go to NA. I had a small slip just over a year ago. But, in 2010, I gave birth to a healthy baby girl.

My children and my husband keep me going every day, and I will always be grateful to Dr. Ruth Elwood Martin for all she has taught me and for all of the women's support. In April 2015, my first daughter Alysha found me. I had no idea where she was, but I guess she ended up back in foster care. We are working on bringing her home. We have a close and beautiful relationship and I honestly can't put into words the love and healing I have done. I have three beautiful children and an amazing husband. He loved me when I couldn't love myself. Today, with my family and Women in2 Healing and NA, I am a whole person again.

NOTES

[1] See *Macleans,* Appendix, Media Reports and Interviews.
[2] See *StarMetro Vancouver*, Appendix, Media Reports and Interviews.

Soar

MAURA GOWANS

death found you
I don't know how or why
I was the one living on the edge
ready to die

together forever
was our motto
our love song

if I could see your smile
touch your face
ensure every memory of you
they said was erased
I would give my soul so they could see

your Dance through my feet,
hear your laughter through my voice
know all your dreams through my eyes

you are the wind that gently pushes me to continue
the voice that speaks through me when I feel silent
the love when my heart feels so broken
the light within me that fills the darkness

if death gave me life so I could live
I promise you I will live for you
so your voice lives forever in the wind
that pushes me gently forward
the wind within my children
that allows them to soar

Final Reflections

But today none of us are the women who left that prison; today we are productive members of society.
—Amber Christie

All I asked for was an ending; I begged for it to be over. Instead I was blessed with a new beginning that ironically started with "happily ever after."
—Colby

When I Was a Little Girl

MO KORCHINSKI

When I was a little girl, I lived a life of trauma.
I stood on the battlefields of parental damnation,
slowly losing my innocence never to be found again.
I faded into seclusion, tried to remain hidden from the world.
> *No words*
> *No cries*

Unprotected, I began to build an arsenal of destructive mechanisms
that shielded me from the pain of neglect, abuse, and mistreatment.
I developed an education of lies, deceit, silence, and manipulation.
Those who should have cherished my heart and soul dismissed me.
I became a casualty of addiction, warped love, and dashed dreams.
> *No peace*
> *No relief*

I am tired of searching for peace. I have no control over my life,
going in and out of jail. What has my life become? No one tries
to find me. No one cares that I'm lost. There has to be more
to my life. This cannot be what God has planned for me.
> *Wishing I could change*
> *Wishing I could make it better*

No one comes. Life and time unfold. I become a soldier.
I arm myself with kindness, empathy, and love.
I now stand tall, proud of the woman I have become,
yet humble with the knowledge of my past. I offer
new hope for future women who have faced
a traumatic childhood, by lending an open mind
and listening with an open heart.
> *Knowing I can change*
> *Knowing I can make it better*

No longer am I a casualty of a traumatic history. I am a mother, sister, aunt, and grandma. I survived, and I am stronger today because of my past. Don't let the darkness from your past block the light of joy in your present. What happened is done. Stop giving time to what no longer exists.

There is always so much joy to be found.

Transformation and Action

RUTH ELWOOD MARTIN

I WAS RECENTLY INVITED to give a keynote presentation on community-based participatory health research at a conference in which "patient engagement in research" was the overall theme. I suggested that the conference organizers also invite a woman with incarceration experience to co-present with me, in keeping with the conference's focus on patient engagement. Hence, Mo Korchinski and I travelled together to the Cochrane Colloquium that took place in Edinburgh in 2018. We split the keynote presentation, each of us telling our story of *Arresting Hope*. People in the audience responded to Mo's presentation with a standing ovation, some with tears streaming down their faces.

I have seen this happen repeatedly. The stories of Mo, Amanda, Amber, Cat, Chas, Christine, Colby, Kelly, Lora, Marnie, Maura, Odessa, Pam, Wendy—whether in a classroom or conference auditorium, church or community hall; in a documentary film, on TV, or on the radio; in a newspaper article or book—connect deeply with audiences. People are moved. I am moved. Moved to tears, to self-reflect, to write advocacy letters, to visit people in prison, to switch careers in order to focus on prison health, and much more. Transformation and action.

When we published *Arresting Hope*, I was unsure if people would read a book like this, given the current era of electronic information and social media, and I questioned what impact a book would have. What I did not appreciate then, and what I now understand, is that *Arresting Hope* has developed a vibrant life of its own. Women portrayed in the pages of *Arresting Hope* continue to share their lives, and their hopes, dreams, fears, and passions with readers. Women are speaking, and readers respond. Transformation and action. Here are a few things that have happened since the publication of *Arresting Hope*:

- A UBC colleague applied for a community grant to buy copies

of *Arresting Hope* for all members of her book group; the group then dialogued with Mo and I about ways to advocate for women who are leaving prison.
- Mo gave *Arresting Hope* to her city mayor, who read it and suggested that every member of city council should buy and read it.
- We mailed copies of *Arresting Hope* to every federal government minister on Parliament Hill with responsibility for the wellbeing of incarcerated women; a federal policy advisor told me that *Arresting Hope* is influencing her policy decisions.
- An executive leader of a provincial health authority who will assume the responsibility for healthcare delivery in provincial correctional centres explained that he was unable to finish reading his copy *Arresting Hope*, because his teenage daughters were reading it.
- A church leader explained that the message of *Arresting Hope* has catalyzed four church communities to learn about prison social justice. Two of the churches in the prairies have set up a car-pool system for the provincial women's prison, which is located out of town where bus services had recently been eliminated.
- A healthcare administrator in a large Brazilian prison kept *Arresting Hope* under his pillow at night and dipped into it for encouragement and inspiration; he is now working with a local publisher to translate *Arresting Hope* into Portuguese.
- And, most recently, a grandson introduced *Arresting Hope* to his grandfather, an octogenarian epidemiologist, my uncle living in Wales, who was deeply moved and wrote a letter to the government correctional ministry calling for more humane conditions for women in UK prisons.

Arresting Hope and its companion, *Releasing Hope*, are offerings by women whose lives have been deeply impacted by choices: the choices that have been imposed upon them; the choices made by institutions, policy makers, and community members in shaping the correctional system; and the choices of individuals, many of whom are willing to listen, to reach out, to witness, and to be allies in the long journey that is ours to share. In *Releasing Hope*, our hope is that women's voices and stories will touch you in a deeply transformative place, that they will inspire you to make choices, and that they will ultimately inspire you to action.

Here, In This Moment

LYNN FELS

AT THE EDGE OF THE PACIFIC OCEAN, Mo and I call back and forth.
"The water's cold!"
"Go for it!"
"Arghhh!"
We are spending a weekend at Galiano Island, at the farm, where we are participating in a writing workshop.
"Let's go swimming!"
"What? Now? It's dark outside!"
Mo invites me to join her, promising a surprise, and gratefully, I follow. I have been struggling to find a toehold in this group of women whose life experiences trouble my heart. This I can do, swim in the ocean.
Slipping, splashing, sliding, we enter the water, froth of sea at our ankles. Knee-deep, I hesitate and look back at Mo, who waves me forward. "Go on! Do it!" I enter the black sky that is the ocean, speckled with stars. The rush of cold water chills my skin. My heart stutters in syncopated beats. I move my arms in a cautious breast-stroke, and, to my amazement, phosphorescent creatures create swirls of light. I am painting light in water! A galaxy of light in an underwater sky. In this moment, we are no longer a university researcher and former inmate, but two women sharing a midnight swim; here and now, Mo gifts me with an ocean dancing light in our presence.
How shall I receive her offering with grace?

Here and now we meet, and something happens. (Fels 51)

"Do you want a panic button?" asks the guard as I sign my name into the visitors' book. I look up, wide-eyed.
"What's that?"

"You wear it on your shirt. If you get into trouble, you just push it, and a guard will come running." I pause. If I'm wearing one, I'm saying I don't trust the women; how will they trust me?

"No, thanks." Gulp. *How dangerous are they?*

The journey of *Arresting Hope*—through the years from the first time I walked through the prison gates to the editing of our second book, *Releasing Hope*—called me to attention, tugged on my sleeve, revealing my fears of those who dwell outside my circle of familiarity, my reluctance to get involved, to be committed, to become responsible. What happens after I walk through those gates? Who will receive me? I am uncomfortable in places of pain, grief, and loss. Women locked up. Murderers? Drug addicts? Mothers? Sisters? Daughters? Women who walk through darkness, through trauma, through sickness, through despair, through illness, through violence. *What do I know of their pain? What am I doing here? I am so privileged. And what happens when they are released? How will I welcome them?*

We are gathered around a table, sharing angel words we have chosen from a box. Surrender. Hope. Joy. Transformation. Listen. Each word is received and spoken to with careful reflection, stories revealed between the silences, the pauses, the hesitations, the smiles, and the nods of recognition. We share experiences that these words evoke. We recognize resonant moments in between the strangeness of our lives.

There is a crack in everything / that's how the light gets in.
—Leonard Cohen, "Anthem" (373)

Sometimes, someone unexpected finds you and calls you into action.

Inside these walls are women whose childhoods were stolen. Young girls who dropped out of school by the age of fourteen. Children who suffered child abuse, family abuse, relationship abuse, sexual abuse; who self-medicated with drugs, even though they were promised love, who were required to turn corners past themselves into a darkness that I cannot imagine. Women who turned a trick, pocketed a lipstick, lost a child, were lost themselves. *Arresting Hope* and *Releasing Hope* share their stories, awakens us to who they truly are. Women. With stories.

Outside these walls, the barriers and acts of injustice persist. Drugs laced with fentanyl. Women's lives lost. Broken marriages, broken children, fragments glued together, in desperate search of repair, of healing; all this is written in between the lines of those whose stories speak of release, of new beginnings.

Where have I been in the midst of all this suffering unfolding through time? As an educator? As a fellow citizen? What is my responsibility now?

What the women want is to give back.

They offer stories, moments, that arrest me, that break my heart.

I recognize that I do not have their courage. Nor persistence. Nor resilience. Nor their gift of generosity.

Philosopher Hannah Arendt challenges educators to engage children in the world's renewal:

> And education, too, is where we decide whether we love our children enough not to expel them from our world and leave them to their own devices, nor to strike from their hands their chance of undertaking something new, something unforeseen by us, but to prepare them in advance for the task of renewing a common world. (196)

Arresting Hope shares the journey of the reimagining of a prison for women; *Releasing Hope* challenges us to question and reimagine our actions of hospitality and inclusion. We are invited to engage in our communities' re-visioning, to welcome those who arrive in our midst as experts of their experience, as witnesses, as activists. What had begun as a research health initiative has slipped over the edge into a pedagogical life-offering project, in which women are re-imagining the renewal of the world.

Surfacing, gasping for breath, I shout, "This is amazing! Thank you, Mo!" And she laughs, a husky laugh that drifts on the night wind....

What can I offer in return to Mo, to the women who have touched my life, who share their pain, their sorrow, their hopes, in their writing, trusting me with their words, *cracks in the wall,* welcoming me into the magic of painting light in the watery depths of a midnight ocean?

Originally published in Ruth Elwood Martin, Mo Korchinski, Lynn Fels, and Carl Leggo. "Arresting Hope: Women Taking Action in Prison Health Inside Out." Cogent Arts & Humanities *4.1 (2017): 1-15. Web.*

REFERENCES

Arendt, Hannah. *Between Past and Future: Six Exercises of Political Thought.* New York: Viking, 1961.

Cohen, Leonard. "Anthem." *Stranger Music: Collected Poems and Songs.* Toronto, ON: McClelland & Steward, 1993.

Fels, Lynn. *In the Wind Clothes Dance on a Line*. Doctoral dissertation. University of British Columbia, British Columbia, 1999.

We Need to Rise Above

MO KORCHINSKI

COLLABORATING ON WRITING *Arresting Hope* and *Releasing Hope* taught me so many things about myself and others. In many ways, I closed myself off to life and to others as a form of self-defence. The pain of my childhood taught me to hide myself in different ways: don't let others in, use walls to keep others at a distance, hurt others before they hurt you, and hide the pain to show that no one can hurt you. Opening myself up about my life and writing it all down for the world to read was very intimidating but at the same time very healing.

As I wrote my life out on paper, I slowly learned that I was no longer that little girl who was beaten down in all aspects of life—from parents who should have loved me unconditionally but didn't to losing my innocence in so many different forms of abuse. As I wrote poems, stories, and memories, I found the inner strength that kept me from never giving up on life. Having a UBC prof (Carl Leggo) edit my writing was nerve-wracking at first, but I soon learned that he was a caring, non-judgmental, compassionate person. I felt safe to dig deeper into the dark shadows of my childhood.

Today, I give a voice to the women who still don't know that they have one. This is the driving force behind my determination to continue in my work with prison health. In some ways, all our stories have the same themes of darkness and shame. These led us to seek ways to escape the dark shadows of our pasts, to leave behind the street drugs we used to numb the never-ending pain that rips the soul from the inside out. I found inner peace through writing my story, and I no longer feel the guilt and shame of my past. I know that writing my story will help give other women who are still stuck in the revolving door of hell hope that they too can fight their way back and learn to find themselves. *Releasing Hope* gives other women hope that they don't have to stay stuck, that they can make it out of the street trenches of addiction.

My driving force is to give truth to people who others see on the streets as homeless addicts. My goal is to get them to see others as human beings—someone's grandmother, mother, daughter, aunt, or sister—and to humanize the sad reality of childhood trauma that leads most to escape into addiction. All humans want to be loved and accepted, not judged and beaten down. We beat ourselves up way more than anyone else in society can. We need to rise above the stigma of addiction and love others who are lost souls looking for a way to escape life.

A Lingering Resonant Note

CARL LEGGO

IN *WRITING BEYOND RACE: LIVING THEORY AND PRACTICE*, bell hooks calls for "the development of critical thinking and critical consciousness" (18) as essential to creating "a new foundation based on a revolution of love" (12). She readily acknowledges that, "diversity is the reality of all our lives. Diversity is the very essence of our planetary survival. Organically, human survival as a species relies on the interdependence of all life" (26). She also notes that, "no contemporary movement for social justice has changed the nature of how we live other than the feminist movement" (35). It is not surprising that *Releasing Hope: Women's Stories of Transition from Prison to Community* is primarily the work of women. It is a book about women by women who are teaching one another and learning from one another. *Releasing Hope* sings with women's voices, and to hear women's voices is to hear a song rooted in love, a song devoted to personal and social transformation, a song full of hope.

As co-editors, colleagues, writers, and companions, we are committed to living with hope. We live with the anticipation that we can learn to live well together in the world. In *Becoming Human*, Jean Vanier notes that, "we human beings are all fundamentally the same. We all belong to a common, broken humanity. We all have wounded, vulnerable hearts. Each one of us needs to feel appreciated and understood; we all need help" (37). Each of us needs "an accompanier ... someone who can stand beside us on the road to freedom, someone who loves us and understands our life" (128). As Vanier explains, "the word 'accompaniment,' like the word 'companion,' comes from the Latin words *cum pane*, which mean 'with bread.' It implies sharing together, eating together, nourishing each other, walking together" (129). Vanier concludes: "We do not have to be saviours of the world! We are simply human beings, enfolded in weakness and in hope, called together to change our world one heart at a time" (163).

Like Vanier, we understand that "belief in the inner beauty of each and every human being is ... at the heart of being human" (23). And we also know, as Vanier does, that patience is essential: "It takes time to grow to a maturity of the heart" (58). And in a world that daily roars with reports of war, hatred, fear, and violence, we recall Paulo Freire's words in *Pedagogy of the Heart*: "human beings could not be without the impulse of hope" (44). Therefore, like Herbert Kohl, we are hope-mongerers who echo Freire's words: "As I speak with such hope about the possibility of changing the world, I do not intend to sound like a lyrical, naïve educator" (58). We live always with (and in) hope, tenaciously and faithfully living out the conviction that we can learn to live together well in the world. In her memoir *Gently to Nagasaki*, Joy Kogawa writes, "For my part, I hold with a fierce and painful joy my trust in a Love that is more real than we are" (42). As a child, Kogawa was interned as a Japanese Canadian. In her life, she has experienced numerous traumas. She writes, "My story is from the belly of the dark. I am forbidden to tell it and commanded to tell it. I am told that to speak is to slay and not to speak is to slay" (47). She decides that she must tell the stories. She decides that trust is the right action. She chooses to begin with trust. She tells her hard stories. Kogawa sees "the world as an open book embedded with stories. We hear them if we have ears to hear" (149). *Releasing Hope* is an offering of hard stories from the heart, full of love and hope, rooted in the understanding that there will be both disappointment and astonishment.

During the many cycles of planning, writing, and editing *Releasing Hope*, we were frequently reminded of the radical and transformative power of creativity. *Releasing Hope* is a resounding testimony to creative collaboration and activist change. Like Wendell Berry reminds us, "to be creative is only to have health: to keep oneself fully alive in the Creation, to keep the Creation fully alive in oneself, to see the Creation anew, to welcome one's part in it anew" (8). *Releasing Hope* is especially the story of remarkable women who imagined creative possibilities for transforming how we understand experiences of incarceration and life after incarceration, and how we attend to issues of humanity, health, hardships, and hope. Frederick Buechner writes that, "the world is full of darkness, but ... at the heart of darkness ... there is joy unimaginable" (240). *Releasing Hope* is a testament to joy, love, and hope. *Releasing Hope* is also a testament to the power of story-making. In her moving memoir, *This Is Happy*, about growing up in a dysfunctional family and coping with depression, Camilla Gibb claims that, "stories are how we make sense of our lives" (xi). *Releasing Hope* offers a compelling witness to the power of stories for helping us make sense of our lives.

In *Thirst*, the poet Mary Oliver writes about her experience of living with grief after the death of her partner, Molly Malone Cook. In the first line of the first poem titled "Messenger," Oliver professes, "My work is loving the world" (1). We are all called to love the world. In *Book of Longing*, Leonard Cohen sings about desire in an old man's song of praise and lament. He advises us to "press your lips/to the light of my heart" (120). To know the light of another's heart, or to know the light of one's own heart, or to know the heart's light, or to know the light heart, we need to learn how to hear the heart's rhythms. To engage with the heart of light, we need to be engaged with an ongoing practice of story-making. As we share with one another our stories, all our stories, we grow in wisdom and intimacy and joy. We can tell our true stories and we can tell them truthfully, and in turn we can testify to the joyful hope that holds us fast.

In *Storycatcher: Making Sense of Our Lives through the Power and Practice of Story*, Christina Baldwin reminds us that, "it takes courage to tell our stories" (18). We need to hear one another's stories. We need to embrace the healing efficacy of sharing stories. Baldwin understands that "when we reveal details that we think are excruciatingly personal, we discover that the personal is universal" (85). We are all human beings together. To tell a story is to place the story in the space between us, so that we might look at the story and ask each other, "now what…? How shall we now engage?"

Releasing Hope offers an invitation to open our hearts, to imagine how we are all inextricably connected, to acknowledge that we all need one another. In *Becoming Human*, Jean Vanier offers five principles that guide his work, and these principles are at the heart of *Releasing Hope:*

"First: all humans are sacred, whatever their culture, race, or religion, whatever their capacities or incapacities, and whatever their weaknesses or strengths may be" (14). Until we acknowledge the sacredness of all humans, we will fall into demeaning and destructive binary oppositions such as: us/them; good/bad; successful/unsuccessful; winners/losers. *Releasing Hope* reminds us that we all have remarkable gifts for supporting one another, for infusing one another with hope and courage and conviction.

"Second: our world and our individual lives are in the process of evolving" (14). We are all in process. Poets know a poem is always in unfolding. A poem, like a story, is never completed; a poem, like a story, is always available for revisiting. *Releasing Hope* recognizes how our being in process also means that we are frequently looking backward and forward, even while learning how to forgive and forget, always filled with a desire for hope.

"Third: maturity comes through working with others, through dialogue, and through a sense of belonging and a searching together" (14). No one will grow wise and mature on their own. We need collaboration, conversation, and communion in order to grow as individuals in community with others. We can never be whole without understanding how the unique sense of identity expressed in the pronoun "I" is always in relationship with the often mysterious identity of the other, expressed in the pronoun "you."

"Fourth: human beings need to be encouraged to make choices and to become responsible for their own lives and for the lives of others" (15). Since we are all becoming, we are all constantly making decisions, taking action, within contexts and environments and relationships that shape us. Some of those decisions will be wiser than others. We need to learn how to respond with compassion and care to the emerging stories of our lives as well as the emerging stories of others. We must all be engaged in the responsibility of responding.

"Fifth: in order to make such choices, we need to reflect and to seek truth and meaning" (15). *Releasing Hope* is a witness to the meaning-making efficacy of story-making. In writing about the lived and living experiences of human beings, we understand how we are all seeking to "become human," (Vanier) to discern the possibilities for living well on the earth. We all live with broken and fearful hearts. We need "to grow to a maturity of the heart" (Vanier 58). Amber Dawn recommends that one way to nurture the heart is to embrace "that buoyancy that comes when" you observe your life "as art" (65).

As an editorial team, Ruth, Mo, Lynn, and I gathered around Ruth's dining room table on many occasions. Like the writing staff of a television series, we generated ideas that called back and forth to one another, ideas that bounced wildly in our imaginations, ideas that fired our hearts with innovative possibilities. We were always committed to honouring the process. In composing *Arresting Hope*, we realized that we wanted to narrate the story of Alouette Correctional Centre for Women so others could understand the remarkable sequence of events that had unfolded. We knew that we did not want to tell a straightforward story with a beginning and conclusion, a story with a traditional plot line—rising action that culminated in a climax and falling action. We wanted to recreate the sense of wonderful energy, even mystery that erupted when women in ACCW began to research their experiences and take responsibility for helping one another. When we began composing *Releasing Hope,* we knew with confidence that we would follow the discursive structure of *Arresting Hope.*

In addition to the many important themes we have learned in our extensive research together, we have also learned that the dissemination of the research must be pursued with creative intentions. In her memoir, Camilla Gibb explains that telling a story "demands the creation of something coherent out of disparate bits and pieces and gaps in knowledge" (xii). In both *Arresting Hope* and *Releasing Hope,* we have created texts that invite the reader to encounter a diverse chorus of voices. The reader is able to make connections, links, and patterns among disparate fragments. Jeanette Winterson explains how she writes by "collecting the scraps, uncertain of continuous narrative" (41). Winterson notes that, "life is layers, fluid, unfixed, fragments" (156). Like Winterson, we are committed to telling stories that honour lived experiences as fluid and fragmentary.

Releasing Hope narrates a story that is part of a complex and ongoing conversation, a story that evokes tenacious tension and haunting memories and indefatigable hope. The story is personal and political, individual and institutional, idealistic and ideological, ethical and economic. In the process of doing participatory health research, we learned to trust the voices of incarcerated women. In the process of researching, writing, and editing *Arresting Hope* and *Releasing Hope,* we also learned to trust one another and to trust the creative process that seeks serendipity, possibility, and innovation. In these processes, we have all been surprised. Above all, we have been surprised by hope. In the title *Arresting Hope,* we play with the participle "arresting," which can be read as an adjective or a verb.

We seek to arrest hope in order to linger with hopefulness, and we seek to acknowledge how hope arrests us so that we are always committed to radical transformation of individuals, institutions, communities, and social networks. Similarly, in the title *Releasing Hope,* we offer the participle "releasing" as both an adjective and a verb. As we have worked on this new book, colleagues and friends have asked, "What does releasing hope mean?" For us, releasing hope includes the life-changing possibility of hope that can release us from our fears, traumas, and wounds. Hope releases and opens up possibilities for attending to the power of hope for transformation—personal and communal. Hope can release us from the stories of depression, defeat, and destruction that almost all of us live as a significant part of our human stories. Not only does hope release us when we seek to live with hope, but we are eager to release hope, to set hope free, to allow hope to flow freely in the lives of people and institutions. Etymologically connected to the Latin *relaxare*, "to release" is to stretch out again. In our research, writing, and activism, we seek to stretch out again and again in efforts to promote hope, and, above all, to live hopefully.

We offer *Releasing Hope: Women's Stories of Transition from Prison to Community* as a manifesto full of hope for change in the lives of people as well as in the lives of communities. The word "manifesto" is derived from the Latin, meaning to make obvious or public. It holds the notion of making something manifest, clear, and recognizable. *Releasing Hope* is steeped in hope. Activist change is possible, especially when we engage together in creative collaboration with a conscientious commitment to asking critical questions and listening carefully with the heart's attention. We draw our book to a close with a poem composed from wisdom recorded in various research projects when women with incarceration experience were invited to tell their stories.

REFERNCES

Baldwin, Christina. *Storycatcher: Making Sense of our Lives through the Power and Practice of Story*. Novato, CA: New World Library, 2005.

Berry, Wendell. *What are People For? Essays*. New York: North Point Press, 1990.

Buechner, Frederick. *Secrets in the Dark: A Life in Sermons*. New York: HarperCollins, 2006.

Cohen, Leonard. *Book of Longing*. Toronto: McClelland & Stewart, 2006.

Dawn, Amber. *How Poetry Saved my Life*. Vancouver: Arsenal Pulp Press, 2013.

Freire, Paulo. *Pedagogy of the Heart*. Trans. D. Macedo and A. Oliveira. New York: Continuum, 1997.

Gibb, Camilla. *This is Happy*. Toronto: Doubleday Canada, 2015.

hooks, bell. *Writing Beyond Race: Living Theory and Practice*. New York: Routledge, 2013.

Kogawa, Joy. *Gently to Nagasaki*. Halfmoon Bay, BCC: Caitlin Press, 2016.

Kohl, Herb. *The Discipline of Hope: Learning from a Lifetime of Teaching*. New York: Simon and Schuster, 1998.

Oliver, Mary. *Thirst*. Boston: Beacon Press, 2006.

Vanier, Jean. *Becoming Human.* Toronto: House of Anansi Press, 1998.
Winterson, Jeanette. *Why Be Happy When You Could Be Normal?* New York: Grove Press, 2011.

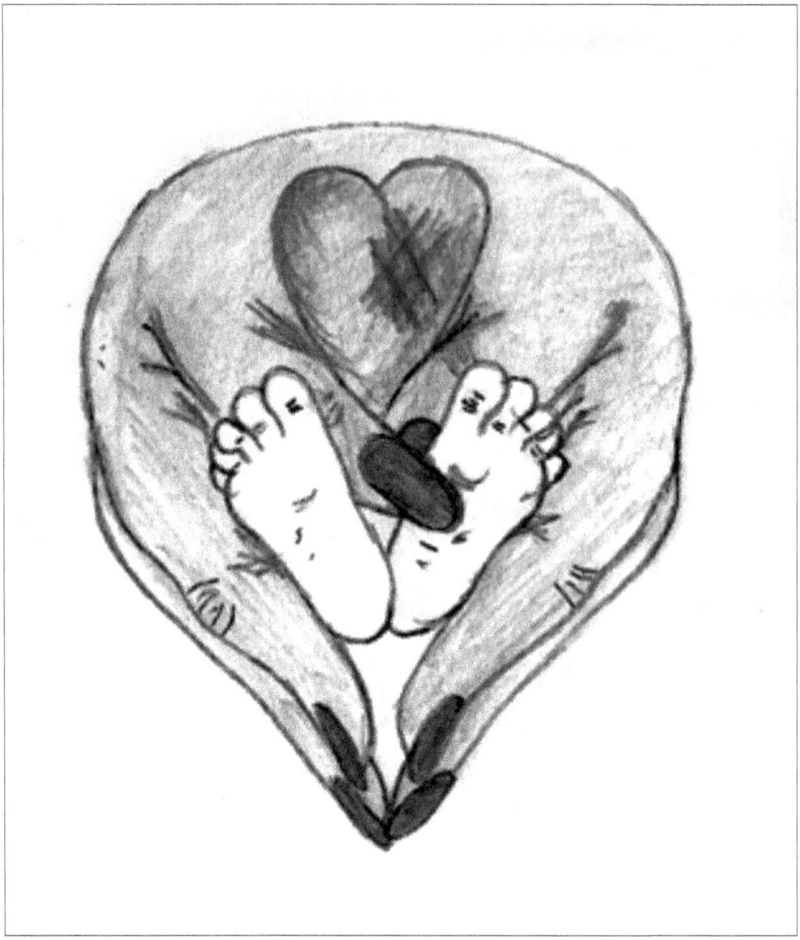

Twenty-Six Ways of Listening to Hope

1

imagine you've just been released
with the clothes on your back
and no family behind you
and no self esteem
only shame

2

we all have responsibility
to respond

3

we are talking about the value of story
language is a way of healing
when we work with words,
they sow hope and love

4

when I wake up,
over my morning tea,
I look onto Facebook
and I see RIP on the women's page

five women died
of fentanyl overdoses

in Maple Ridge
in twenty-four hours just before
Easter 2017

5

when we first started
the peer health mentor program
we wanted to know how
to stop women from relapsing and using

now we want to know how
to stop women from dying

6

we are sending out postcards
we are sending out pleas for help

7

some people are so broken
nothing can be done

nobody is disposable
never give up on them

8

as a society, we are too judgemental
too unloving, some people will be lost
but that only stirs us to more action

9

being the strong one
is tiring

all of us know
we are all in process

we are all broken
 we are all called

10

wasted thirty years in addiction
can't feel guilty about my past

part of my life was to be an addict
it makes me who I am

11

how do we learn how
to respond to others
in their precious uniqueness?

how do we learn how
to become in the presence
of others?

12

learn to tell
your story

learn how to hear
others' stories

13

we know what
we need to do

14

the deputy warden
of ACCW
is giving women
Arresting Hope
to read

15

give space
for the voices
of women

16

individual action and hope
can only dance with
social and political action

17

hope is like grass
growing in the cracks
of concrete

18

hope is another woman
sitting outside the prison gate
waiting to greet you

19

what can I learn
from your story
of success?

20

when you get up
think about ten things
you are hopeful for

21

growing hope
healing hope
keeping hope

living hope
taking hope
releasing hope
sustaining hope

22

the space of hope
heartbreak and hope
home and hope

23

going to the edge looking
into a hopeless chasm
with resilient hope

24

the women are released
with almost no hope
the women are released
with the expectation

they will return

25

the cost
of homelessness
is hopelessness

26

each day brings
opportunities
tomorrow is another
opportunity

this is our hope[1]

NOTE

[1] Carl wrote this Found Poem by lingering over the words of the *Releasing Hope* co-editors' (Carl, Lynn, Mo, and Ruth) discussions, which Ruth scribed in her computer during our frequent working meetings.

Who We Are

EDITOR AND AUTHORS

Ruth Elwood Martin
I worked as family physician in Vancouver from 1983 to 2009; I also worked part time in the medical clinics of BC correctional centres for men and women for seventeen years. I am a clinical professor in the School of Population and Public Health, University British Columbia, and an associate faculty member of the Department of Family Practice. My experiences as a prison physician and participatory health researcher during the time period of *Arresting Hope* changed me, such that my goal became to foster the improvement of prison health and to engage patients' voices in the process. I co-founded the Collaborating Centre for Prison Health and Education, which is a group committed to encouraging and facilitating collaborative opportunities for health, education, research, service, and advocacy, in order to enhance the social well-being and (re)integration of individuals in custody, their families, and communities. From 2011 to 2017, I served as chair of the Prison Health Communities of Practice Group of the College of Family Physicians of Canada. I so much love spending time with my four grandchildren.

Mo Korchinski
Since writing *Arresting Hope/Releasing Hope*, I am now a proud member of society. I never thought it could be so good living a clean and sober and maintaining a crime free life. I continue to build a relationship with my three children, and we are healing from me being an absent mother for eleven years. I am a proud grandmother to two beautiful granddaughters, who have taught me what unconditional love is. I graduated in 2014 from the Nicola Valley Institute of Technology

with my Bachelor of Social Work degree. I work as a project manager for the project Unlocking the Gates to Health in the peer health mentor program at the University of British Columbia. I spend most of my spare time helping others in my community, and I feel that the key to turning one's life around and keeping it moving in the right direction is to help others turn their lives around as well. I co-directed several documentary films about individuals' release from prison, when the prison gate is unlocked, but the doors to society are kept locked. My passion is to take my experience of addiction and the justice system and show people that changes are needed; to get the voices of women who are still inside prison heard; and to get policy-makers to understand that change is needed in the prison system and in the communities.

Lynn Fels

I am a writer and professor in arts education at Simon Fraser University in British Columbia, and a former academic editor of *Educational Insights*, an open-access journal that reimagines curriculum, research, and education (www.educationalinsights.ca). With George Belliveau, I co-authored *Exploring Curriculum: Performative Inquiry, Role Drama and Learning* (2008). My research focuses on performative inquiry, arts across the curriculum, mentorship, performative writing, and curriculum as lived experience. Alongside Ruth, Carl, and Mo, I was co-editor of *Arresting Hope: Women Taking Action in Prison Inside Out* (2014). I was also a co-investigator in a six-year SSHRC Partnership Grant, researching arts for social change in Canada. I am truly grateful for the learning and friendship shared during our journey together.

Carl Leggo

Carl Leggo was a poet and professor at the University of British Columbia. His books include: *Come-By-Chance*; *Lifewriting as Literary Métissage and an Ethos for Our Times* (co-authored with Erika Hasebe-Ludt and Cynthia Chambers); *Creative Expression, Creative Education* (co-edited with Robert Kelly); *A Heart of Wisdom: Life Writing as Empathetic Inquiry* (co-edited with Cynthia Chambers, Erika Hasebe-Ludt, and Anita Sinner); *Sailing in a Concrete Boat*; *Arresting Hope: Women Taking Action in Prison Health Inside Out* (co-edited with Ruth Martin, Mo Korchinski, and Lynn Fels); *Arts-based and Contemplative Practices in Research and Teaching: Honouring Presence* (co-edited with Susan Walsh and Barbara Bickel); *Hearing Echoes* (co-authored with Renee Norman); *Poetic Inquiry: Enchantment of Place* (co-edited with Pauline Sameshima, Alexandra Fidyk, and Kedrick

James); and *Provoking Curriculum Studies: Inspiration/Imagination/Interconnection* (co-edited with Erika Hasebe-Ludt).

CONTRIBUTING AUTHORS

Alison Granger-Brown
It has now been twenty years since I landed in the Alouette Correctional Centre for Women (ACCW). I had so much hope for what was possible in those years when we were able to be creative and inspired in our support for women to recover. Nothing has diminished my belief in the determination and courage of the women. However, I am uncertain about the current direction our world is moving toward, one that seems to care less and less for those with multiple barriers from early trauma, who break the law. My humbling recognition is that the women will recover despite the lack of resources and without the correctional systems support; all that we can do is share our unwavering belief in the possibility and step gracefully out of their way. Thank you to all of you who have shared your stories, your courage, and your laughter with me.

Amanda Staller
Life has taken on new meaning since I was released. At forty-two, I went back to school and earned a diploma in Addiction Services, and today I'm a certified addiction counsellor. For the past five years, I've been in the helping field, where my lived experience has been my greatest asset. Running has saved my life, and with a few marathons behind me, I now lead others to celebrate crossing finish lines. I devote my life to love and service. I have been given a life beyond my wildest dreams, and I have a new happiness, new joy, and a new freedom.

Amber Christie
I am a Cree First Nations woman. I was first incarcerated in 2000 at the age of twenty, and I returned to prison thirty times over the next five years. In my most recent incarceration in 2005, I spent six months inside Alouette Correctional Centre for Women (ACCW). I suffered from a severe heroin addiction for many years and lived on the streets. Today, I am a mother and a contributing member of society. I was a research assistant for the University of British Columbia, working in community-based participatory research, employed by the project called Doing Time and I was part of the Women in2 Healing team. I also worked with a community-based participatory health research project called Aboriginal Healing Outside of the Gates. My goal is to support

women in the reintegration process so that they can safely reintegrate into their chosen communities.

Brenda Tole
I retired after a thirty-seven-year career with BC Corrections Branch. I graduated with a Bachelor in Education from the University of British Columbia and started my career as a community probation officer/family court counsellor. I worked in various communities in the Lower Mainland over the next fifteen years, and then I held a variety of management positions in different correctional centres in the custody division. The last position I held was as the warden of Alouette Correctional Centre for Women from 2003 to 2007. I live with my husband Mark and spend time with eight grown children and six grandchildren between Cultus Lake and Galiano Island.

Cat Wilson
I am aka CAT, and I was born in Inverness, Scotland. I moved with my family to Canada in 1977. I grew up in North Delta. I left home at the age of seventeen and got introduced to substances. I struggled over the years and now live a healthy, productive, substance-free life in Fort McMurray, Alberta. I had some post-secondary education in social services. I was an active participant in the Doing Time project and Women in2 Healing, drawing on my own life experiences to help other women.

Chas Coutlee
My YeYe (grandmother) gave me the name Sulinek, which translates into "starry night." I am a forty-two-year-old mother to a fantastic daughter. I am Nlaka'pamux First Nation on my mother's side and Irish on my father's side. Growing up, I have spent a lot of time incarcerated in youth detention centers, and as an adult I received two federal sentences, which I served at Fraser Valley Institution for women. In addition, while in Alouette Correctional Center for Women (ACCW), I was part of the group that started the participatory research program with Dr. Ruth Martin. Then I worked as a research assistant on the Doing Time participatory research project as a peer mentor in Kelowna. Since my final release from FVI, I have worked hard to create a beautiful life for myself and my daughter. For the first few years I had a job at Talitha Koum Society, working with women who were actively working to escape addiction and find new way to live in recovery. I am passionate about working with women who are living the way I once

did. Therefore, I have gone on to share my story in different intuitions to give hope to others who want a way out of addiction and are seeking a better life. I am currently in my final year of my Bachelor of Social Work degree at Nicola Valley Institute of Technology while working as a child and youth care worker. For me, education has always been a way to work toward the life I want. My YeYe was a language instructor and an on-campus elder at NVIT. My mom also completed her BSW at NVIT, and now I, too, am completing my BSW at NVIT along with my daughter who is currently a student at NVIT. I am a huge fan of people helping people, lifting up and loving each other. We really are all in this together. *Kwukwscemxw* (Thank you).

Christine Hemingway
Since writing *Arresting Hope/Releasing Hope*, my life has been amazing. I have been very active in trying to help change health care inside the prisons for other women. I'm also a member of the Unlocking the Gates to Health Peer Mentor Program, which helps women on this side of the gates. My son, who is now twenty-five years old, is a first officer with a major airline. I am so proud of all his hard work and super glad that today I can be part of all his milestones in life. I love to travel and see the world; being a part-time travel agent gives me the freedom to have this opportunity. I own my own business and today employ other women to give them the empowerment to take back their lives. I am very grateful that I became involved with the research team and Unlocking the Gates to Health; it has helped me get my life back and become a productive member of society.

Colby contributed her writing for *Releasing Hope*, and then we lost contact with her.

Henry "Henk" Smidstra
Justice issues were close to Prison Chaplain Henk Smidstra's heart, especially Aboriginal and women's issues. Henk immigrated to Canada from the Netherlands in 1949. He initially worked as a mechanic but later attended Calvin College and Seminary. Following seminary, he interned for a year in San Francisco at a Native outreach centre before going to the Philippines as a missionary and church planter with Christian Reformed World Missions from 1978 to 1985. After returning to Canada, he worked for several years with the Victim Offender Reconciliation Program and M2/W2 Ministry, a restorative Christian prison ministry named for its man-to-man, woman-to-woman

approach. From 1991 until his retirement in 2012, he served as prison chaplain at Aloutte Correctional Centre for Women and Fraser Valley Institute. During those years, Henk participated in restorative justice initiatives in the Christian Reformed Church. Henk's commitment to his family (wife Grace, four children, and four grandchildren), friends, and colleagues, and his passionate pursuit of justice, equality, and shalom will be his enduring legacy. Henk passed away in September 2017, nine months after being diagnosed with glioblastoma, a type of brain cancer.

Kelly Murphy
While incarcerated in 2005, I participated in the prison participatory health research project in Alouette Correctional Centre for Women (ACCW). Starting in 2008, I was employed with University of British Columbia on various community-based research projects, which collaborated with women to improve their health as they were being released into the community. I have arisen out of abuse and adversity, and I am passionately involved in helping other women find their voices and rise out of oppressive circumstances. I now live and work in Vernon with my husband, Ric. Our two daughters and two grandsons (ages two and three), and my niece and her child (age two), also live in Vernon, and I spend a lot of time childminding. I even have a car seat in my car! I love being a grandma.

Lara-Lisa Condello
I am currently a faculty member with Nicola Valley Institute of Technology (NVIT)—BC's Indigenous public post-secondary institute. I have facilitated university transfer Criminology courses at NVIT's Vancouver campus since 2004, and I founded NVIT's prison education program at Alouette Correctional Centre, which ran from 2007-2010. I am also an associate faculty member of the University of British Columbia's Collaborating Centre for Prison Health and Education. As a collaborative educator, I am passionate about interdisciplinary issues such as health, and applying arts and film to address the provocative yet often misunderstood concepts of penal abolition and transformative justice.

Lora "Koala" Kwandibens
Lora Kwandibens was an Ojibwa woman who faced adversity since before her birth. Born outside of Collins in Ontario, her family was always involved in an alcoholic, violent lifestyle. Lora was first imprisoned as a youth and spent many years in custody, including

prolonged periods in segregation. Following her release from prison in 2005, Lora gave birth to her son, Stewart. After he was apprehended, Lora fought to regain custody of him. Lora's criminal history and prior gang affiliation contributed to the gap in communication and understanding with the social workers. Lora and Stewart then had a home of their own and built a healthy loving life together. Lora was a role model for determination; she never gave up hope to regain her child. She was constantly concerned for the wellbeing and support of women in similar situations to hers and was particularly interested in helping women who are feared and misunderstood by service providers and the justice system. Lora worked part time as a community-based participatory researcher with Women in2 Healing and volunteered her time with Sisters in Action and Solidarity. Lora's life ended tragically and too early when she died of metastatic breast cancer in 2013.

Marnie Scow
I am a thirty-one-year-old First Nations woman. I was born and raised in Port Hardy, a small town located on the northern end of Vancouver Island. My family comes from both Kwakiutl and Heiltsuk Nations. I found myself immersed in addiction and involved in a pro-criminal lifestyle after experiencing multiple traumas and the death of my parents as a teenager. I came into recovery in 2008 and have spent the majority of the last ten years clean and sober. I pursued post-secondary education and studied Criminology/Legal Studies at Douglas College. I've dedicated the majority of my adult life to working with others and to helping other addicts and people of marginalized demographics, using a harm-reduction approach. I have worked for several organizations in the Downtown East Side and Surrey; my heart belongs to this work. As an Indigenous woman, I believe in sharing my experience, strength, and hope with others so they too may also find their voice and experience a new way of life. In my spare time, I love to play slow pitch, engage in culturally rich activities such as smudging and sweat lodges, and volunteer within my community. All my relations.

Elder Mary "Holy Cow" Fayant
I am a Cree descendent from Saskatoon, Saskatchewan. I have two beautiful sons, six grandchildren, and one great-grandchild. I have worked with our Métis Society in Surrey, with the children and families of the Kla-how-eya community, and for a short time as a counsellor at the Native Education Centre. I also take part in Ceremonies whenever requested at Langara College and Simon Fraser University. I was

involved with the First Nations Breast Cancer Society as a director. I started to work in the women's correctional centre when two wonderful co-workers, as well as one woman in prison who had cancer, convinced me that they needed an Elder/Spiritual Advisor. I work in provincial and federal centres, and I volunteered for many years in the male correctional institutions. I have invited inmates to come to sweats in the community with their families when they are released from prison.

Mattie Campbell
When I wrote this piece about visiting my mom, I was sixteen remembering back to when I was thirteen. She had been addicted to drugs since I was three years old, and this was the last time she had been incarcerated. Writing this piece made me realize that writing is an amazing coping tool, whether it be just a journal entry, a reflection, or even a story. It cleared my mind and helped me deal with a lot of the pain and suffering throughout my life. Along with writing, I have worked very hard in school to get where I am. I'm now eighteen years old and going to university for my associate degree in Psychology to work with youth and mental health.

Maura Gowans
I am a proud mother of five boys. I was born in Yellowknife, Northwest Territories, but I have lived in the Vancouver area for the past twenty-five years. I am passionate about working towards ending violence, I am a registered social worker and an active member within my community, and I enjoy reading.

Odessa Marchand
I'm a Cree woman. I was raised in Prince George, BC. I've been in and out of jail since I was twelve years old. Now I am thirty-two I got my first real big bit when I was twenty-two. I did three years in provincial corrections awaiting trial. I started taking schooling inside. I got my Dogwood Diploma in the first two years. I started to look at the different options for filling my mind with knowledge. I did fundraisers. I found my culture. I felt free in my mind. Being locked up is a rough place for people—but for me, I found knowledge, I found myself. For many years I was lost in addiction, and I didn't know who I wanted to be. But when I went to jail, I started learning about who I was and what I wanted in life. When I got my sentence—I got a ten-year sentence—I was shocked, but then again, I was just happy that it was over, and I was able to do my time in my new mind. After I did

my prison sentence, I got out on parole. I was out for maybe a year, and I got my daughter back. I was so happy. At the same time, it's hard to reintegrate into the life. I wanted to only because I didn't have much knowledge about how to live a legit life. All I knew was what I wanted, and I wanted to succeed. I got pregnant with my second child, and while I was pregnant I went to the BC Institute of Technology (BCIT). I got my Construction Safety Officer (CSO) ticket. I got my Level 3 First Aid Certificate. I've had a job now for about three years being a first aid attendant and a CSO. I have two kids. I pay my own bills. I'm living a very good life, dating a very good man who loves me and believes in me. I also go to schools and talk about my life and how it affects me and where it has brought me. I appreciate you for giving me this time to share a little bit about myself.

Pam Young
I am a research lead for University of British Columbia on the Unlocking the Gates to Health project, which offers a peer mentor to women leaving prison to assist them in overcoming the obstacles that many women face during the first seventy-two hours after release. Prior to coming to work on the project, I was also a peer health mentor offering support through my own lived prison experience, twenty-year battle with addiction, and success at making my way back to the community. I currently also work part time in a transition house in my community. I have now been substance free for over nine years, and I have studied chemical addictions at Nicola Valley Institute of Technology. My life now revolves around bettering my life and the lives of my children, grandchildren, and the women I work with.

Wendy Sproule
I was a community-based project assistant with the University of British Columbia Collaborating Centre for Prison Health and Education, working on two projects: A Participatory Approach to Developing Preventive Health Tools for BC Individuals with Lived Incarceration Experience (P4H), and A Participatory Approach to Improving Cancer Screening and Early Detection Among Individuals with Incarceration Experience (P4C). I have over seven years of incarceration experience and am an active advocate for people who are released from prison, to help improve their opportunities for success and reduce recidivism. I am a proud grandmother of two girls, and I am now managing a large housing program for Raincity Housing in Vancouver. I am still in touch with many women who have come away from the cycle of addiction,

prison, and trauma, and I am passionate about teaching others to find positive learning in negative life experiences by openly sharing my experiences and assisting others to see possibilities for success.

Appendices

FUNDING SUPPORT

We are grateful for all of the funding that we received, including the following:

In 2009, Women in2 Healing received designated funding donations from academic friends and supporters to fund five members' travel to present their research findings at four academic conferences:

National Network for Aboriginal Mental Health Research (NAMHR), Annual Meeting, August 13-14, 2009, Montreal. Amber Christie gave an invited keynote presentation entitled "Aboriginal Healing Outside the Gates."

World Health Organization-Prison Health Protection Conference, October 2009, Madrid. Jen McMillan presented posters on Aboriginal Healing Outside the Gates and Women in2 Healing project overview.

International Corrections and Prisons Association Conference, October, 2009, Barbados. Mo Korchinski presented on "Post Incarceration Syndrome."

North American Primary Care Research Group (NAPCRG) Annual Meeting, November 2009, Montreal. Mo Korchinski, Debra Hansen, Kelly Murphy, and Dr. Ruth Elwood Martin presented on: "The Inmate Rec. Program" and "Women in Prison Develop Participatory Research"and led a pre-conference workshop on "Community Based Participatory Research."

Operating Research and Program Grants to support participatory health research with women who were incarcerated, include:

Fraser Health Authority, Tula Foundation and Vancouver Foundation. R. E. Martin, T. Corneil, T. G. Hislop, J. A. Buxton, C. Leggo, K. Meyer, L. Fels, V. R. Ramsden, M. Buchanan, A.C. Macaulay, and G. Ogilvie, "Community-Based Participatory Action Research: Women in2 Healing, Women Who Were Incarcerated," 2008.

Canadian Institutes of Health Research (CIHR). P. Janssen, R. E. Martin, K. Shannon, J. Frankish, J. A. Buxton, V. R. Ramsden, A. C. Macaulay, D. Wardman, T. Corneil, C. Leggo, L. Fels, M. Buchanan, and G. Ogilvie, "Doing Time: A Time for Incarcerated Women to Develop and Evaluate a Community-Based Action Health Strategy," 2008.

National Network for Aboriginal Mental Health Research (NAMHR). R. E. Martin, A. Christie, L. Kwandibens, and members of the Women In2 Healing research team, "Aboriginal Healing Outside the Gates," 2009.

Vancouver Foundation. BCMSF Community Engagement Grant. R. E. Martin, L. Fels, C. Leggo and M. Smith, "Book Proposal: Prisons that Heal," 2010.

Vancouver Foundation. R. E. Martin, J. A. Buxton, V. R. Ramsden, L. Fels, C. Leggo, J. Kaczorowski, J. Oliffe, and L-L Condello, "A Participatory Approach to Developing Preventive Health Tools for BC Individuals with Lived Incarceration Experience," 2011.

Canadian Institutes of Health Research (CIHR). R. E. Martin, P. Janssen, M. Buchanan, J. A. Buxton, L-L Condello, L. Fels, A. Granger-Brown, C. Leggo, A. Macaulay, and V. R. Ramsden, "Knowledge Translation Grant. Unlocking the Gates to Health," 2011.

Public Health Agency of Canada. R. E. Martin, J. A. Buxton, V. R. Ramsden, L. Fels, C. Leggo, J. Kaczorowski, J. Oliffe, and L-L Condello, "A Participatory Approach to Improving Cancer Screening and Early Detection Among Individuals with Incarceration Experience," 2012.

Koerner Foundation. "Peer Mentoring Program," 2012.

Peter Wall Foundation. International Roundtable Discussion Award. S. Sarra, R. E. Martin, J. A. Buxton, T. Zupancic and K. Hargreaves, "Bonding Through Bars: How Can an Equity-Focused Approach Protect the Bond Between Incarcerated Mothers and their Children?" 2012.

Anonymous Foundation and Mary Pence Foundation. M. Korchinski and R. E. Martin, "Women in2 Healing's Unlocking the Gates Peer Health Mentoring Program," 2014.

First Nations Health Authority, Women's Health Research Institute & Interior Health Authority. R. E. Martin, B. Tole, A. Granger-Brown, A. Salmon, J. Darnforth, and M. Korchinski, "Collaborative Meeting to develop Guidelines for the Implementation of Mother-Child Units in Canadian Correctional Facilities," 2014.

First Nations Health Authority. "Unlocking the Gates to Health: Peer Health Mentoring for Women Leaving Prison," 2015-2018, 2018-2020.

Anonymous Foundation. "Unlocking the Gates to Health: Peer Health Mentoring for Women Leaving Prison," 2017, 2018.

SELECTED MEDIA REPORTS AND INTERVIEWS

StarMetro Vancouver. "Expensive dental problems are holding back people in addiction recovery," by Perrin Grauer. Interview with Amber Christie, Mo Korchinski, and Leeann Donnelly, 13 May 2018.

Macleans. "Women need health and dental care to stay out of prison." Interview with Patti Janssen, Mo Korchinski, and Ruth Elwood Martin, 23 October 2017.

The Conversation. "Women need health and dental care to stay out of prison." Interview with Patti Janssen, Mo Korchinski, and Ruth Elwood Martin, 22 October 2017.

WE-*Web-based*. "Cradles in prison cells: Mothers behind bars," by Craig and Marc Kielburger, 6 May 2017.

The Globe and Mail. "For BC's female prisoners, this peer mentor program is a leg up on the outside," by Vanessa Hrvatin. Interview with Colby Kristjønson and Mo Korchinski, 13 March 2017.

Vancouver Metro. "Babies in Prison." Three-part series by Sidney Cohen. Interview with Mo Korchinski, December 2015.

Newstalk 770, Corus Radio, Edmonton and Calgary. "Bonding through Bars," by Dan Riendeau, November 2015.

CBC *News—British Columbia*. "BC should keep more babies with their moms in prison," by Rick Cluff, 16 September 2015.

CKNW. "Arresting Hope." Interview with Lynn Fels, December 2014.

Vancouver Sun. "Arresting Hope." Interview with Lynn Fels, December 2014.

Global TV. *Babies Behind Bars*. Documentary, by Mia Sheldon, 25 October 2014.

Global News. "Incarcerated mothers and their children," by Jill Krop, 9 May 2013.

Readers Digest. "Babies Behind Bars," by Diane Selkirk. Interview with Jennifer Smith and baby Sierra, May 2009.

Vancouver Co-op Radio at 102.FM. Live interviews with Kelly Murphy, Jennifer McMillan, Lora Kwandibens, Christine Hemmingway, Jennifer Smith, Alison Granger-Brown, and Catherine (Cat) Wilson, 2008-2009.

CBC AM *Radio, the Early Edition*, with Rich Cluff. Live interviews with Kelly Murphy, Jennifer Smith, Alison Granger-Brown, and Catherine (Cat) Wilson. Oct 2008–April 2009.

Women's Health Research Network. "Giving voice to prison mothers." Podcast interview with Kelly Murphy and Jennifer Smith, Oct. 2008.

The Vancouver Sun. "Female Inmates Fight to Keep their Babies," by Lori Culbert. Interview with Jennifer Smith and baby Sierra, March 5, 2008.

The Vancouver Sun. "Ex-cons give hope to those in need," by Lori Culbert, 21 February 2008.

SELECTED JOURNAL PUBLICATIONS

Buchanan, Maria, Kelly Murphy, Megan Smith Martin, Mo Korchinski, Jane Buxton, Alison Granger-Brown, Debra Hanson, Greg Hislop, Ann C. Macaulay, and Ruth Elwood Martin. "Understanding Incarcerated Women's Perspectives on Substance Use: Catalysts, Reasons for Use, Consequences, and Desire for Change." *Journal of Offender Rehabilitation* 50.2 (2011): 81-100.

Granger-Brown, Alison, Jane Buxton, Lara-Lisa Condello, D. Feder, Thomas G. Hislop, Ruth Elwood Martin, Amy Salmon, Megan Smith, and J. Thompson. "Collaborative Community Prison Programs for Incarcerated Women in BC." *British Columbia Medical Journal* 54.10 (2012): 509-513.

Janssen, Patricia A., Mo Korchinski, Sarah L. Desmarais, Arianne Y.K. Albert, Lara-Lisa Condello, Marla Buchanan, Alison Granger-Brown, Vivian R. Ramsden, Lynn Fels, Jane A. Buxton, Carl Leggo, and Ruth Elwood Martin. "Factors that Support Successful Transition to the Community Among Women Leaving Prison in British Columbia: A Prospective Cohort Study Using Participatory Action Research." *CMAJ Open* 5.3 (2017): E717–E723.

Martin, Ruth Elwood, Mo Korchinski, Lynn Fels, and Carl Leggo. "Arresting Hope: Women Taking Action in Prison Health Inside Out." *Cogent Arts & Humanities* 4.4 (2017): 1-15.

Martin, Ruth Elwood, Debra Hanson, Christine Hemingway, Vivian R. Ramsden, Jane Buxton, Alison Granger-Brown, Lara-Lisa Condello, Ann Macaulay, Patti Janssen, and Thomas G. Hislop. "Homelessness as Viewed by Incarcerated Women: Participatory Research." *International Journal of Prisoner Health* 8.3-4 (2012): 108-16.

Martin, Ruth Elwood, Sue Adamson, Mo Korchinski, Alison Granger-Brown, Vivian R. Ramsden, Jane Buxton, Nancy Espinoza-Magana,, Sue Pollock, Megan Smith, Ann Macaulay, Lara-Lisa Condello, nd Thomas G. Hislop. "Incarcerated Women Develop a Nutrition and Fitness Program: Participatory Research." *International Journal of Prisoner Health* 9.3 (2013): 142-50.

Martin, Ruth Elwood and Brenda Tole. "Mother-Child Unit Supports

Infants Born to Incarcerated Mothers." The Vanier Institute of the Family, 2016. Web.

Martin, Ruth Elwood, Kelly Murphy, Rene Chan, Vivian R. Ramsden, Alison Granger-Brown, Ann C. Macaulay, Roopjeet Kahlon, Gina Ogilvie and Thomas G. Hislop. "Primary Health Care: Applying the Principles Within a Community-Based Participatory Health Research Project that Began in a Canadian Women's Prison." *Global Health Promotion* 16.4 (2009): 43-53.

Martin, Ruth Elwood, Kate Murphy, Debra L. Hanson, Christine A. Hemingway, Vivian R. Ramsden, Jane A. Buxton, Alison Granger-Brown, Lara-Lisa Condello, Marla Buchanan, Nancy Espinoza-Magana, Gillian Edworthy, and T. Greg Hislop. "The Development of Participatory Health Research Among Incarcerated Women in a Canadian Prison." *International Journal of Prisoner Health* 5.2 (2009): 95-107. Web.

Meyer, Karen and Lynn Fels. "Breaking Out: Learning Research from the Women in Prison Project." *International Review of Qualitative Research* 2.2 (2009): 269-290.

O'Gorman, Claire M., Megan Smith Martin, John L. Oliffe, Carl Leggo, Mo Korchinski and Ruth Elwood Martin. "Community Voices in Program Development: The Wisdom of Individuals with Incarceration Experience." *Canadian Journal of Public Health / Revue Canadienne De Santé Publique* 103.5 (2012): E379-E383. Web.

Ramsden, Vivian R., Ruth Elwood Martin, Jennifer McMillan, Alison Granger-Brown and Brenda Tole. "Participatory Health Research within a Prison Setting: A Qualitative Analysis of 'Paragraphs of Passion.'" *Global Health Promotion* 22.4 (2015): 48-55.

BOOKS AND BOOK CHAPTERS

Ann, Danita, Devon, Julie, Lynn and Shelley. "'Can You Imagine... What if Women Were Sentenced to Education?' Women Speaking Out Inside the Gate." Poetic inquiry: Vibrant voices in the Social Sciences. Eds. P. Sameshima, M. Prendergast and C. Leggo. Rotterdam, The Netherlands: Sense, 2009. 201-306. (Last names withheld due to confidentiality.)

Fels, Lynn, Karen Meyer, and Ruth Elwood Martin. "Angel Words Inside Prison Gates: Participatory Action Research as an Action of Restorative Justice." *International Perspectives on Restorative Justice in Education*. Eds. J. Charlton, S. Pavelka and P. J. Verrechia. Kanata, ON: JCharlton, 2011. 69-88.

Martin Ruth Elwood, Joshua Lau and Amy Salmon. "Incarcerating Mothers: The Effect on the Health and Social Well-Being of Infants and their Mothers." *Incarcerated Mothers: Oppression and Resistance*. Eds. Gordana Eljupovic and Rebecca Jaremko Bromwich. Bradford: Demeter Press, 2013. 197-209.

Martin, Ruth Elwood. "Participatory Health Research in Prison. Case Study, Canada." *Companion Website for 'Health Promotion— Planning and Strategies 3e'*. Eds. J. Green, K. Tones, R. Cross and J. Woodall. London: Sage, 2015.

Martin, Ruth Elwood, Kelly Murphy, and Marla Buchanan. "Inside and Outside of the Gates: Transforming Relationships Through Research." *Feminist Community Research, Case Studies and Methodologies*. Eds. G. Creese and W. Frisby. Vancouver: University of British Columbia Press, 2011. 168-188.

Martin, R. E., Mo Korchinski, Lynn Fels and Carl Leggo. *Arresting Hope: Women Taking Action in Prison Health Inside Out*. Toronto: Inanna Publications, 2014.

DOCUMENTARY FILMS

All documentary films can be viewed at the Collaborating Centre for Prison Health and Education webpage.

Bonding through Bars. Made with financial support from Peter Wall Institute for Advanced Studies. 2013.

Cancer Walks Free. Collaborating Centre for Prison Health and Education and Public Health Agency of Canada. Producer and Director Mo Korchinski. Vancouver. 2014.

Life on the Streets. Interview with Pam Young. Made with financial support from the Public Health Agency of Canada. 2014.

Revolving Door (animation). Creator, Producer and Director Mo Korchinski.

Revolving Door: *Women in2 Healing*. Pull Focus Film School and Canadian Institutes of Health Research. Producer and Director Mo Korchinski. Vancouver. 2010.

Unlocking the Gates. Pull Focus Film School. Producer and Director Mo Korchinski. 2012.

SELECTED CONFERENCE PRESENTATIONS

Martin, Ruth Elwood, Mo Korchinski, Pamela Young, Christine, Lara-Lisa Condello, Lynn Fels, Jane A. Buxton, Patricia A Janssen, Alison Granger-Brown, Vivian Ramsden, Marla Buchanan, and Carl Leggo. "Unlocking The Gates To Health: Peer Health Mentoring For Women Leaving a Correctional Facility." The Academic & Health Policy Conference on Correctional Health. Atlanta, Georgia, March 16-17, 2017

Janssen, Patricia A., Mo Korchinski, Sarah L. Desmarais, Arianne Y. K,Albert, Lara-Lisa Condello, Marla Buchanan, Alison Granger-Brown, Vivian R. Ramsden, Lynn Fels, Jane A. Buxton, Carl Leggo, and Ruth Elwood Martin. "The Impact of Health and Social Factors on Re-Incarceration Among Women After Release from a Canadian Provincial Correctional Centre." The Academic and Health Policy Conference on Correctional Health. Atlanta, Georgia, March 16-17, 2017.

Granger-Brown Alison and Ruth Ellwood Martin. "Babies Born Behind Bars." Healthy Mothers and Healthy Babies: Advances in Across Clinical Practice and Research the Continuum. Vancouver, BC, March 11-12, 2016.

Martin, Ruth Elwood. "The Collaborative Generation of Guidelines for Prison Maternal-Child Units in Canada." 8th Academic and Health Policy Conference On Correctional Health." Boston, Massachusetts, March 19-20, 2015.

Korchinski, Mo, Ruth Ellwood Martin, Lynn Fels and Carl Leggo. "Arresting Hope: Participatory Health Research in a Women's Prison in BC." Public Health Association of BC, Richmond, BC, December 4-5, 2014.

Korchinski, Mo, Ruth Elwood Martin, Pam Young, Patti Janssen, Marla Buchanan, Jane Buxton, Lara-Lisa Condello, Lynn Fels, Carl Leggo and Vivian Ramsden. "Unlocking the Gates to Health–A Peer Mentorship Health Navigator Program for Women Who Are Transitioning From BC Provincial Correctional Centres." Canadian Public Health Association Conference, Toronto, Ontario, May 28-29, 2014.

Korchinski Mo, Debra Hanberg, Lara-Lisa Condello, Lynn Fels and Ruth Elwood Martin. *Cancer Walks Free*. Documentary Film Viewing. Canadian Public Health Association Conference. Toronto, Ontario, May 28-29, 2014.

Martin, Ruth Elwood, Debra Hanberg, Renee Turner, Larry Howett, Marnie Scow, Sproule W, Nunn A, Lara-Lisa Condello, Janusz Kaczorowski, Carl Leggo, John L. Oliffe, Marla Buchanan, Vivian R. Ramsden, Jane A. Buxton and Lynn Fels. "A Participatory Approach to Improving Cancer Screening and Early Detection among Individuals with Incarceration Experience (P4C)." Canadian Public Health Association. Ottawa, ON, June 2013.

Hanberg, Debra, Martin Ruth Elwood, Renee Turner, Larry Howett, Marnie Scow, Wendy Sproule, Alex Nunn, Lara-Lisa Condello, Janusz Kaczorowski, Carl Leggo, John Oliffe, Marla Buchanan, Vivian R. Ramsden, Jane A. Buxton, and Lynn Fels. "A Participatory Approach to Developing Preventive Health Tools for BC Individuals with Lived Incarceration Experience (P4H)." Canadian Public Health Association. Ottawa, ON, June 2013.

Martin, Ruth Elwood, Lora Kwandibens, Amber Christie, Mo Korchinski, Cindy Worsfold, Dawn Fraser, Rose Hesketh, Cat Wilson, Lara-Lisa Condello, Ann Macauley and Vivian R. Ramsden. "Aboriginal Healing Outside of the Gates." North American Primary Care Research Group Conference. Seattle, WA. November 13-17, 2010.

Murphy Kelly, Debra Hanson, Christine Hemingway, Vivian R. Ramsden, Jane A. Buxton, Alison Grange-Brown, Lara-Lisa Condello,

Marla Buchanan, Nancy Espinoza Magana, Gillian Edworthy and Ruth Elwood Martin. "The Development of Participatory Health Research Among Incarcerated Women In a Canadian Prison." North American Primary Care Research Group Conference. Montreal, QC. November 14-18, 2009.